THE HILL OF FLUTES

BY W. G. ARCHER

Poems
The Plains of the Sun

Indian Tribal Poetry
The Blue Grove
The Dove and the Leopard

Indian Sculpture and Painting
The Vertical Man
Indian Painting in the Punjab Hills
Bazaar Paintings of Calcutta
Kangra Painting
Garhwal Painting
Indian Painting
The Loves of Krishna
Central Indian Painting
India and Modern Art
Indian Painting in Bundi and Kotah
Indian Miniatures
Paintings of the Sikhs
Kalighat Paintings
Indian Paintings from the Punjab Hills

With Mildred Archer
Indian Painting for the British

With Robert Melville
Forty Thousand Years of Modern Art

With S. Paranavitana
Ceylon: Paintings from Temple, Shrine and Rock

With Edwin Binney 3rd
Rajput Miniatures

A hill of flutes

THE HILL OF FLUTES

Life, Love and Poetry in Tribal India

A Portrait of the Santals

W. G. ARCHER

UNIVERSITY OF PITTSBURGH PRESS

First published in Great Britain 1974 by George Allen & Unwin Ltd

Published in the U.S.A. 1974 by the University of Pittsburgh Press

Library of Congress Catalog Card Number 73-13311
ISBN 0-8229-1112-4

Printed in Great Britain
in 12 point Barbou type
by W & J Mackay Limited, Chatham

To
my son Michael
who also loved
the Santals

———————

'The ever singing, ever flute-playing Santals.'
T. H. Lewin

'Their bodies were strong and unfettered; their eyes
were bright and intelligent but I think it was an in-
expressible dignity that most affected me, a purely
natural dignity untinged by any shade of affectation.
They were alive and I sensed their vitality. I could feel it
and I felt that it made me live too.'
Clement Egerton

'It is perhaps in the blending of the directly sensual
with the romantic and in the wide and weighty
sociological consequences of what, to start with, is the
most personal event – it is in this richness and multi-
plicity of love that lies its philosophic mystery, its
charm for the poet and its interest for the anthro-
pologist.'
Bronislaw Malinowski

'Squeamishness is out of place in India.'
Nirad C. Chaudhuri

'On the hill of flutes
A flute is sounding.'
Santal Song

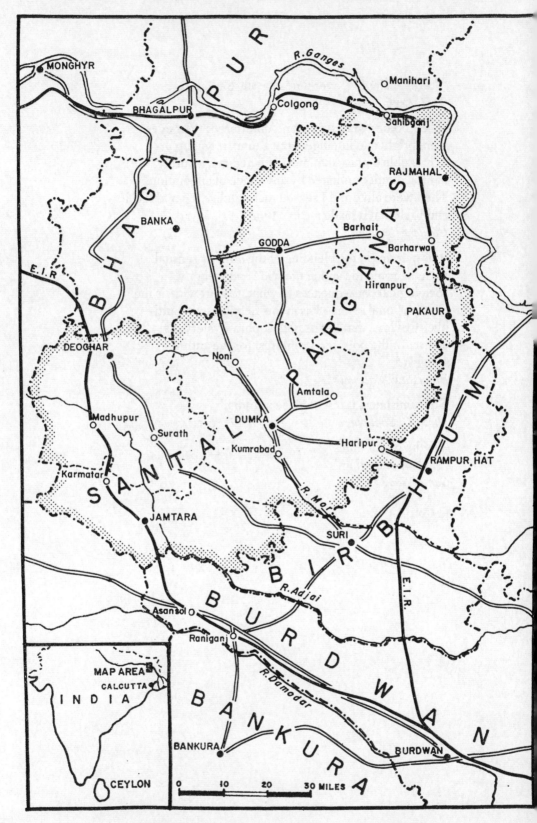

MAP OF THE SANTAL PARGANAS DISTRICT, BIHAR

PREFACE

The purpose of this book is to give a descriptive account of the Santals and their poetry as they existed in the Santal Parganas district of Bihar in the years 1942 to 1946. At that time the Santals were the largest, most integrated and possibly the most resilient tribe in Eastern India. Indo-Melanese by race and speaking a non-Aryan language, Santali, they had antedated in India both Aryans and Dravidians and were still, to a great extent, unaffected by either Hindu or Muslim practices. Their love of dancing and singing, their splendid physiques, the airy freedom with which both men and women went about and their belief in bongas or nature-spirits reminded the observer of ancient India; and their love poetry – simple, sensuous and passionate – shared with that of Kalidasa, Amaru and Jayadeva the early Indian attitude to sex. Totalling over two million at the census of 1941, they numbered 800,000 in the Santal Parganas and comprised half the district's population. A variety of historical factors had led the Bihar Government to uphold their tribal way of life and in many parts of the district, Santals governed Santals. In December 1942 I was appointed Deputy Commissioner of the Santal Parganas and after two and a half years was placed on special duty to record and codify Santal civil law. This post I held until June 1946. It is on the basis of three and a half years' life and work among the Santals during which I learnt the Santali language, organised the collection of Santal poetry, legends, stories and addresses, attended Santal ceremonies, dances and festivals, and assisted in the settlement of cases that this book has been prepared.

To the many from whom I received generous cooperation, unseen influence or active encouragement, I am deeply grateful. No scholar can ignore the work of his predecessors and, especially in my early months, I was guided and stimulated by the works of such Santal admirers as Man, Carstairs, Bompas, Campbell, Macphail and the great Bodding. Bodding's reference to the Santals' chief spirit, Maran Buru, as 'the Devil' and his description of Santal poetry as 'often pure gibberish' were later to outrage me but his huge Santali-English dictionary staggered me by its encyclopaedic learning and gave me indispensable help. I must also pay tribute to the pioneering initiative of Skrefsrud who in the nineteenth century induced an old and knowledgeable Santal, Kolean Haram, to dictate an account of Santal traditions and customs. *Hapram Puthi* – 'The Book of the Ancestors' as it came to be termed – alerted one to many things that the Santals valued while its Santali prose style had the grace and lucidity of Caesar's *Gallic Wars*. As a printed book, it resembled Cyril Connolly's *The Unquiet Grave* and like that bedside breviary, could be taken up at any time and read with keen enjoyment. From these and other works I learnt the pattern of Santal life.

But it was the Santals themselves and in particular village elders, gurus, intelligent headmen and experienced parganas who instructed me in their living customs, cited examples of tribal behaviour, explained the emotional crises and conduct of Santal lovers and the deep feelings which underlay the fearsome ritual of bitlaha. To list them all would be impossible but I cannot refrain from naming seven honoured personalities – Sangram Hembrom, pargana of Katikund, Kisun Soren, pargana of Durgapur, Sibu Hansdak', guru of Dhamna, Megrae Kisku, jogmanjhi of Kalajore, Lokhon Hansdak' of Dumka, Chotu Ramu Murmu of Amtala and Dhunu Hembrom, dihri of the Nuni Buru hunt. Above all, I must record my permanent indebtedness to Gopal Gamaliel Soren, Seth Choron Hansdak' and Stephen Hidim Murmu who assisted me in many enquiries and translation and played a vital role in collecting and discussing poetry. Without their lively zest and pride in Santal life and culture, I might never have recorded these memorials of 'the ever-singing Santals'.

W. G. ARCHER

CONTENTS

CONTENTS

ILLUSTRATIONS

16

Frontispiece and illustrations 1, 3, 4, 27, 57 and 58 by courtesy of Professor Christoph von Furer-Haimendorf. Remaining illustrations from photographs by the author

CHAPTER I

The Santals

Flanked by rows of tall palmyra palms, Santal villages have an air of genial comfort. In the middle of the Santal Parganas district they nestle at the foot of hills, protected from the hot gales of March and the windy rains of August. To the south and east they lie near mango groves, open to the sun, but free from wind and storm. In the north, the forest goes sweeping to the sky and the view closes on a line of hills. Elsewhere the country is a vast and slightly falling plain, the eye ranging over red uplands and dipping rice fields. From November until January the climate is bland and mild, never hot but rarely cold. In February the 'winter' ends and from then onwards until May the whole countryside basks in a dry exhilarating heat. Forest trees burst into flower – the spiky cotton tree with its flopping crimson petals, the palash with its flaming coral, the sal with its delicate sprays of greenish yellow, the mango with its heavy sticky scent. At night, lines of flame can often be seen advancing up the hillsides, casual sparks having ignited the dry leaves. In June great monsoon clouds gather in the sky and days of pouring rain alternate with periods of startling brightness. The rice fields become a brilliant green and the whole land revels in liquid freshness. In September the rain slackens, to be succeeded by days of steamy heat. October then ushers in the three to four months of mild and dry winter weather, the moon pouring down at night from a clear and dust-free sky.

Within each village, it is the street that dominates the scene. Along its thoroughfare the crops and firewood come and bullock carts go off to market. It is up and down its sandy surface that the women dance. It is in the street that the villagers share their feasts and collect for talk and councils. When a tribal crime has been committed or a matter needs to be discussed, the men gather at the headman's house and sit outside. The street is not merely a link between the houses. It is at once a dance floor, a council chamber and a court of justice.

While the street expresses Santal unity, the houses give the village its uniquely Santal air. The mud walls have a hard cement-like precision, a suave and solid neatness, and the roofs, softly thatched or ribbed with tiles, compose a vista of gently blending curves. As the setting sun catches the thatch and the light loses its hardness, the walls take on a grey dove-like softness and the village exudes an air of mellow peace. At night, the houses loom stark and clear in the moonlight and even in the rains the walls contrive to keep their trimness. Of all the other tribes of eastern India, none has quite the same relish for neatly ordered buildings, the same capacity for tidy spacious living or the same genius for domestic architecture.

Within each house the rooms centre on a courtyard. This is often ten yards square and several times a day is carefully swept and tidied. Here rice and mahua flowers are dried, clothes are aired, and grain is husked in a mortar. During the hot weather, the men no longer hurry to the fields, but sit about in the courtyard making string, baskets, ploughs and the handles of tools. When a boy or girl is married, it is here that a wedding booth is erected and the village girls and women dance violently round and round.

From the courtyard, doors lead to the rooms. These are built as separate houses and are ranged along the courtyard sides. A room has often a broad verandah that is either open to the air or shut in by an outside wall. The room itself is sometimes divided by small partition walls. Windows are rarely provided and apart from a little light which leaks in from the eaves, the interiors have a cosy gloom. In this darkness, snug in winter, cool in summer, the greater part of the family work is done. Each room is a granary, a store room, a kitchen and a bedroom. Clothes and ornaments are kept in wooden boxes. Cobs of maize hang from the rafters while rice and mahua are stored in huge bales of plaited straw. A fire glows in a corner, hens strut through the doorways, and pots of water, eating utensils, bows and arrows, sticks and flutes clutter the floor and shelves. Breakfast of stale rice and salt is warmed on the fire and eaten in the early morning. Rice is boiled and eaten with a curry at noon and a similar meal is cooked and eaten in the evening. Especially at weddings and festivals, a meal is washed down with rice-beer brewed from boiled rice mixed with a ferment known as ranu and then left for three to five days to mature. When the meal is over, married sons are given separate rooms or verandahs in which to sleep with their wives, while the rest of the family beds itself down throughout the house. A pig-sty, cow-shed and hen-roost are set either to one side of the courtyard or at the back beside the garden. Along one verandah a heavy rice-pounder is installed and its sullen thud sounds throughout the morning. Certain villages possess a common pounder and first one girl and then another takes her place at the machine jerking the heavy beam with vigorous movements of the leg.

Behind the houses, fields of open upland commence. A patch nearest the house is often treated as a garden and a number of vegetables are carefully tended. Pumpkins, marrow-like creepers and swelling bottle-gourds are planted, a patch of sugar cane is sometimes grown and in many villages a group of plantains with smooth stems and glossy leaves bear bunches of green fruit. Occasionally a family also plants a fruit tree – a jack-fruit, a tamarind, a munga or a bel – to swell its diet.

The uplands proper adjoin the gardens. These lie fallow from January to March but with the showers of April ploughing starts and if the rain is regular, a crop of maize is quickly sown. A man drives a plough round and round the field. A woman strides behind him, dropping the seed into the furrow and behind her comes a boy driving a second plough and filling in the earth. Side by side with maize, raher – a kind of pulse – is sometimes sown and the plants poke up together. Two or three weeks after sowing, men and women take their mattocks and with brisk stabbing cuts, go over the whole field loosening weeds and pulling out grass. Often the women do this by themselves and as you go through the villages, you notice strapping Santal girls, their clothes pulled high up their shins, chopping at the earth or strolling languidly home carrying their mattocks. In sixty days the crop ripens and bunches of cobs are hung up on the rafters to await the next cold weather. If the rain is scanty, sowing is put off until June and the crop harvested in August.

Besides maize, a number of other crops are also grown in the uplands. The giant millet or bajra is planted close to the village, while smaller millets – iri, gundli and kode – as well as erba, a small grain, are grown in fields further away. These ripen early in the cold weather and form a valuable supplement to the incoming rice-crop. Late in the cold weather some small pulses – horec' and ghangra – ripen into beans and are threshed on separate floors.

Uplands have yet another part in Santal economy. Almost every village possesses mahua trees which are divided out among the various families. The trees flower in March and every day the ground is littered with their soft corollae. It is these which make a tasty dish and every hot-weather morning sees a number of girls stooping under the trees and gathering up the fleshy flowers. These are taken home in baskets, dried in the courtyard and either fried for the day's meal or stored in bales. From fermented mahua flowers liquor also is distilled.

Somewhere in the uplands is a stretch of ground reserved for grazing. Here the village cattle are taken when other land is under crops. Boys and girls stand about gently prodding the animals while the cows and buffaloes crop the grass and the air is loud with flutes.

Beyond the uplands lie the rice fields on which the welfare of the village chiefly depends. These are built along the main lines of drainage and descend in even terraces, each field being composed of puddled mud firmly rimmed by earth embankments. For six months these are blistered by the sun while the cattle bite down the short stubble. With the first showers, however, seed-beds are sown and by June the seedlings are showing brilliantly green among the terraces. Later the same month, ploughing starts and the buffaloes toil round the moist earth or stagger through the liquid mud. Each morning the men commence work before the sun is high and after returning for breakfast continue through the morning. A month later huge clouds loom, heavy and swollen, in the sky and the fields swim with water. The seedlings are now taken out and transplanted by the girls and women. They go in bands to the fields, pull their clothes up to their knees, and as they busily dart the plants into the soft mud, address the seedlings in song.

I

Wealth, wealth
Where is your mother?
Where is your father?
My mother and father
Are wind and rain
My milk is water trickling.

2

Wealth, wealth
O mother wealth
Where was your birth?
I was born
In the splash of rain.

3

The paddy is weeping
The paddy is asking
When will be my wedding?
When the water of the sky
Drenches the earth
Then will be your wedding.

4

In our fields
In our lands
Is a house of wealth.

When the seedlings are in the fields, the men keep a careful eye on the ridges lest a sudden rush of water should breach the embankments and wash the plants away. They also set up reed containers and little bamboo traps so that as the water trickles down from field to field, small fishes are caught. The crop comes into ear in September and by October if both sun and rain are good, the heads begin to sway and sag. Cutting starts in November and a month later the paddy is heaped on the threshing floors. These are made on dry ground somewhere near the village, and as the cattle are driven round, they trample out the ears. In certain areas the paddy is threshed by dashing it against a stone. As the straw is separated out, it is either piled on platforms or plaited into long ropes. With these ropes the great bales are made in which the dry paddy is stored.

Near the rice fields or sometimes in their midst are one or more springs edged with flat stones. The spring is the source of drinking water and every day in the late afternoon the girls and women file down to it to draw a day's supply. Each balances a large round pot on her head and tucks another on her hip. As they wait their turns, they discuss each other's business and while away the time with joking gossip. A little later as the sun begins to set, the girls again go to the spring either to draw more water or to clean the kitchen utensils. If a stream is available, it is used for washing clothes, for bathing and for part of the funeral ceremonies. In some villages, an artificial pond or tank provides yet another supply of water.

If rice fields are vital to the village, another portion of the landscape is even dearer to the Santal heart. This is the forest – in southern villages a tiny patch, but in the north a vast expanse of trees surging to the lonely hills. These supply the villagers with twigs and branches for fuel, timber for rafters and tools, and leaves for plates and cups. During the hot weather the girls and women lay in the year's fuel, going to the forest in little chatting bands and returning with the long poles waggling on their heads. If the year is bad, the forest is scoured for roots, leaves and berries and certain plants are cooked for curry. These plants are an insurance against famine as well as a mainstay of the kitchen. But above all, the forest is a place of secret recreation. In it the men can discuss their tribal ways in privacy, they can talk sex away from women, and they can hunt. 'The crisis for a girl,' it is sometimes said, 'is childbirth; the crisis for a boy is the chase.'

The beat may nowadays yield only a hare or a peacock. Deer, leopards and bears are only rarely encountered, but an air of faint romantic danger persists. Like Frenchmen enjoying 'la chasse' on Sundays, Santal men relish nothing more than a hunt in the forest. At the greatest occasion of all – the annual hunt – they assemble from far and near, spend the day scouring the hillsides and uplands and then at night debate tribal matters and regale themselves with 'music-hall' entertainments. It is the big fixture of the year, when, like a Wembley Cup Final, Santal men 'let off steam'. Finally, the forest is a trysting place for lovers, a setting in which boys and girls can meet in private, sing love songs, form attachments and prosecute their affairs. Here old or divorced women instruct girls in the special love songs which, on account of their use of 'four-letter' words and open allusions or references to sex, are banned in the village. Girls who have learnt such songs teach them to the boys and in this way a whole repertoire of forest love songs is acquired by each successive generation. It is no surprise that long after marriage has brought adult responsibilities, the forest should retain for most Santals vivid associations with early romance.

2 SANTALS AND THE TRIBE

Within this neat and ordered setting most Santals lead calm and happy lives. Each family usually possesses fields and while there are differences in economic status, the tribe is renowned for its sense of democratic equality. Wealth matters little and to such an extent are riches discounted that servants are often on a par with their masters.

There is a similar lack of social distinction between the various clans. According to myth, Santal clans originated as a means of avoiding incest. They began as seven, each of which was strictly monogamous but a little later, the number rose to twelve. After that, in the manner of Ten Little Nigger Boys, one of them, the Bedea clan, was lost and now there are only eleven. In the beginning, it is said, each clan was occupational – the Kiskus being chiefs or rajas, the Hembroms courtiers or princes, the Murmus priests, the Sorens fighters or soldiers, the Tudus blacksmiths and drummers, the Marandis merchants and the Baskes traders. The remaining four – the Besra, Core, Pauria and Hansdak' clans – were hunters and cultivators. Class distinctions, however, rapidly disappeared for there are no Santal legends that show them operating. On the contrary, in all the stories dealing with recent history, clan bears no relation to occupation and chiefs are never despots. Every Santal village includes members of different clans and there is nothing in ordinary life to set one clan above another. In the case of Tudus and Besras, marriages are avoided because of traditional enmity but in other respects the members of one clan are regarded as the friendly equals of another. Similarly, although each clan has a number of sub-clans or khunts – the Murmus possessing thirty-five, the Hembroms eighteen, the Kiskus seventeen – it is only in exceptional circumstances that the sub-clan has any practical significance. The son, for example, of a Murmu father and a Soren mother may marry a Soren girl but if his mother's sub-clan is Nij Soren, the girl's sub-clan must be different. Apart from minor matters such as these, a sub-clan has no marked role. It is the tribe, rather than the clan or sub-clan, that is significant in Santal life.

This loyalty to the tribe is expressed through various institutions – the annual hunt, often known as the Santal 'Parliament' or 'High Court'; a local council which comprises the headmen of five villages and is a court of appeal from village decisions; and the village meeting which determines day-to-day affairs. For deciding disputes or village matters, male Santals of the village meet as one. The manjhi or headman acts as president and may often give the meeting a firm lead. But the accepted principle is that no one may overrule any one else, that agreement is vital and that the sense of the meeting should prevail. Santal officials in fact are the servants, not the masters of the village and their role is purely functional. The headman summons village meetings, organises the annual festivals and administers communal property. The paranik or deputy headman collects rents and taxes, and the godet or village messenger is a means of summoning villagers to a meeting. The naeke or priest conducts the sacrifices but only on the villagers' behalf and even the jogmanjhi, or superintendent of youth, has little independent power. His duty is to prevent scandals and arrange marriages. But if a boy or girl offends against the tribal code, they are brought before the villagers as a whole, and it is these whose judgement settles the matter. At the Mag festival each year, village officials surrender their offices and, although this is mainly a matter of form, it is a pointed reminder that their tenure depends upon the village will. If an official dies, the villagers choose his successor. A member of his own family is normally appointed but in theory there is no bar to the choice of someone else. Within the village, Santals govern Santals.

3   THE SANTAL WORLD VIEW

If this assumption underlies the greater part of Santal life, there is none the less a vital area in which it is only partly true. Although fields, houses, men and women seem to constitute a Santal village, Santals regard them as at most a portion of their total world. From a dwelling 'somewhere in the sky', the Creator, Thakur Jiu, allots each Santal a term of life, rarely interferes and maintains a calm indifference. Sin Cando, the sun, with whom he is sometimes identified, has the same listless majesty. He organises the days and nights and is responsible for heat and cold, rain and sunshine. In most other respects he is unconcerned with human affairs and provided he is worshipped once in a lifetime, can be counted on to promote health and happiness. It is underneath the sun, beneath the clouds, that Santal rule is challenged. Here bongas or spirits roam and only by coming to terms with them can Santals be happy.

These bongas are said to inhabit three distinct kingdoms. The first is largely an underground replica of the upper land and in fact, for purposes of hunting, its forests blend with those of the ordinary world.

The second kingdom is the realm of the dead, a region vaguely located in the sky above the village. When his final funerary feast has been performed, a Santal becomes an ancestral bonga or hapram, enters this airy region and so long as he is remembered in the village, continues to influence its affairs.

But the third and most significant bonga territory is the village itself – its fields and houses, trees, hills, rocks and air. Here reside the sima or boundary bongas, bir or forest bongas, buru or mountain bongas, dadi or spring bongas, and khuntut' or tree-stump bongas. Within the street itself, each dwelling contains an orak' or house bonga. All these bongas are 'spirits of particular places', which the spot itself has partially suggested.

Other bongas, on the other hand, have a much wider role and special places are provided for them. Inside each house, a tiny compartment, known as the bhitar, contains the abge bongas – the bongas of the sub-clan to which a particular householder belongs. Beyond the village street a remnant of the original forest is jealously preserved as a jaher or sacred grove. Within its circle, three sal trees in a line are dedicated to Maran Buru (the Great Mountain), Moreko Turuiko (the Five-Six), and Jaher Era (the Lady of the Grove). A mahua tree is reserved for a fourth bonga, Gosae Era, a lonely figure stationed a little distance apart. Two other trees are assigned to Pargana bonga, the spirit of the regional chief, and Manjhi Haram, the bonga of the village manjhi or headman. The latter is also located in a small shed beside the headman's house, known as the manjhithan. Two stones are imbedded in a mud plinth, a sal post is set beside them, and a second and smaller pillar supports a pot of water. Here the villagers assemble and the founder's spirit is honoured. Far out in the forest is a special arbour reserved for the Rongo Ruji bonga – a bonga who expresses the mysteries of sex and whose 'head' is indicated by a stone.

There remains another class of bonga, not connected with any special place but vaguely associated with particular individuals, occasions or functions. These include the bonga husbands of witches, the nameless bongas who cause sickness, the bongas who assist an ojha or medicine-man, the naihar bonga who sometimes accompanies a woman when she joins her husband's house, 'Hindu festival' bongas, and finally a kisar bonga or brownie who is the means by which a man gets rich quickly. These either lurk in close proximity to their Santal wards or roam rest-lessly about.

All these bongas are, in a special sense, a Santal creation, monopoly or prerogative. Their prime concern is with Santals only. Indeed to the bongas, Hindus, Muslims, Christians or the British simply do not exist. Yet despite their purely Santal character, their attitudes to the tribe are curiously mixed. They constitute on the one hand an independent race, living a life of their own, but on the other hand, vitally involved in every-thing Santal. Nothing a Santal does can escape their attention and while it is only in special circumstances that Santals can visit their underground kingdom or actually stumble on bongas in the village, the bongas, for their part, are always mingling with Santals and interfering in their lives. They resemble, in fact, invisible associates of three distinct kinds – those who are capable of sudden vicious behaviour, those who are either protec-tive or at any rate well-disposed, and those who are intimately, even desperately concerned with tribal welfare and integrity.

The bongas who are naturally spiteful and from whom inaction is all that can be hoped, include the bonga husbands of witches, the anonymous dispensers of sickness, the sima or boundary bongas, all the bongas of forests, rocks, springs and tree-stumps, whether within or outside the village frontiers, the Rongo Ruji bonga, 'Hindu festival' bongas and finally, the bonga of the house. Of this vast and miscellaneous crew, a boundary bonga is particularly feared. 'It causes snakes and leopards to attack men in the fields.' The house bonga is not so hostile but is like a touchy, 'testy' woman, quick to take offence and apt to cause disease. The Rongo Ruji bonga is regarded as a female obsessed with sex. She resembles the leading character in Beardsley's 'Story of Tannhauser and Venus' but vents her restless impulses more in promoting hunting failures than in causing sexual troubles. The bongas of the forests, hills and springs are liable to spoil the crops or cause accidents, and the bonga of a Hindu festival may induce a sudden feeling of mysterious insecurity.

The second type of bonga on the other hand is altogether beneficent. Ojhas or medicine-men have special retained bongas through whose aid the forces of evil can be countered. Bonga girls occasionally fraternise with Santal boys or take them as husbands or lovers. But it is the abge bongas who count most. Each sub-clan has special bongas, the names of which are known only to the head of the household. If a Santal dies without telling them to his son, the latter must take another member of the sub-clan into his confidence, go quietly to a lonely place and there be briefed. Only after he has learnt the bongas' names can he solemnise the annual sacrifice which every household is expected to perform. Yet even as a junior member he is not denied their firm protective backing. To be admitted to the sub-clan is to be associated with its bongas and from the date of his birth ceremony onwards, a Santal lives and moves, fortified and protected by their watchful care.

If the abge bongas protect Santals as individuals, it is above all the bongas of the sacred grove who supervise them as a tribe. The greatest of these is Maran Buru (the Great Mountain). Under the pseudonym of Lita, he is supposed to have dwelt with the first Santals, instructed them in sex, introduced them to rice-beer and escorted them on their first wanderings. When the Santals were trapped in a 'stonehouse', perhaps a landslide in a narrow pass, Lita broke through it with his axe and brought them all to safety. Finally in the country, termed Sikhar, he disclosed his true identity as Maran Buru and instructed the Santals how to establish their sacred groves, install their tribal bongas and make proper offerings. He then disappeared but ever since has been loved and venerated as a genial, kindly grandfather.

Slightly inferior to Maran Buru in Santal regard but still of great importance are Jaher Era (the Lady of the Grove) and Moreko Turuiko (the Five-Six). These two bongas are closely associated and at the Baha or Flower festival they share a single shed with Maran Buru himself. Their identity and relationship, however, is full of mystery. Buchanan writes of the Santals, 'the most common objects of their worship are Marang Burha, an old man, Marako his younger brother, and their sister Jaher Burhi, an old good-natured creature, who never does them any harm'. Man describes them as 'the five brothers and the one sister', while Hunter writes Maniko for Moreko Turuiko and describes him as 'the husband as well as brother of the female deity in the triad, Jaher Era'. Neither Kolean Haram nor Bodding throw any light on the curious numeral – Five-Six – which comprises their name, but C. L. Mukherjea notes from Mayurbhanj, 'Another village deity is Moreko Turuiko who is now a single entity but addressed in the plural. The Santals believe that there were five brothers (*more*, five) who were wedded to six sisters (*turui*, six) named Dangi, Pungi, Hisi, Dumni, Chita and Kapra. They are supposed to preside over the welfare of the village. His younger sister, Gosae Era, constitutes a separate deity of the Jaherthan; Jaher Era, another sister of Moreko is the goddess of the Jaherthan named after her.' In other myths which I myself recorded, the Five-Six are either five brothers with Jaher Era as their mother; five brothers, plus five brothers over again with Gosae Era, a girl, making six, and finally five *or* six brothers.

Associated with these three spirits but in a slightly inferior position are three other bongas – Gosae Era, the girl connected with the Five-Six, Pargana bonga, the first pargana who still rules the local region, and Manjhi Haram, the original founder of the village or the current headman's immediate predecessor. The latter is worshipped at the manjhithan and in the sacred grove, the village is in his charge and he acts as the spiritual adviser of the current headman.

This third group of bongas constitutes the prime concern of Santals. Other bongas may vex and trouble them but if the great or 'national' bongas are ignored or outraged, the very foundations of Santal life are threatened. To pass their days happily, to experience to the full the joys of tribal existence, Santals must not only attune themselves to village customs but unite in honouring their ghostly protectors.

Such a double world, a world at once visible and invisible, has a number of repercussions on Santal behaviour. So long as life proceeds without disturbance, the bongas are treated very much as if they were only another kind of Santal. They are accorded the normal courtesies of Santal life and steps are taken to show that even if they are not in the immediate forefront of Santal minds, they are far from being ignored or forgotten. To honour the bongas of his sub-clan, and ensure their continuing care, each house-holder sacrifices a pig at the harvest festival of Sohrae. Whenever rice-beer is drunk, a little is spilt on the ground for Maran Buru. Whenever a meal is taken, a small fragment is put aside for the house bonga, the immediate ancestors and the bongas of the sub-clan. Finally if sickness comes and a bonga is diagnosed as the cause, a special sacrifice is made.

These expedients are individual concerns. Other courses of action, however, lie with the village. At every crisis in the agricultural year, a festival is held, fowls are subscribed for, and with these offerings the priest appeases malignant bongas and beseeches the major ones to continue their blessings.

The first of these occasions – the Erok' festival – occurs in July when seeds for sowing are broadcast. The priest visits the sacred grove and squatting by the three trees offers a chick in turn to Maran Buru, Jaher Era and the Five-Six. Gosae Era, Pargana bonga and Manjhi Haram are next approached and the offerings end with the sima or boundary bongas and the various bongas of the fields. As the priest offers, he says to each bonga, 'Take this in the name of the Erok' festival. Where we sow, may twelve shoots come. Let there be rain and storm. May the fields be flooded. Let no illness, no ache of belly or head enter this village. Bear all sickness away. Bear it on a pole of gold. Carry it with strings of gold. If there are widows and women of bad omen who tear and fold the leaf, who doom and mark down, frown on them and destroy their good omens. Show them no favour. If they lurk in hiding, save us from them. Keep us from all harm. May the cattle roam at will. Protect them with your covering hood.'

After Erok', the Hariar festival is performed so that the paddy may grow green. Fowls are offered as at Erok' and the same invocation is made.

The next occasion is Iri Gundli in early September. This is for eating the first millet after harvesting. No fowls are killed but the first millet is offered in the sacred grove and at the manjhithan. The priest invokes the same spirits and, addressing first the major bongas and then the boundary ones, prays 'May no ache of belly or head come from eating this crop. Keep all illness away.'

A little later comes Janthar. This is also a festival of first fruits. A pig or goat is chased for sacrifice and the kudam naeke or special supplementary priest offers it with the first paddy to Pargana Bonga. 'Accept this pig,' he says. 'May no ache of belly or head assail us as we eat. When we reap the paddy and thresh it, make it more than it is. Increase the bongas' share. If there are rats and mice, stop them from eating it.'

When all the harvest is in, and the threshing floors are piled with straw, the Sohrae is celebrated in late December or January. This is a 'harvest home', a period of relaxation, a time of drinking and dancing. But here also the bongas are not forgotten. Fowls are offered in a rice field to the same bongas as before and the priest prays that the feast may pass 'without ache of belly or head, and in coming and going, all danger may be far away'.

The next festival is Mag, for cutting thatching grass. The same friendly and hostile bongas are given fowls and the priest prays that the thatching grass may be abundant. The village children take a little thatch, make toy bullock carts and run laughing and shouting through the village.

Finally before any fresh flowers are worn or mahua flowers eaten, the Baha or Flower festival is performed in March. This is a celebration of the sacred grove itself. Two sheds are put up, one to Maran Buru, Jaher Era and the Five-Six, and the other to Gosae Era. Fowls are offered and the same bongas are asked to free the village from sickness and witches, preserve the crops and cattle and ensure children.

In addition to these festivals which are celebrated every year, a special festival of Mak' More is performed whenever sickness is raging in the village. The headman vows animals to the Five-Six in return for their removing the disease. When the epidemic is over, goats and fowls are bought by a house-to-house levy and sacrifices are made in the grove.

If all these festivals are duly performed, the worse expressions of bonga malice may be averted and the major bongas will be induced to maintain their daily care.

But besides being accorded these honours, the national bongas must on no account be polluted. At birth and death, pollution is unavoidable and so long as they remain in this state, their care is withdrawn. The cleansing ritual must therefore be promptly performed so that the village may again enjoy their aid. At other times pollution may be due to the faults of individuals. If the tribal rules of sex are infringed, the leading bongas are defiled. Here also appropriate ritual must remedy the lapse and until it is performed the whole village is devoid of bonga care. The bongas, in fact, are no mere alien hierarchy. When hostile, they are not unlike the demons of medieval Europe – a Santal reaction to the mysteries of existence, its sudden calamities, its abrupt hazards and chances. When benign, they represent all that the tribe acutely values. The national bongas are 'guardians of the faith, the army of unalterable law'. They assist Santals to be themselves and by their active intervention sustain welfare and morale.

CHAPTER II

Early Years

I BIRTH

'When a Santal woman is with child' Duli Murmu said, 'her flowers stop. Her nipples go black. Her belly grows big and her face and body get thin. Her neck becomes a stick. In six months she feels the child stirring within her.'

During this time, she is subject to strange cravings. She will want to eat meat and fish, or puffed rice and laddu – a form of sweet. She may also crave for soil from an ant-hill and for the special kind of earth with which Santals wash their hair. At the same time, she must take a number of careful precautions. While daily intercourse with her husband is not only permissible but advocated – 'It will make the child big and strong' – she must on no account have relations with any other man. 'If she does the child will be born with pain. She may even die in child birth.' If there is a thunderstorm she must put her fingers in her ears and if a death occurs in her house she must keep out of the way when the corpse is carried out. If a death occurs in the village she must on no account catch sight of the dead body. If by accident or in spite of taking every care she sees a corpse and its eyes are open the eyes of her child will be 'wide and staring' and move 'like the eyes of an owl'. If, however, the eyes of the dead person are shut, the child's eyes will either be small or never open at all.

Should there be an eclipse of the moon or sun while she is carrying a child, she must go inside her house and sit quietly until it is over. Were she to break a piece of wood or stick while the eclipse was still in progress, an arm or leg of the child would be broken or it would be born with bent limbs. If she is making leaf-cups and tears or pins the leaves together, the child will be born with a split lip. If an eclipse catches her while she is digging up or planting turmeric roots the child will either be born with two fingers joined together or his hands may have an extra finger. If at this time she notices the sight of a medium in a state of possession the child's head will wag to and fro and he will never be able to keep it still.

Apart from these, however, there are few restrictions on her movements. She can continue to assist her husband at sacrifices and can go to all the festivals. She can also join in dances and attend weddings. She does not have to avoid any field with growing crops. A pregnant woman must, however, never go to a lonely place in a forest or to a river or spring where there is a bonga and if she has to cross a river she should always see that others are with her. 'If she goes near a bonga, the bonga is enraged and the child will at once come out.'

Provided these warnings are heeded, a birth is rarely attended with any difficulty. The mother lies on a cot, a midwife is called and after delivery, the umbilical cord is cut with an arrow and the placenta is buried. Within two days the mother is up and about but the midwife continues to attend her for five days from the birth. If she is a Santal she eats her meals with the family and on the final day is presented with a cloth, a pot of rice-beer and a few annas – eight for a boy, four for a girl. If she is from the Hindu caste of Dom, she is given the same rewards but draws her food uncooked. If the delivery is protracted and the midwife is compelled to pull the child out with her hand, she is given five rupees more and may sometimes demand and get a goat.

When the baby has come, the news is announced by saying, 'Some new guests have arrived' while its sex is learnt by asking a member of the family whether it carries on the head or on the shoulder. If the baby is a boy, the answer is 'On the shoulder'. If it is a girl, the reply is 'On the head', alluding to the way in which girls and women carry water-pots.

As the neighbours learn the news, someone from the family is sent to tell the priest and give him some oil for washing with. Since the bongas of the grove are polluted by the birth, the priest is also defiled. On receiving the news, therefore, he at once goes and bathes – doing so 'in the name of the child and its father'. Later, on the third, fifth or any subsequent uneven day, the cleansing ceremony of nim dak' mandi – mixing nim leaves with rice-water – is performed. This ceremony is of special importance for until it is done, the whole household remains polluted. Its members cannot offer to their bongas or eat and drink with others. The bongas of the grove are also defiled and village worship is for the time being at a standstill.

If the birth occurs on the eve of a wedding or a festival or even after they have started, emergency action must be taken. The rule of allowing at least two days to elapse is abruptly rescinded. Flour, nim and rice-water are hurriedly got ready and the ceremony is done forthwith.

Khare Hembrom of Telni gave birth to a girl the night before the Sohrae festival. No one wanted to delay the celebrations so the ritual was performed the next morning and after that the festival began.

33

Similarly in Nimakalan, the wife of Surai Hansdak' gave birth to a girl the night before a wedding. The whole arrangements would have been disturbed if there had been delay so the ceremony was done the next morning and the wedding went on.

If the child is born the day before a new moon, this also involves immediate action. 'After bathing the child', Bompas states, 'they place an old broom in the mother's arms instead of the child; then the mother takes the "child" and throws it out on the dung heap behind the house. The midwife then takes an old broom and old winnowing fan and sweeps up a little rubbish onto the fan and takes it and throws it on the dung hill. There she sees the "child" and calls out "Here is a child on the dung heap". Then she pretends to sweep the "child" with the broom into the winnowing fan and lifts it up and carries it into the house and asks the people of the house whether they will rear it. They ask what wages she will give them and she promises to give them a heifer when the actual child is grown up. If this is not done the baby will be unlucky; if it is a boy, however often he may marry, his wife will die, and if it is a girl, her husbands will die also.'

When the day for nim dak' mandi arrives, five persons must be present – the priest, the parents, the midwife and the child itself. If the priest is absent, either the deputy priest or his son officiates and if these are also absent, either a villager acts as priest by proxy or a dummy priest is made by planting a stick in the ground. If for any reason the child's father is absent, its grandfather, a relative or a proxy acts as substitute.

The cleansing ceremony begins with the shaving of the priest. This is done by a villager who acts for the occasion as a barber and is confined to dressing the cheeks and chin. After this, the headman, the other villagers and the child's father are shaved. The barber then cuts a little patch on the child's head, carefully collects the hair in a leaf-cup, pours some oil on it and hands it to the midwife. The latter rubs the child's head with oil, washing-earth and turmeric. After that, the men go to a tank and wash.

While they are away, the midwife takes the arrow which cut the umbilical cord, winds two threads of cotton round it, gathers up the cut hair and goes with the women for bathing. At the tank she plants the arrow in the water, makes marks of lamp black and vermilion on the ground, puts the child's hair and a thread in the water and lets them float away. Then the women wash and go back to the house and the midwife soaks the other thread in turmeric and ties it round the child's waist.

When everyone is back, the mother sits on the verandah with the child in her lap and some leaves of the atnak' tree in her hand. The midwife mixes cowdung in water and lets it trickle into the left hand of the mother.

34

The mother dabs it on her head and also sips a little. After that three leaf-cups of the mixture are handed to the midwife who punctures each cup with a finger and tosses them away. The child is then taken inside. Here two little cakes are pressed against its cheeks, legs and chest. The midwife makes a thin white paste from powdered rice, marks the four legs of the mother's cot and then goes round the courtyard dabbing first the chest of the priest and then the other villagers in the order of their shaving. She ends with the child's father. When the men are finished with, she begins with the priest's wife and marks the other women in the same order as their husbands.

The child's name is then announced. Its clan and sub-clan are always those of its father and provided the marriage is not in ghar jawae form, a first son is always named after its father's father and a first girl after its father's mother. This announcement of the name formally admits the child to its clan and gives it the protection of the abge bongas. The mid-wife then salutes the priest and after that, the other villagers. Rice is boiled with nim leaves and after the head of the house has offered some to the immediate ancestors, the villagers drink the remainder and disperse.

2 GAMES

From the age of five or six, Santal boys and girls begin to make themselves useful. Girls are taught to husk rice and fetch water. They do small jobs in the house and go about with babies tied in a cloth nodding on their backs. They learn to watch the goats and herd them in the fields. They accompany their mothers to the jungle, lend a hand with the cooking and get accustomed to the long striding walk to market. When they are taller, they take out the bigger cattle, graze them on the uplands or in the forest and bring them home at sunset.

Santal boys are also occupied. Until they are old enough to plough, they spend the greater part of the day herding buffaloes and cattle. They learn to make and play the flute and to shoot birds with blunt-tipped arrows. They also trap quails and go about with the birds gently whistling in their cages.

It is from this time that boys and girls begin to know each other. During the leisured grazing of the cattle, they often meet and play games and in the early evening come together in the village street and sometimes play till supper. Most of these games are jolly romps but some provide oppor-tunities for gentle fumbling embraces. All of them accustom the children to each other's ways. They scramble together and from their very early years handle each other with natural familiarity. Through this play the children establish the easy joking friendships out of which their later romances mature.

Among these games a favourite is pusi pusi. The boys and girls hold hands in a circle. The 'master of the house' goes round filling the hands with dust. The dust is 'fish', 'curds', 'milk', 'cow's meat'. He goes away to get water and a 'cat' with a cloth tail comes and dashes the dust down. The master returns and asks where all the food has gone. The circle replies 'The headman's cat has eaten it'. The master sees the cat and goes round the circle calling 'Gunun gunun' to it. At each archway, the cat and the master slap hands. Suddenly the master chases it, the two run in and out of the circle, the master whacking the cat with a cloth. The chase goes on and on and then the circle rushes in. It catches and 'kills' the cat and throws it outside the village. Finally the circle becomes a ring of vultures which huddle round the 'cat' and pick and pinch its flesh.

Another pantomimic game is sim sim or 'chicken, chicken'. In this game the boys and girls form a line holding each other, while a boy flaps his arms like a kite. The kite has to pick off the endmost player without itself being caught. As it dives first one way and then another, the line sways violently about and tries to check it. Finally when only one 'chicken' is left, there is a great struggle between the two and they throw each other down and wrestle on the ground.

A game which always excites delight and mirth is kan kotra. This is named after a weevil which makes a creaking sound in wood. Boys and girls stand in a circle while one goes round with a forefinger in each ear. He says to each player, 'Would you like an insect in your ear?' They answer 'Pig's excrement', 'Goat's droppings', 'Watery stools'. As he goes round, various pairs try to change places. If one is caught he takes the place of the questioner.

In marak' bele or 'the peacock's egg', boys and girls squat round in a circle, facing inwards. One of them picks up a stone with his big toe and goes walking round. He quietly leaves the stone behind one of the girls and goes on round the circle. If the sitter does not notice it, she gets her bottom spanked and has to walk round with the stone herself. If she detects the stone behind her, she pounces on it and springs away.

A variant of this is thoc' thoc'. In this game, instead of walking round with the stone between the toes, the walker creeps round with the stone in his hand. He pretends to leave it behind each sitter. He leaves it behind one, goes on round the circle and then tries to spank the victim before the stone is discovered.

Another common game is sakam binda or 'tying the leaf'. The boys and girls form a long line. The two at the end make an arch and the 'head' brings the line round. It reaches the tail and dives under the waiting arms. When it has gone completely through, the third player from the end turns round, locks his or her arm to the 'tail' and the line again comes round, and dives between the second and the third. In this way more and more of the tail goes 'dead' until there is only the head which doubles round itself. The line is now linked up with all the arms criss-crossing. It then curls in on itself until there is only a tight struggling mob laughing and jumping. When the jumping is over the cluster straightens out and the line moves on. The boys and girls now separate and end with a game called jambro bin, 'the snake which was in the leaf'. They form a long line like a snake. The 'head' starts to move and the line runs waggling down the village. Two girls 'who found it in the forest' rush along behind, whacking at the others with sticks.

Another game, bikhai birkhai, is a form of 'Blind Man's Buff'. The boys and girls form a circle and each of them takes the name of a fish. A boy is blind-folded and as the circle goes round he hops about like a frog dashing at the line to make a catch. If he catches and guesses the 'fish' correctly, he takes its place. Otherwise, he goes on catching until a fish is guessed.

Merom bhet' bhet' or 'goat's bleat' is a form of 'Oranges and Lemons'. The boys and girls form a double line and make an archway of hands. The line then turns in on itself and each pair goes creeping down the tunnel clapping its hands as it goes. When everyone is through, the arch reverses and the line goes creeping back.

A game that always ends in laughter is caki dar. The boys and girls squat down in a line, one behind the other holding each other's shoulders and gripping the hips with the knees. Then the line leans forward and heels from side to side. As it rocks it chants, 'Caki dar dahu dambat' dombok'.' When the chant is over, the line hops forward like a vulture. It goes on in great clumsy jerks until at last it collapses.

In durup' tengon or 'sitting, standing', a boy or girl stands up while the others sit around. The sitters try in turn to get up without being touched by the stander. If anyone fails, he or she is 'out'.

A counting-out game, which is confined to Santal girls, is icin bicin. The girls squat down in a circle with their hands pressed out in the centre. They start to sing and as they chant, a girl counts them out. A 'hand' that the chant ends on goes out. At last it is a tussle between a 'hand' and the earth itself. When the counting out is over, the girls form a bedstead by sitting in two lines with their legs in rows. The girl who did the counting lies down on the 'cot' and the others pinch and prick her like bugs. The girl kills the 'bugs' with the help of a 'light' and edges gingerly over the legs. As she goes she asks each player, 'Is your pounder new or old?' If it is new she picks the leg up and taps it smartly on the ground. If it is old she gives it a dull thud. Then she asks, 'Is your grinder new or old?' and rubs each heel on the ground.

Finally there is a game, also played only by girls, which often produces great excitement – horo tase or 'spreading rice'. Girls sit down in a line with their legs out. Two girls then go down the line. The first has a stone which she slips under a hand while the second shakes each fist to see if the stone is inside. They go down the line and the second girl guesses. If she guesses right, she has the turn of slipping the stone under a hand. When this has gone on for some time, the sitting girls put one foot on another and pretend to be drying paddy on a fire. The two leaders put some cloth on their heads and pretend to be old women going to fetch water. Suddenly the girls cry out 'Old women, your paddy is burning'. The two rush back, take down each foot and give it a twist. They then spread the 'paddy' out between the legs and go away for water. Again the girls cry out 'Old women, the pigeons are eating your paddy'. Again the two come hurrying back and pretend to drive the birds away. They go away once more. The girls cry out 'Old women, the paddy is all scorched up'. They come back and go along the line sampling the paddy by putting an ear between their teeth and knocking chins. The paddy is at last ready and they pound it by knocking one foot on another. As they pound they say 'How does your mother pound?' The girl answers 'Dhakur kuduk'. 'How does your mother winnow?' 'Petec' petec'' and each girl waves her hands like a fan. 'How does she clean the grain?' 'Aithan paitan khode jala khaijur khaijur' and the leader catches her right ear with her left hand and right toe with her right hand and swings her up and down. 'How does your mother grind pulse?' 'Rigdai rigdai rigdai' and she catches her big toe and moves it round like a grinder. 'How does she winnow the pulse?' 'Petec' petec'.' 'How does she clean it?' 'Cobhar cobhar' and she pounds her foot up and down. Then the leader forages about for some sticks and puts them in the toes of the girls. These are 'lights' and the two lie down on the legs like a cot. As they lie the girls pinch them and they cry out, 'How badly the mosquitoes are biting!' They leap up, take the 'lights' and 'kill' the mosquitoes. Once more they lie down. Again the girls pinch them and they get up for their lamps. Then all the girls run away. The two follow, calling 'There go the mosquitoes'. They smack them with their hands and with the slapping the game ends.

3 RIDDLES

As a change from grazing cattle, playing games, or assisting in the house, Santal children amuse themselves with riddles. These forms of verbal play do not have special functions but spring from euphemisms and kennings which liberally besprinkle tribal talk.

Certain symbols for example are constantly being used for avoiding the unpleasant or disguising the sad and painful. A Santal who sees that an old man's teeth are decaying does not refer directly to the teeth but says 'the white pebbles are falling' or 'the grinding stones are wanting'. When someone dies, the villagers do not mention death but say 'he has gone down to the ground', 'he has gone to herd the alligators', 'he has got tired', 'he has fled', or 'he has gone across'. A Santal, who goes out in the dark hours of the morning, does not say that he intends to urinate. He simply says that 'he is going to the courtyard' or 'to open the outlet of a tank'. If he goes to excrete, he says he is 'going to pay a moneylender', 'to meet a marriage party' or 'pay his rent'. Santal women, noticing that a girl is pregnant, do not directly allude to her condition but employ phrases such as 'her body is in bud', 'she is sitting heavy at home', 'her body has altered', 'she is carrying a bundle', 'she is going with a full form'.

Other phrases are simple pleasantries. At a wedding or a feast the guests are 'tethered' when their legs are washed and 'tied with a new rope' when they are given rice-beer. Those who are tired of waiting say that 'the flour ants are eating them', while hosts who are conscious that a meal is late offer mock apologies and say 'we are spreading our friends out to dry'. A boy who is particularly hungry complains that 'a standing fever is on him' or that 'his middle boy has still not got a wife'. Distributing leaf-cups is 'sending round the boats', cooking maize is 'a leopard growling', while waiting for a second course is 'getting the threshing floor ready'. When the meal is over and the guests get up, 'they straighten the ends of their spines' and 'convert their bodies from baskets on the ground to palmyra palms'. If they have fed well they say they have 'covered their kettle drums' and 'loaded the carts' but if they have been given only a little parched rice they complain of getting only 'a few ants' drums'. During the 'hunger' period of the year when Santals often dilute their rice with water, they say they are 'looking at the stars'. Finally at the end of all meals when the women are cleaning the utensils, they 'make the big and little axes shine'.

Similar verbal stratagems refer to other aspects of life. The penis, for example, is often known as 'babu' (the young gentleman), 'the bent pestle', 'the mallet of bar wood', 'the bunch of lopon fruits' or 'the goats' tail'. The testicles are referred to as 'the two eggs' and 'the pumpkin of the underworld', while semen is described as 'marriage water'. The vagina is called 'mai' (girl or daughter), 'the buried bonga', 'the little cockroach', 'the small bear', 'the husking mortar', 'the scorpion hole', 'the flesh of a mussel' or 'the hollow where men fall'. In a similar way, sexual intercourse is often referred to in words such as 'they laughed and joked together', 'she put a flower-bud in her hair', 'they went off to eat figs', 'the girls are spreading out their tail feathers', 'she swept his courtyard', 'the boy took her to drink water', 'he is always stealing skin', 'the girl has been smelt'. Santal parents seeking a match-maker say 'we must find a golden oriole' and when the marriage is arranged, they announce that 'they have shut up the girl' or 'tied her to the boy'. Fixing the wedding date is 'sending the knot', while calling off a marriage is 'stopping the waterway'. A goat killed for a wedding feast is 'the mountain vegetable', a pig is 'an elephant' and women at a wedding are 'the beardless rajas'. When the wedding is over and the girl has gone to a rich husband, the villagers remark 'the girl has perched on a thick branch', 'she has found a shelter under a big tree', 'she has got a creeper's pole to support her', and after an ordinary wedding, they say 'the calf has been tied'. If a family wants a widow or a divorced girl as a bride, they ask for 'a vessel with a cracked base'.

There is a similar set of phrases for childbirth. When a woman is about to bear a child, Santals remark that 'she has gone to watch a corner of the house', 'her sitting days have come', 'she has collected a bundle of seeds'. When labour pains start 'her water is hot' and women assisting at the confinement may say of the child 'it is reaching the socket but has not yet passed the door'. When the mother is delivered, the villagers remark that 'she has had a flower-bud fall', 'she has come down from the dry tree', or 'the paddy bale has burst'.

But besides these sentences which gently or jokingly dispose of difficulties, Santals also employ a number of kennings. These are used when too direct a reference to the subject is believed to harbour danger. In the forest, for example, the mention of a leopard may bring the animal charging on the hunters. They therefore refer to 'the wild cat', 'the hornless bullock' or 'the red ox'. If bears are known to be about, they do not say 'bears' but talk of 'hairy caterpillars'. Similarly when a man is bitten by a snake, the snake is referred to as 'a fibre', 'a twig' or 'the long man'.

Even more widely used is the 'false' kenning. Here there is no particular danger to be avoided and a symbol is resorted to simply as a form of jesting speech. In this way a husband is known as 'the umbrella shadow', 'the one who stirs the curry', 'the woman's bridle' or 'the jaher tree'. A wife is 'the old house site', 'the ruling bonga', 'the basket bonga', 'the load' or 'the yoke'. Children are described as 'the ears of paddy', 'the paddy seedlings', 'the young calves', 'the whimpering ones', 'the young parrots', 'the fruit of the tree', 'the yolks of eggs' or 'the little pumpkin fiddles'. A mother becomes 'the milk-tree', a raw girl 'the unopened flower', water 'the frog's platform' and a goat 'the leaf-tearer'. A stone is 'the soap of centuries', a thunderbolt is 'sky fire', while an enemy is 'a thorn in the eye'. Rice-water is 'black cow's milk' and a pot of rice-beer is 'the black girl'. A small man is called 'the field mouse', hands and legs are 'leaves and branches' while a full-grown girl is 'a clucking hen'. A woman with fuzzy hair is 'an owl'. A stay-at-home is 'a well frog'. Women talking are 'the noise of drums'. A pig is 'the earth rooter', a cock 'the fence owl' while maize cobs are 'bats hanging in the house'. Clothes are 'feathers', milk is 'white water' and a stick 'a faithful companion'. A drum is sometimes 'a gay girl' and sometimes 'a tortoise egg'. An angry man has eyes 'red with blood'. Tears are 'eye water' and cloth a 'fence'. A Hindu is a 'cat'. A lazy girl who only gossips is 'a swimmer'. A jealous lover is a 'man with burning eyes'. Rice-beer is 'furrow water' and magic is 'a fiery arrow'.

These turns of riddle-speech are such a common part of Santal practice that formal riddles or kudum are sometimes barely distinguishable. Their main difference is one of form. Whereas a riddle-phrase or a kenning comes naturally into conversation, a formal riddle is always supposed to be a question and to need a slick and rapid answer. Boys and girls use them, in fact, as tests of wit, as ways of demonstrating each other's cleverness. Yet although amusement is the primary object, riddles are not without importance for later life. They bring 'remote concepts into mutual irritation'. They reveal fantastic similarities and emphasise unusual parallels. They accustom the children in fact to thinking in images and when in due course they learn the village songs, they are immediately at home with their complicated symbolism. The kudum is the Santal child's unconscious introduction to poetry.

In the following riddles, details of landscape, day-to-day sights and sounds, aspects of village life and general Santal behaviour are widely invoked.

I

They grow it in a field and thresh it on the skin.   Tobacco.

41

II

The father is in the mother's bed and the children have gone to sell clothes.

The cotton plant.

III

The lapwing in the rains with only one leg.

A bamboo umbrella.

IV

A little bird flies about in the thicket of slim bamboos.

A louse.

V

A rabbit runs without a tail.
A dog goes after with no legs.
A man without a head looks on.

Frog, snake and crab.

VI

It enters the house but is not a thief.
It enters the cowshed but is not a leopard.

A mosquito.

VII

Two brothers and both are black.

Eyes.

VIII

The water of five rivers will come out through a single hole.

The udders of a cow.

IX

The black sahib of Calcutta has hair within his bones.

A coconut.

X

A pair of fans on the top of a hill.

Ears.

XI

An earthen pot upside down in the rivers.

A turtle.

XII

The raja's plate which you cannot wash.

A coiled-up snake.

XIII

All the jungle burns but the tail of the quail is not burnt.

The root of a tree.

XIV

Sweet the blood but not the flesh.

Rice-beer and its dregs.

XV

The man who runs around the little hillock.   A razor.

XVI

The man with the single leg and the twelve ribs.   An umbrella.

XVII

Old teeth that waggle.   Tamarind pods.

XVIII

The black string on the path.   Ants.

XIX

I aimed an arrow at the ground and it hit my nose.   A fart.

XX

The young buffalo squats while its rope grazes.   A kind of pumpkin.

XXI

A moon weeps in the middle of a tank.   A cake of flour
simmering in oil.

XXII

A man who is always lying down but gets up
when a thread is put in his bottom.   A needle.

XXIII

When the dead ox lows, the fence begins to shake.   A tumdak' (drum)
with girls dancing.

XXIV

The man who vomits rice when they kick
his bottom   A rice pounder.

XXV

Silver the branch, little the fruit, big the tree.   A pipal tree.

XXVI

The tank that overflows when dirt falls in it.   An eye.

XXVII

A white goat is tied with a black rope.   A silkworm.

XXVIII

The bird that makes a nest with its buttocks.   A needle.

XXIX

Can you climb an old woman's back?   A wall.

43

XXX
Coiled-up bowels.   Paddy rope.

XXXI
Hullo, you black one, where are you
galloping? This way, you bearded paranik,
trailing in the water.   A leech and shrimp.

XXXII
The cow that chews with its belly.   A grinding stone.

XXXIII
The big house with the single pole.   A bamboo umbrella.

XXXIV
A white flower blossoms on a dead tree.   A feather on a bridal
                                                       drum.

XXXV
The two men who are always beating each other.   The lips.

XXXVI
The fried white pulse in the little pot.   Teeth and mouth.

XXXVII
A bamboo with seven eyes.   A flute.

XXXVIII
The white rolling pin is drowned and the
cotton floats.   Rice and bubbles.

XXXIX
The black deer that drinks red water.   A louse.

XL
He has a crown but is not a king.
He wakes men but is not a watchman.   A cock.

XLI
The elephant's eggs that are like a drum.   Coconuts.

XLII
The black dog that loiters in the rivers.   A leech.

XLIII
The woman who always ties her black goat to
the back of the house.   A way of doing
                                                       the hair.

XLIV

The hobby-horse from the jungle on whom the
women soldiers canter.

A rice pounder.

XLV

When young they keep apart.
When old they come together.

Thatching grass.

XLVI

Two men who sit on one stool but do not
touch each other.

Pots on a hearth.

XLVII

I press you when sleeping at evening. I rise and
desert you in the morning. A little later I drag
you out.

A cot.

XLVIII

In a dry tree the cockscomb flowers.

A fungus on a tree
stump.

XLIX

The pale-skinned soldiers who lie head
downwards.

Bats.

L

The water of four rice lands in a single field.

The udders of a cow.

LI

The bird with a tail on both its sides.

A leaf-cup.

LII

A bullock lows in a narrow street.

A fart.

LIII

A buffalo that sits in the rivers.

A boulder.

LIV

The dove's pot at the back of the house.

An earring.

LV

The man who speaks when his belly is tickled.

A violin.

LVI

The grubby mouth of an old woman.

A niche in a wall.

LVII

The old man's tooth that dangles.

A mango.

LVIII

When the dead ox lows, the goat bleats and draws near.

A drum and pair of small cymbals.

LIX

When the string round his loins is pulled, the boy weeps.

The pole of a well.

LX

A man below a ridge stays with his mouth open.

A fishing trap.

LXI

The boy who cries when he is kissed.

A flute.

LXII

The woman who has a child every month.

A fig tree.

LXIII

They trail in a line. On their heads are two horns. They have no wings. They lay eggs on the leaves of trees.

Red ants.

LXIV

Without a drum it dances and every time it eats it bathes.

A kingfisher.

LXV

On a hillock a glinting fish is roaming.

A razor.

LXVI

The cow lows and the calf scampers away.

A gun.

LXVII

On the bank of a river a thick rope is stretched.

A line of black ants.

LXVIII

The leveller that crosses the thickly wooded mountain.

A comb on the head.

LXIX

On the banks of the rivers it flaps its wings.

A fishing net.

LXX

The bird that eats twigs and leaves, drinks rain water and has droppings like a ring.

A green pigeon.

LXXI

A hundred fathers-in-law with only one belly.

An onion.

46

LXXII

The flashing haunches of a cat. The eyes.

LXXIII

The wriggling tail with the branching antlers. A scorpion.

LXXIV

A sickle hangs in the sky. The new moon.

LXXV

A field is full of a goat's droppings and a handful of cowdung. The sky, the stars and moon.

LXXVI

Guns that lean against the sides of the rivers. Shrimps.

LXXVII

The ox that gorges its navel. A fishing net.

LXXVIII

The bullock that raises its tail when it has fully eaten. Scales.

LXXIX

The dark girl who never has a bath. A pot for frying maize.

LXXX

The boy who weeps when he is taken to the end of the village. A flute.

4 PROVERBS

'The proverbs of a people,' Westermarck has said, 'are valuable documents concerning its character and temperament, opinions and feelings, manners and customs. They are not only reflections of life; they also play an active part in it. Most proverbs are expressions of feelings or opinions or are intended to influence people's wills and actions.'

The majority of Santal proverbs are similes that either point a moral or enshrine a tribal experience. 'Mocking words itch like burrs.' 'Plenty and a pestle, famine and an axe.' 'A dog barks at an elephant's arse.' 'Cunning dogs are bitten in their tails.' 'Gossip stings like cold water.' 'A tune and a flute wander everywhere.' 'Children are as mothers make them.' These are so explicit that comment is unnecessary. 'Pigs go to their wallows.'

Natures do not change. 'Thieves have no legs.' They act so quietly that no one ever hears them. 'A cowdung fire smokes.' Secrets cannot be kept hid. 'A blind man loses his stick only once.' Experience teaches. 'A jungle fowl, another's child.' They are never your own. 'What does the yolk of an egg know?' Wisdom does not spring from children. The fact that disasters do not come unannounced, the importance of memory in preserving tradition, the way that little things rankle, the fact that patience has an end – these are also expressed in pungent phrases. 'Visitors tap the floor.' 'A mouth is better than a book.' 'Fish bones stick.' 'Even rock wears thin if pots are always put on it.'

Certain proverbs on the other hand satirise the ways of individuals. 'Even the mice dance and die in his house.' He is such a miser. 'An old hyena crunches a dry bone.' A moneylender will leave you nothing. 'If a cowherd becomes a chief and a serving girl a headman's wife, will twelve cart-loads hold their conceit?' It is necessary to keep your proper station. A vain boy is castigated – 'A frog with a fat belly always croaks' – while the man who pretends to more than he possesses is disposed of with the words, 'He cannot excrete but he has called the pigs'.

Sometimes a group of proverbs attempts to see both sides. 'You cannot cook a cake one side up.' In deciding a dispute, the village must hear the other man. Similarly, 'You cannot clap with one hand'. The headman alone cannot decide a quarrel but the whole village must assist. At the same time even a village may make itself ridiculous. 'A dog in moonlight, a meeting at night.' Just as a dog bays the moon, how often a night council wears itself away in aimless talk!

A few proverbs review the tribe as a whole and these are valuable pointers to Santal feelings. Santal improvidence is aptly summed up. 'When they have nothing, they sigh and die. When they have something, they give it out in fans.' The tribal experience of Dikus (non-Santals) is tersely put – 'A Diku cat, a bush of thorns' – while Santal unity is proudly asserted 'A million Santals have a single word.' It is the tribe that counts and whatever the individual, he is first and last a Santal.

Finally there are a few proverbs that comment on sex and marriage. These are of great importance since their symbolism provides an every-day link with poetry. A proverb such as 'A feathered arrow drives straight' is almost unintelligible without a reference to the songs. Its meaning is that marriage keeps a husband constant, but in order to express this point it has recourse to poetry. Not only is the arrow a stock poetic symbol for a potent lover but by referring to a wife as 'feathers' the proverb conjures up two other Santal images – 'the peacock with its tail' (the image in

...ntal houses
...reading paddy out to
...y
...ntal village street

4 Santal woman spinnin
cotton
5 Making leaf-cups
6 Santal daughter servi
her father

Santal co-parents-in-law
completing their greeting
Santal girl greeting her
mother and aunt
Santal co-parents-in-law
greeting each other

10 Santals playing flutes
11 Santal boy shooting a
   arrow
12 Santal son greeting h
   father

poetry for a young unmarried girl) and an image from ordinary life, the clothes of a girl hunched like feathers over her haunches. A proverb 'Every leopard must have its goat' makes a similar use of poetic symbolism to describe the need of boys for girls, and in the saying 'A village once visited, a tree once climbed, both are easy', the sexual symbolism of the tree is used to suggest that a girl, once won, can be had at will. Yet another symbol occurs in the phrase 'In a rocky country there are springs in all the rice fields'. The meaning of this proverb is that even in the poorest village, there is a girl for every boy, but in order to convey this observation the proverb refers to springs – a symbol which commonly appears in Santal poetry to suggest the act of love. In three other sayings, the 'snake woman' appears in circumstances that are parallel to songs. 'Fat pythons never stir.' A lazy daughter-in-law never works. 'Women, like snakes, bite one in the dark.' Girls use the night for seducing boys. 'Tame snakes still have fangs.' Married girls can still do mischief. In the phrase 'A cow with a calf always kicks', the symbol of the cow is used to stress the fact that a young mother does not take a lover. Finally behind the proverb, 'A sad heart, a smouldering fire', there is all the poetry of a girl 'who is lovely as a flame' and the frenzy of lovers ardent as fires.

These proverbs do not convey the whole Santal attitude to love and sex. Some of them are not even accurate summaries of general behaviour. They represent, as it were, the cynic's view, the comment of the wiseacre. But they are not without importance. They illustrate some fundamental Santal assumptions. They emphasise certain practices, and by using the symbolism of poetry achieve an added authority.

5 MANNERS

During their early years, Santal boys and girls insensibly acquire the village code of manners. This is of even greater significance than a girl's instruction in domestic hygiene and a boy's apprenticeship to agriculture. The latter qualifies them for earning a livelihood. The former enables them to fit easily and smoothly into the general pattern of village life.

The first requirement is respect for elders and reverence for relations. When a son meets his father, he bows low, touches his right elbow with his left hand, raises his right fist to the level of his forehead and slightly pauses. His father receives the greeting by touching his right arm loosely with his left hand, moving the right fist downwards and opening his hand. A daughter in a similar way greets her mother by bowing low and touching the earth. Her mother acknowledges the salute by putting out her hands, turning the palms up, flexing them two or three times and bringing them over her head. These gestures are not confined to parents and children but are the standard forms of salute for all inferiors and superiors.

Certain relations employ more complicated greetings. The bahonharea johar or form of greeting is when a man meets his younger brother's wife. The man bows, shading his eyes with his right hand, while the woman bends low in return peering at him through her hands. This greeting is intended to stress the fact that each is sacrosanct to the other. Balaea johar on the other hand is used by co-parents-in-law of the same sex and expresses their sense of familiar intimate union. The men catch each other's arms and draw them backwards and forwards three times, lifting their hands up and butting each other's shoulders. The women lower their hands with their palms up and move them three times like a mother receiving a johar. They then catch each other's arms by the elbow, and work them backwards and forwards three times, butting each other's shoulders.

This attitude of mutual respect is extended to the use of language. It is not that invectives are never employed but the terms which are permitted and those which are forbidden are carefully distinguished. References to the bongas, to bestiality, to impotence or homosexuality are completely ruled out while the terms that Santal men employ are often only threats of simple injury. 'I will kick, slap, beat, or eye you.' Such threats are usually a substitute for actual violence and are so mild that no one takes the slightest notice. There are also two sexual terms which are often used with impunity. 'I will fuck your mother' is a threat that never calls for comment, while endic' – 'you offspring of a penis' – is merely used as a strengthener to talk. 'Without it', said Sibu Hansdak', 'a man's words have no blood.' Yet common as they are with men, no one may in any circumstances use these terms to women or in their presence. Siru of Kurum abused his own mother saying, 'You offspring of a penis, I will fuck your mother.' His mother complained to the village and he was fined five rupees for using the word to a woman.

Certain terms of abuse are sometimes used by men but are always condemned. These fall into three groups. The first is the threat to kill your opponent, the second is to allege that he is a bastard, a thief or permanent outcaste, while the third is to state that a woman is a witch or a loose woman. If a man uses any of these words the village almost always condemns him and he is punished with a fine.

Chaitan Murmu of Bargama was ploughing his field when by accident he overploughed his brother's boundary. At this his brother shouted, 'That bastard Chaitan, he has over-ploughed my field.' A quarrel started and at the village meeting Chaitan's brother was fined one rupee and four annas.

In Raksi, Barka Soren accused another Santal of enticing away his wife. 'You thieving son of a penis,' he said, 'you have hidden my wife here.' The charge was actually not true, but because he had called him a thief, Barka was fined five rupees.

In Telni when the widow of Sam Hansdak' was one day going to the well for water, she stopped to chat with a Santal of her village. Her husband's elder brother was slightly drunk and seeing her talking to a man, he bawled out, 'Widows are no better than stallions. You strumpet, I will give you a good thrashing.' The girl was very hurt and annoyed so she told the headman and the villagers fined the man twenty-five rupees for calling her a loose woman.

While I was at Bokrabandh in May 1944 a quarrel involving the use of the term 'witch' was still going on. Two male friends, Loksa Baske and Chunu Soren of Pipra, had been going on a visit when they started to discuss the affairs of their village. During their talk Loksa said that Barki Hembrom was a witch. When the news got round to Barki she was very angry and asked for proof. Loksa denied that he had said it and accused his friend. The matter then went to the local pargana and five headmen who fined Loksa one rupee and his friend eight annas. A week later Loksa went to Barki and called her a witch to her face. The matter went to the manjhi and as Loksa could not prove it he was fined fifteen rupees and told to pay five of it to Barki. When I left Bokrabandh, he was saying he would pay her five rupees and give the villagers two goats.

Among women, a reference to urine is the normal form of abuse and this can be employed to either sex without offending village rules. If a boy is pushing into a group of girls, one of them may say, 'You little pisser'. If a woman is angry, she says, 'Piss me, if I listen to you'. In addition a woman can apply the terms 'blind' or 'slut' to either sex, and both of these are taken in fairly good part. If she is wild with fury, she can say 'Even a bear or a tiger would not eat you' or 'A dog has eaten all your shame'. If, however, she calls a person a thief, a bastard or a permanent outcaste she is liable to the same punishment as if she were a man.

In Gardi, at the Hook-swinging festival Kanhu Tudu caught hold of the breasts of a girl. The girl rounded on him and called him a bastard. At this the boy was so insulted that he told his village headman. The villagers were called and at the meeting they held that even the boy's advances did not warrant the girl's using such a term and it was the girl and not the boy who was fined one rupee four annas.

Even stronger notice is taken if a Santal woman uses words such as 'I will eye you', or 'May you burst'. Although a man can say to another, 'I will eye you', a woman cannot say this for every woman is regarded as a potential witch and there is great danger in allowing her to use phrases that imply 'the evil eye' or the wish and power to kill. Two brothers shared the same house in Dhamna. One day the children of the elder brother took water from a pot that the wife of the younger brother had filled. The woman lost her temper and scolded them, saying, 'You little bastards, may you die or burst yourselves.' The children told their mother who reported it to the manjhi and the wife of the younger brother was fined a rupee.

In Telni, Durga Hembrom was ploughing his field when his buffaloes got caught in some beans which Barki Kisku had grown. When the girl saw the damage she accused Durga of theft. 'You blind one, of course you have taken them away. You wretch, you bastard, so that is why you are not growing any. Burst your eyes.' Such a stream of abuse was too much for the boy and he caught her by the hair and slapped her three times. The girl complained to the headman but when the boy narrated the invectives she had used, the meeting fined the girl two rupees and four annas while the boy had only to pay one rupee as the cost of the sitting.

Moreover no woman may in any circumstances call another a witch, and in this respect Santal usage is completely parallel to Baiga. 'I have listened,' says Verrier Elwin, 'to quarrels in which women have been getting along very bouncingly with the most violent reflections on their own honour and the morals of their families, in which the obscenest expressions have been used with entire good humour; but no sooner has the fatal word "tonhi" been uttered than there has been screaming, passionate tears, and the initiation of a life-long feud. For the word "tonhi" is not only disreputable, it is dangerous; witchcraft and its punishment are still far too real to be referred to lightly.'

In Chutia, Pagan Marandi called another Santal woman a witch while the woman retorted by calling her an outcaste. Both were fined but it was Pagan who paid fifteen rupees and the other only seven.

Again no woman may call another a besram, backar, chinar, saidhin, or jhaeki. These are all terms that imply a number of lovers and strike at the roots of Santal assumptions about the home. No woman also can use male abuse to men or indeed employ any sexual expressions in public.

Chunki Hembrom of Dasorae was a particularly quarrelsome person and after her husband had gone to the war she annoyed the whole village by continually abusing people in sexual terms. In the end, the villagers lost patience. The headman asked for examples and after hearing them, he fined Chunki five rupees.

6 PROHIBITIONS

As they grow bigger, Santal boys and girls become aware of acts that one or other sex is prohibited from doing. We have already seen that certain places are connected with the bongas – the sacred grove, the manjhithan, the roofs of dwellings. All of these must be treated with the greatest circumspection. No one, whether man or woman, may plough the sacred grove or cut its trees. When the son of Raghu Murmu of Simbra dragged his plough across the grove, his sister suddenly died. In Belbhita, Galu Hansdak' cut a tree in the sacred grove and used it for his house. About a year later, although it was the height of the Rains, the house was struck by lightning and burnt to ashes. Women in particular must never climb a tree in the grove or break its branches. 'The bongas do not like women on their heads. If a woman climbed a bonga tree, rain would fall for as far as she could see.' Two women of Bodacaper went to the grove, broke the branches of a tree and took them to their houses for fuel. One died within two days and the other within eight.

The kulhi or village street is equally sacrosanct for it is here that the manjhithan is erected. 'The village street is the chest of Manjhi Haram. He will leave the village if its surface is broken.' Accordingly no one of either sex may plough the street, drag a leveller across it or even pull a thorny branch from side to side. Balea Soren of Bhatonda dragged a plough across the street and within a month murraine broke out among the cattle. In Telni, Karu Hembrom dragged a leveller along the village street. The next night jackals howled by the village and a little later cholera broke out.

Similarly, no girl may mount a roof in order to thatch it. 'Bongas dwell in the roof. They will not allow a woman to walk on them. They will stop rain and blight the crops.' In Simaltola there was no rain. The villagers discovered that a widow and her daughter had mounted a roof and thatched it. Thereupon they made the two women put lotas of water on their heads and walk the village street from end to end. They also took a goat and sacrificed it at the manjhithan. Shortly afterwards, heavy rain fell.

Even uncooked rice must be avoided in most of Dumka subdivision for 'it is the food of bongas and if anyone eats it, he will cause a famine'.

Besides these prohibitions which immediately concern the bongas, Santal girls must avoid a number of acts that boys themselves are permitted or even expected to do. No girl may shoot an arrow, use a razor, chisel a hole, strike with an axe, or fish with line and hook. She is also debarred from weaving cloth, stringing a cot, wearing male clothes or playing on a flute. If she ploughs a field, the act may stop rain. The son of Ramsin Hansdak' of Simbra was ploughing when his mother brought him his early morning food. He left a bullock yoked but as he ate, the animal strayed and his mother fetched it. She caught the plough by its handle, drove the bullock back and in so doing ploughed some land. The villagers took a brown fowl and a black goat from her and sacrificed them at the manjhi-than.

In certain areas, besides a goat for sacrifice, extra penalties are also imposed. In villages round Kundahit, for example, if a woman ploughs a field, 'she must be tethered like a cow and made to eat some grass', and at Rajabhita she must circumambulate the village carrying a leaking pot of water. It is also dangerous for a woman to touch the handle or carry any part of a plough otherwise than on the head for this also causes drought and renders sacrifices necessary. In Kala Dumaria the daughter of Anu Tudu carried a plough on her head and touched its handle. The village intervened and the girl was yoked to the plough and made to pull it five times round a field. In Katikund, the wife of Ludu Murmu carried a plough from a field to her house. The villagers took a pot, made four holes in it and filled it with water. Then they dressed her like a man and sent her round the village watering the earth as she went. When it was over they took a goat from her and sacrificed it at the manjhithan.

A girl is also forbidden to use a leveller. In Kalhajor the daughter of Hopna Kisku mounted a leveller while her father drove the bullocks. The villagers feared that the rains would fail, so they took a goat from Hopna and sacrificed it at the manjhithan. In Majdiha a Santal was ploughing while his wife stood on a leveller and the buffaloes pulled her round. Here also the woman's husband was fined and had to pay twenty-five rupees.

All these acts are in varying degrees suggestive of the male role in sex and it would be regarded by the bongas as a kind of symbolic perversion if a girl resorted to them. In most cases rain would cease and even if nothing for the moment happened there would be a sense of grim disquiet.

7 THE ONSET OF ADOLESCENCE

As Santal boys and girls grow up, two rites are performed to mark their changing natures. A boy who has reached the age of seven is branded on the left arm, above the wrist. He is given one, three, five or seven marks according to his father's fancy and is expected to stand the operation without evincing pain. The marks have no connection with his clan and are rather an indication of his tribal status, a sign that he is truly Santal. 'If a boy is not branded, he will suffer in the after-world. He will be given a caterpillar as large as a log and will be made to hug it.'

The same calamity awaits a Santal girl who for any reason has failed to be tattooed. As soon as she is ten or twelve, her left arm and left breast are pricked with a variety of marks. The patterns vary with the village and like the marks of a boy they are not intended as a clue to her family or clan. It is rather as a means of identification as well as an aid to beauty that the marks are given, to add a bluish tinge to the dark chocolate of the glossy skin. Until a girl is married only her left side is tattooed and it is when she has joined her husband that her right arm and right breast are also pricked.

It is about this time that Santal children make their first attempts at sex. 'Boys', said Dhunu Hembrom, 'start when they are ten or twelve, girls when they are eight or nine.'

5

When her hair was short as an oriole's
And still there was no pubic hair
He took and took her.

There is, however, no conscious organisation of their sexual life. Unlike Uraons, Hos and Mundas who from an early age segregate their boys and girls and bed them down at night in separate houses, Santals keep their children in their families. Until they are six or seven years old, they sleep near their parents. After that, they are put in separate rooms. If their parents sleep on the walled verandah, their sons and daughters go inside. If a boy lies on the verandah, his parents shift to the courtyard or occupy an inner room. It is when the children are asleep and then in the darkness of the house that their parents cohabit and it is only by accident that a child surprises them together.

It is from slightly older children that a Santal boy first learns the facts of life. 'Boys learn how to go to girls' said Dhunu 'by talking about it. They pick it up in the fields. Other boys do not show them how. They only tell them.' Occasionally a boy learns it from an older woman. 'A grand-mother takes a grandson. She has not done it for a long time. She makes him do it to her.' Sometimes a great aunt takes a young boy. Or his elder brother's wife shows him. 'His brother does not know but it is only for a day and if he knew he would not mind.'

Girls on the other hand do not usually learn from girls. 'It is the boys who teach them.'

The scene of a first encounter is often the forest. While they are grazing the cattle, boys and girls play 'Houses'. They appoint village officials. 'You are the manjhi. She is manjhi budhi.' They make little hearths and pretend to cook rice. 'It is then that they are yoked. Later, after dark, the boy and girl come together.'

'Sometimes a boy and girl play together. The boy goes on all fours. The girl rides on him. Suddenly he turns on his back and holds her. A girl pulls her away. He seizes her legs. If the girl likes it, the boy does it.'

A common game which is sometimes a prelude to encounters is played in the evening. This is oko oko or 'Hide and Seek'. A boy covers his eyes with his hands. All the boys and girls run away. A girl is waiting for him. He rushes to her and while the others are hiding they hurry down the village street.

These encounters do not necessarily end in passionate friendships. They are petty, childish introductions to the act of sex and it is not in fact until the ménarche that Santal girls begin to long at all avidly for 'the play of boys'. 'It is when the flower has blossomed that desire seizes her.'

This bodily change with all its repercussions begins about the age of twelve but is not at first accompanied by any precautions. Sometimes a girl takes a flower, puts a little of her menstrual blood on it and drowns it in a pot of oil. If after three days she takes it out, her period will never continue for more than three days.

Precautions of another kind are taken during her subsequent periods. A girl is always very careful to hide any rags that are smeared with her menstrual blood for if a boy lights upon them, he gets the girl in his power. If the rags reach a stream or any flowing water, her blood will flow for days on end. If the rags come into contact with a granary, they contaminate the family store and the whole house may lose its wealth.

Moreover menstrual blood is obnoxious to all the bongas except the Rongo Ruji and if a girl chances to approach a bonga while her period is on, the latter may make her blood flow for a month. She must then consult an ojha or medicine-man and appease the bonga by offering a fowl. The Rongo Ruji bonga on the other hand sometimes demands a girl's menstrual blood by way of offering.

In other respects, menstruation has little significance. A woman's acts and movements are unrestricted. She can fetch water, cook food, cowdung a floor, pass through standing crops, join the dancing, use a rice pounder. There is no taboo on intercourse but if a man takes a woman during her period, he cannot sacrifice to any bonga the following day.

Apart from this, intercourse during menstruation has no dangers and Santals do not attribute any disease to a contact with menstrual blood. 'At the most,' they say 'her blood will flow a day or two longer.'

CHAPTER III

Induction to the Tribe

I THE CACO CHATIAR CEREMONY

With the approach of adolescence, the responsibilities of adult life loom gradually larger. The naming ceremony admits a boy or girl to the outer fringes of the tribe. It is kind of baptism which serves as a necessary prelude to fuller recognition. But before a boy can assume the role of parent or be granted all the privileges of a separate house, he must undergo a ceremony of confirmation. At the naming ritual he was, as it were, placed under the protective surveillance of certain bongas. He must now be accorded adult status so that he may himself approach them with the customary offerings and share in the sacrificial feasts.

Similarly a girl must now be brought into closer union with the bongas. Until her confirmation she is eligible for bonga care but is debarred from assisting in the ceremonies. When she has been formally confirmed, she can clean the bhitar or family shrine and cowdung a place for the offerings. She can help in making the cakes that are offered in the cowshed at Sohrae. If an animal is killed for sacrifice, she can help to cook all the meat except the head. She can also eat such meat unless the bongas concerned are the abge ones. Moreover when she marries she can now have vermilion smeared upon her forehead and thus exchange her own bongas for those of her husband. Prior to confirmation she is little more than a baby. After confirmation she is virtually a woman.

But besides involving a new relationship with the bongas, adolescence makes even more necessary a sense of tribal discipline. We have seen that in their early youth children grow accustomed to village manners and to certain prohibitions. They must now be instructed in the tribal tradition and made to realise what it means to be a Santal.

The ceremony that combines these various functions is known as Caco Chatiar and is usually performed when a child is eight to ten years old. When several children in the family are ready, the father or sponsor visits the headman and tells him he has brewed some rice-beer. The headman asks what ferment he has used, and the man replies, 'The ferment is this.

I have heard some little parrots crying in the hole of a tree. Their feathers are sprouting. We are bringing them down. Fix a date for me.' The headman then enquires in how many holes there are parrots and the man tells him how many children are proposed for confirmation. The headman then announces a date and commands all the villagers to be present.

On this day the village assembles. The children are washed by the midwives who assisted at their births. All the married women are given fresh vermilion for their foreheads, and after rice-beer has been circulated, the headman starts the ritual.

'Early today,' he says, 'I was passing this house when I heard some little parrots in a hole. They were trying to fly out. For bringing them down we are drinking this rice-beer. Let those who can make ladders, make them. Those who can climb trees, climb them; those who can hold a cloth, hold it. Not a single parrot must break its legs or wings.'

An old man or guru then launches on the Caco Chatiar sermon. He begins by recalling the early history of the race and reminds the Santals of the vital role played in parturition by the midwife. He describes how the early Santals discussed their customs for twelve years and how none could be finalised owing to the accidental omission of the midwife's dues.

2 THE MYTH OF THE BASTARD

He then passes in rapid review the first migrations of the Santals, describing how first they went from Hihiri Pipiri to Khoj Kaman, thence to Sasanbeda, Here, Jarpi, and Kaende, until at last they settled in Cae Campa, close to Hazaribagh in Chota Nagpur. 'There in each village,' he says, 'we appointed headmen, in each area a chief or pargana and above everyone a Raja. The first Raja was Dharapnaran and his seat Champanagar. Near it lived Mandhwa pargana. Mandhwa had two sons, Surjan and Durjan, and when they grew up they went to Champanagar and worked in the Raja's service.

'One day a girl came to Mandhwa's house. He took her in and kept her for sweeping the courtyard. She lived there, grew up and did all the house work. One day she met a Birhor in the forest. She "slipped on the white earth", conceived and gave birth to a boy. Out of fear the girl bore it in the forest. Mandhwa pargana heard of the birth and brought the child home. He did not know who was the child's father so he called it Mandhwa after himself. The boy grew up and lived in his care.

'One day Surjan and Durjan grew tired of serving the Raja so they left him. Dharapnaran asked why they had left. When he knew the reason he

59

said he would give them half the kingdom and sent two soldiers to bring them. Through fear, Surjan and Durjan did not return and sent Mandhwa, the bastard boy, in their place. When Mandhwa told the Raja that he was the son of Surjan and Durjan, the Raja gave him half his kingdom. Thereupon Mandhwa changed his name to Madho Singh.

'At that time the Santals had no bongas and no festivals. Then the first ancestors out of joy started a Buru Beret' (mountain raising) festival and sent news of it to Madho Singh. At the festival people from distant villages had gathered and were enjoying themselves dancing. Madho Singh went to see the dances. Among the dancers he saw a young Hembrom girl and wanted to possess her. But because he was a bastard the first ancestors refused to give her to him. When he heard this, Madho Singh became enraged and desired to take her by force. The first ancestors feared to be defied and preparing the whole night they fled. They shut the main gate and left by the back. They hurried on for five days and five nights until they reached the Damodar river. The river was in flood. They could not cross. Madho Singh was coming after them. They heard the bells on his horse jingle. Then they began to pray, "Let the upper water halt and the lower water flow away. When we have gone across we will make you an offering." Then the upper water stopped and the lower water subsided. They crossed the dry river bed and, as soon as they were over, the water flowed again. Madho Singh came up to the river, but as it was in flood he could not cross it or do them any harm.'

3 'THE CORRUPT LAND'

'The first ancestors on the other side of the river wanted to fulfil their promise and seeing a great mountain and taking it to be the biggest they killed a white fowl in the name of Maran Buru.

'Crossing the Damodar they went to the Gola Kusumba Bhiloja country. "Here," they said, "we are close to the Cae country. Madho Singh may follow and surprise us. Let us move further on." From there they went to the Sir country. They stayed a while. Then they went to Nagpur and thence to Sikhar. In Sikhar they installed the bongas in the sacred grove and for the first time performed the Baha and Sohrae festivals.

'There also they could not stay long. They crossed the Ojoe river and settled here. One day they were going to inspect a girl for a boy. With the boy's father were two friends. On their way they heard a golden oriole calling. They stopped and said, "From what rock is this oriole calling? Is it an omen?" They saw it was singing on a rock and they said, "This is a good omen. If we bring this girl she will make the house like a rock. Let us fetch her." A little further on, another oriole crossed their path. They stopped and said, "It sang to us before. Now it has crossed our path. Let us see where it is singing." They looked. It was sitting on a meral tree. Then they said, "Is it an omen?" They looked and said, "This also is good. As the meral has a fruit on every leaf, so will this girl have children." Then they went on and, a little further, again the oriole sang. They stopped and saw that it was singing on an ant hill. Then they said, "This also is an omen. In future bullocks will have to be yoked by climbing on an anthill." Again they went on and reached the girls' village. The match-maker showed the girl to them and a little later they performed the wedding. From then on their numbers increased.

'When the first ancestors had stayed there for some time, they tied a cow and bullock to a post and sacrificed them. When the servants of the Raja saw this, they reported that the ancestors had killed a bhongomati in the field and eaten it. Then the Turuk (Muslim) Raja ordered them to be brought before him and to be kept in a house with twelve doors. The Raja said, "Let them stay today. Tomorrow we shall crush their heads in a pounder." They were locked up and left. The first ancestors were full of fright and began to think. "Once we saved ourselves from Madho Singh. Now we are in even greater trouble. How can we save ourselves?" Then they asked each other how many bongas they had. Each man disclosed his bongas. A Santal of the Copear clan was with them. He said, "We are Copear. We have seven umbrellas full of bongas." The first ancestors seized him and said, "Go ahead of us and open the doors." Then the Copear Santal went ahead and at a little push the doors opened. As the doors opened, they went out with him. They left the prison with its twelve doors, and ran out into the night. At the Ojoe river they parted with a silver ring. They nailed it to a sal tree and said, "From today we shall not cross the Ojoe because it is O-joe (a place of disaster). The land of the Turuks is a corrupt land. If at any later time we cannot feed ourselves and cross the Ojoe, may our children be defiled even in the womb." Then the first ancestors recrossed the river and at the Sikhar boundary they settled in the Sonaboi upland.'

4 THE REMOVAL OF POLLUTION

From this general account the guru now passes to the actual village where the ceremony is being held. 'And so in early times,' he says, 'there was virgin soil and virgin forest, all of which we cleared. In those days there was a certain country. There the cobs of maize were fat as drums, the horec' fruits were like swords and the yellow ants like monkeys. If you desired to eat a yellow ant, you climbed a tree with a rope, tied it and brought it down. Hearing of such a country, our headman brought us to it. We settled and put up huts. Then the headman cleared a plot for himself. He took seeds in a bottle-gourd. He ploughed and sowed. From the seeds of iri came up erba. From the seeds of erba came up iri. The iri and erba began to ripen. There was fear that the birds would eat them. So the ancestors said, "Let us keep watch. Fowls play about, lizards nod their heads, birds twitter." So taking their women with them the men kept watch. As they watched they played at "climbing the dry tree". Then by the grace of Thakur, rice did not fall down and scatter. It fell unhurt from the dry tree and only when its feet lighted on the ground did it grow dirty.'

From this allegory of child birth, the guru passes to the man who has sponsored the ceremony. He refers to the way in which the birth had polluted him – a pollution only partially removed by the initial cleansing ceremony. 'In past days,' the guru says, 'We did not let that Santal be with us at the spring or enter the pool in the river. We did not let him take water. We told him, "You are defiled". But today we have cleansed him. From now onwards call him to the spring. Take him to brew and drink rice-beer, to pin leaves together on the days of marriage, Chatiar and cremation. Take him to fairs, summon him to meetings. Once he was defiled but now he is clean. Once he was black as a crow. Now he is white as a heron.'

With the ending of the sermon, the sponsoring Santal asks the village to forgive his poor hospitality and the people reply 'We came on our feet but you welcomed us on our heads. Your water pleased us. We brought nothing with us either in a big or a little gourd. Those who could make ladders made them and those who could climb trees climbed them. In this way we brought the little parrots from their hole. We took them in our cloth and did not let them fall or break a leg or wing. In bringing them down from the dry tree, we let them touch only a small piece of the ground.'

This declaration ends the more essential parts of the ritual. After that, rice-beer is drunk in ever-increasing quantities. The guru is asked to say how many of the children are erba or boys and how many are iri or girls, how many are this type of bird and how many are that. Bird after bird is taken up and at each question more and more rice-beer is drunk until the whole gathering is permeated with a gentle fuddled joy.

Finally the guru struggles through a series of songs describing the processes of birth:

6

O my love
What is the pain?
My head is aching
My head hurts
My legs ache
My arms ache
My chest aches
My back aches
My waist aches
My thighs are aching.

Once again he brings the midwife onto the stage, describes her intimate functions, gets the child born once more and finally passes in review the cleansing ritual of nim dak' mandi. The older people now begin to dance and with a few staggering jhika and thapra songs and dances the ceremony ends.

7

The grass flowered
And a girl came
The marar blossomed
And a boy was born
The fat one, the plump one
The little parrot, the starling
They are feeding at the breast
Bring down the small ones
The little parrot, the starling.

5 GRADUATION

All this time the children have been kept for the most part inside the house. They are dressed in new clothes and fidget uneasily while the long narrative proceeds. The ceremony in fact is done for them and at them rather than with them and their chief role lies only in maintaining a passive unobtrusive presence. Yet although the children are 'patients' rather than 'agents', certain important results are achieved.

The ceremony removes the last taint that is supposed to survive from the processes of birth. The children are, as it were, 'born again' and for this reason the midwives attend in person, their role in parturition is

63

formally stressed and the whole drama of birth is re-described. The father who, after the first ceremony of nim dak' mandi has not, in fact, suffered any social disabilities, is again treated as if he were not entirely pure and it is only after a second fictitious cleansing that the pollution is deemed to end. It is this final cleansing that now qualifies the children to assume an adult relation to their bongas.

At the same time the sermon brings forcibly to their notice certain points of tribal importance. The myth of Madho Singh reflects the horror with which Santals regard all sexual intercourse with persons not of the tribe. So enormous is this crime that in order to preserve their integrity the ancestors abandoned their villages and sought another country. Similarly their sojourn in 'the corrupt land' of the Muslims was attended by such grave harassment that contact with Muslims must at all costs be avoided.

Yet despite early troubles which seem to have dogged their wanderings, one fact towers above all else – the protective role of the bongas. At every moment of crisis – whether when harried by Madho Singh or imprisoned by the Muslim tyrant – it is the bongas who succour and save. The tribe, in fact, is made by its bongas and only by preserving this ghostly connection with fervid anxious care can Santal boys and girls maintain their happy laughing freedom.

CHAPTER IV

Social Dances

I LAGRE

If the Caco Chatiar ceremony gives Santal children a new status, it is the village dances that gradually merge them in the society of the adult. From the time a girl can toddle, she joins the line of dancers, while little boys strut round and round aping the antics of the drummers. But besides initiating boys and girls into subtle graceful movement and making them feel an integral part of the village, the dances bring them face to face with poetry. At the Baha and Sohrae festivals, dancing and singing by the women is necessary for the celebrations. During the Karam ceremony, the annual hunt and at the savage spectacle of bitlaha, the men have special songs and dances, and during the performance of a wedding, both men and women dance. All these songs are in the Santali language and are directly or indirectly connected with practices sanctioned by the bongas. During the hot weather when the nights are dry and warm and a cream-coloured moon goes slowly up the sky, a different kind of song is sung. This is in mixed Bengali and Santali – a language that the bongas are supposed either not to know or not to recognise – and accompanies a form of dance intended for recreation only. The village girls and women form a single swaying line while a group of boys bring out two types of drum – the tumdak' with its cylinder of clay and the tamak' with its great hide-covered bowl. The tumdak' is played with the hands while the tamak' is beaten with little sticks. The former sets the rhythm while the latter echoes and adds to it. These drums are of great importance, for it is the way in which they are played that decides the rhythm and style of the dancing. If the drumming is dull and blurred, the line of girls and women waggles in confusion. If it is smart, clear and precise, it gets them firmly moving and the whole dance goes with sharp clarity, each dancer in step with the other, the entire line dancing as one.

The lagre dance which forms the mainstay of these meetings has a standard form called tahri. The girls form a curving line facing the drummers. They begin with a song to 'bind' the akhra or dancing ground and after that they slowly edge along its rims. Then the drums quicken and a jerking oscillation starts. The right foot goes slightly out and edges right. The left foot joins it. Then the right moves a little to the side and the left goes out and edges near it. At the same time the knees bend and straighten, the clasped hands sway gently in and out and the buttocks bob roundly up and down. The heads go nodding to the drums and as the line of bodies sets up a vertical undulation, the songs rise calmly through the din.

These songs have almost always romantic connotations. Birds such as fly-catchers, peacocks, doves and pigeons stand for girls; monkeys and porcupines for boys. Making love is suggested by phrases such as 'drinking a river-full of water', 'crying for water', 'swaying in the dew', 'picking cotton on a hill' and 'losing a ring'. Seduction is implied by the phrases 'striking with a flute', 'shooting an arrow' or 'climbing a fig tree'. An unwanted pregnancy is described as 'making a citron fruit fall', and places of assignation are referred to as 'a gully with the plantain' or 'the foot of the mountain'. Direct allusions to sex are never made. 'Four-letter' words are scrupulously avoided and it is rather by means of symbols drawn from daily life that the singers make their point.

8

There are ten drummers
There are twenty girls
The dancing ground is big and wide
Do not rouse me, drummer
Or I will make you drink
A river-full of water.

9

The fly-catcher, elder brother
Is crying out for water.
All things are bad, girl.

10

At night I slept on a verandah
And in a dream I found you
How lovely you were
Swaying in the dew.

11

O you peacock in the peacock forest
I will make you fly

On your feathers I will put
Golden sindur.

12

To the high lands
Went the cattle
To the muddy swamp
The buffaloes.
Middle brother,
The mud is heaving.
In the gully with the plantains
Is a spring with a bonga.

13

Monkey, from branch to branch you sprang
You strolled from path to path
Take care, monkey
Or the citron fruit will fall.

14

In the middle of the street
Is a dancing ground
Go quickly, girl
For though you are frightened
I shall look inside your heart.

15

With a gold umbrella
You have gone away, my son
But do not cross
The five mountains
Let me go, mother
Go I will
For a girl is standing
Lovely as a flame.

As the dance goes on, with the line undulating and the haunches jerking and jerking, the girls become more and more a set of neutral units. With their slow doll-like swaying, the blank indifference in their staring eyes, their calm singing, their buttocks nodding to the drums, it is as if they are a line of rounded forms whose sole function is to undulate and sing.

In sharp contrast are the antics of the men. As the line goes round and round, each drummer demonstrates his skill. He treats his drum as a toy, tosses it high in the air and rolls with it on the ground, maintaining all the time the basic rhythm. At the same time, boys with flutes go prancing round. These also are out to make a show, to amuse the girls, to break down their bland indifference. Sometimes they adopt comic poses known as sogoe and strut with their clothes coming slightly down while every now and then they romp on the ground or stick a joking article in the hair. Sometimes a boy takes a flower or a twig of leaves and hurries down the line of women, pushing it under their noses. This is called 'sniffing a flower' and gives the boy a chance to see which girls are there.

When the standard form has been danced through and through, the dancers change their style and try out other patterns. One of these, the handwe lagre, goes even more slowly, with a lingering bend of the knees and a languid rounding of the haunches. Another, the bangla or tundun lagre, is somewhat faster and instead of slowly edging round a vast circle, the line goes first in one direction and then in another. Not until the condok' pattern is reached, however, is the girls' poise finally broken. They begin with the same kind of line, clasping hands and oscillating to the drums. Then as the rhythm quickens, the drummers get wilder and wilder, hurling their drums about and jerking their heads with hissing snake-like movements. At the same time, the girls abandon their slow sidling drift. With every step their heels leave the ground and the line goes bouncing up and down, the breasts shaking and the legs springing and jerking. When it is over, the line collapses into laughing talk.

2 DAHAR

Side by side with lagre, Santals also dance the dahar. This resembles a forward-moving lagre, the girls taking two steps to the side and then a pace forward. As with lagre itself, the songs are chiefly concerned with village romance:

16

In a bush of thorns
Two pigeons
Are busy with a nest
Boy
Do not shoot an arrow
For the two
Are calling to each other.

17

On the mountain the flames spread
On the hill the fire
Goes mounting in a line
Look at that old man
Running and stumbling
Look at that boy
And the lily
Straining into bud.

18

Climb on the thatch, girls
See him on his way
For he goes, he goes
To the foot of the mountain.

19

Mother
On the small hill
I gathered cotton
And my ring
Slipped from my finger.

20

Behind an ant-hill is a porcupine
We will stone him from above
We will pelt him till he falls.

21

Beyond the mountain
The ring dove is cooing
Under the mountain
The boys are with the cattle
With a flute they struck the dove
O my friend, go slowly
Very slowly.

22

Durgi
Your brother-in-law
Has climbed a fig tree
Durgi
Your brother-in-law
Is being chased by bees.

3 GOLWARI

If lagre with its nodding poise is the prose of Santal dancing, golwari represents its poetry. This dance occurs either when the night's performances are almost over or before the lagre is commenced. It consists of a series of figures based on scenes of Santal life, each dance being, as it were, a rural pantomime.

The type with the greatest majesty is called the vulture dance and is modelled on different kinds of bird. The women stand one behind the other in single file, their arms held out like flapping wings. Then very slowly and deliberately, they start to move in a circle.

23
The vultures circle in the sky
O vulture, give me wings like yours
And I will fly like you.

24
The peacocks feed on scorpions and snakes
O peacock, give me wings like yours
And I will dance like you.

25
O quail, quail
Give me a song like yours
And I will sing like you.

As they advance, their hands gently paw the air, their breasts are thrust out and with a proud insolent dignity, they bear down on the drummers. At the end, in a phrase of Sir Richard Burton's, they sometimes 'cower down and lay out their buttocks'. Then, squatting in a line, they flutter their arms and edge slowly forward like great ungainly birds.

This form is the most impressive of all golwari dances but the baha sid – 'putting flowers in the hair' – has also the dignity of a graceful march. The girls put out their hands as if they were picking flowers from a tree. They gather the blossom and drop it in their 'aprons'. Then, as the line moves slowly on, each 'picks a flower' from her hip and puts it in the hair of the girl in front of her. Sometimes they turn about and after picking flowers from a bush, they swing sharply round and put them in a dancer's hair.

Another golwari dance is based on catching fish. The women stand on their left legs, while their right legs swing out across their bodies as if they were driving fishes from the mud. Then with a little whisk of the hand, they catch the fish and tuck them into their waists. In the alternative, they form a bending line. Their hands dart out as if plunging into water and with each stroke they seize some fishes and throw them over their heads.

26

Stir the sand round
Stir around the rice
Cup the water with one hand
Cup the water with two hands.

27

Come to the pool, girls
And pick up fishes
We will cook them in a fire
The smoke rises
To the mouth of the dead.

Another variant is 'catching snails'. The girls make a little ruck in their clothes and edge along the circle. At every fourth step they swing the right arm out, bring it back as if it had scooped up some water and then drop a 'snail' into the ruck at their hips. As they do this, they sing:

28

Come to the pool, girls
And let us pick up snails
It is not good to gather snails
My lover went there
And never returned.

Other dances depict the planting of paddy. The girls stoop down, 'pull up the seedlings' and 'twist them into bunches'. Then the torso bends low and the arms dart out as if they were plunging the seedlings into mud. Sometimes, as a change, they reap a crop, one hand grasping the stalks while the other 'cuts' it with a 'sickle'.

29

In the headman's field
The mustard reaches to the waist
The pigeons' hands will blister
As they pick it.

71

30

The sun is on the road
The moon is in the forest
The millet is ripe for cutting
The pulse has grown thick.

Side by side with 'agricultural' dances, several others employ the gestures of greeting. The train of girls begins by slowly oscillating up the line, then every odd girl swings round and looks at her partner and they raise their arms in a johar or formal greeting. Sometimes the dancers split into half and the two lines stand face to face. Each dancer then holds the arms of her opposite number or they peer at each other through raised hands as if they were mothers-in-law.

Finally a few kinds of golwari are distinguished either by hopping or by the clapping of hands. A few girls form themselves into a tight bunch while a line with linked arms confines them in a struggling mass. Then they all begin to hop and the bunch collapses in shrieks of laughter. In a form which is known as polor, each girl lifts her left leg and crooks it in the leg of the girl behind her. The whole line then starts to hop, clapping hands as it goes. In another dance the girls take three little steps forward, running out like mice, clapping their hands, turning smartly about and scampering back. Sometimes the women kneel on the ground and swaying to and fro, clap their hands, and, in yet another form they crouch in a long line which follows the drummers in a wriggling course, clapping their hands, first to one side and then to another.

4 THE DASAE PLAYS

Dances of such pretty grace are confined to girls and women. Boys, however, also indulge in pantomimic dancing for, towards the end of the rains, those who have undertaken a course in tribal medicine under an ojha or medicine-man perform a series of 'plays'. These are part of the Dasae daran ('September wanderings') and are a mixture of dancing, pantomime and trance.

For putting on these plays, current pupils, as well as those already initiated, assemble in the village. They wear a special dancing dress – a long white skirt not unlike a cassock – and taking with them some peacock feathers, cymbals, fiddles and a special kind of drum, the dedger, they go to a lonely spot beyond the houses. Here the medicine-man sacrifices to Maran Buru, Pargana bonga, and others. As he does this, the boys form a small platoon and begin to chant and sing. They advance in swaying lines, clashing the cymbals, brandishing the feathers and lifting their voices with a curious praying fervour. When everything is ready, they leave dancing, tuck up their skirts and squat on the ground.

The 'plays' that now commence are a series of 'impersonations'. Boy after boy is 'possessed', he stands or crouches in a dream-like trance and is then 'impelled' to impersonate a bonga or enact a story. The bongas which possess him bear no relation to actual bongas and seem in fact to be not bongas at all but rather the 'spirits' of different dramatic parts. The first 'character' to assume control is the tiger bonga or baghut. After that, various 'bongas' seem to come and the 'plays' proceed in whatever order the company decides.

Baghut bonga, the tiger For appearing as Baghut, a boy is thrown violently into the circle. He then goes prowling round, nuzzling his nose on the ground and making pouncing jumps. A chick is put in the ring and he bites its head off. The medicine-man then offers it to the bongas and the boy is rescued from his trance by being lifted off his feet.

Hati bonga, the elephant Two boys crouch on all fours, two others ride them and they lumber slowly round with a clumsy swaying gait.

Gai bonga, the cow This is much more elaborate. A 'cow' comes in on all fours, followed by a smaller boy, the 'calf'. They mimic the lowing of cattle. Then a third enters. This is the milkman who goes round calling to the cow. He picks up a stick. Then suddenly a 'tiger' comes. The milkman attacks it with the stick and the 'cow' and 'calf' rush to safety.

Mermetec' bonga, the flea A 'tiger' comes slinking in while a 'flea' bites its flanks. The 'tiger' goes roaring round and the 'flea' jumps nimbly after.

Car cari bonga, the scourge 'These are the bongas of Dibi who will only go away when they are beaten.' Two men come staggering in with wildly waving arms. They reel to a halt while two others hit them smartly with a lash of sabai grass. They are then picked up and are carried struggling away.

Jugi bonga, the sadhu Two 'sadhus' come running in and commence to fall about. The medicine-man forces them down and they sit side by side. Their heads nod violently. A stick is placed in their hands and they toss it up and down. The medicine-man then puts some 'ganja' in a 'pipe' and the two proceed to 'smoke' it.

Bindi bonga, the spider A boy with great straddling legs and arms goes round on all fours rolling on the earth and tossing lightly about. Two boys hold a long flute on their shoulders. The 'spider' clasps it, dangles his legs and turns a somersault over it.

San la bonga, digging roots This is more complex. Two men squat down and shift about, one behind the other. The first has a stick and digs at roots while the second scrapes them up.

Haru bonga, the monkey Here the 'monkey' comes running in, turns catherine wheels and escapes in great bounding leaps.

Backar ar landa bonga, the joker and the tart. A 'tart' comes in on all fours and is pursued by a joker. The joker catches her 'breasts' and follows with hollow laughs. They grapple and wrestle with each other.

Dhubi bonga, the washerman A 'washerman' enters, takes a cloth and beats it on the ground.

When the 'plays' have been rehearsed outside the village and in the presence of Maran Buru and the other bongas, the way is clear for their presentation to the villagers. The boys repair to their teacher's house and for three days the company goes dancing down the street, stopping at the houses, swirling into the courtyards, begging presents and staging its varied shows. As the long white skirts flounce into the courtyards, the dancers sing a variety of songs.

Some of these invite the village girls to enter their joking ranks.

31

Girl, how lovely you look
With your dress clinging
How lovely you look
With your cloth
Rucked in folds.

32

On the path the pipal fruit is ripe
And the pied mainas cry cero bero
The green pigeons twist their heads.

33

Parrot, do not cry
At the pain in your body

Do not mourn
In the bar tree by the road
Your father and mother
Are high up on the mountain
Dove, your father and brothers
Are out in the forest.

34
In the forest the birds twitter
In the village the girls sing.

35
Two girls like sticks
With winding curves
O two girls
Stamp on the pounder
Clean the rice in a fan
O two girls
Listen to the bangles
Listen where the pounder calls
O two girls
Finish your rice
Finish making that curry.

36
O you two girls
In a big house
With rounded thatch
Comb your tresses
Tie them in a knot
The Dasae boys are upon you
You must take their greetings.

37
O you two girls
Bathing in the river
You are scrubbing your hair with earth
The string of a necklace is drifting down
As you catch the string, the sun is setting.

38
In the river, the fish glitter
In the stream, the fish shine
In the big village, the girls are flashing.

39

Going, I went and saw
Looking, and I looked
At the water brimming in the well
The water gushing from the spring.

A few songs poke gentle fun at the dancers themselves.

40

In the river, the alligator
Slashes with its tail
In the village the boys
Swagger up and down.

41

Mother, give me my loin-cloth
Give me my fiddle
I am going, mother
To wander in the country
I am going, parrot
To rove about the land.

42

On the road the traders
Are raising the dust
In the village street
The Dasae boys are romping.

43

At the village end is a bar tree
With a sound of bells
The two teachers met
The bells are jangling
The dust mixes
From the kicking feet.

Finally in yet another group of songs, the guru or his family are jokingly addressed.

44

Guru, for many days
You ruled your pupils

Now I will blind you like a dove
I will trap you like a quail.

45

Guru, your right foot
On a line of gossamer
Guru, your left foot
On a fiddle's bow.

46

In a gold cloth
Is the Guru's wife
She is sitting in a chair
She is looking in a glass
And like a lotus leaf
She moves her head.

When the begging is over, a feast is held and the 'plays' and dances are laid aside for another year.

The Rules of Sex

I ROMANCE BEFORE MARRIAGE

Among the tribes of Middle and Eastern India, romance before marriage is tacitly assumed. N. E. Parry says of the Lakhers, 'Apart from the fact that discretion in love is essential, there is no bar to the freest of intercourse between unmarried persons and no fine is inflicted merely because a young man and a girl have slept together.' Among the Pardhans, Shamrao Hivale states, 'Before marriage both boys and girls live lives of almost complete freedom. Even little children of four or five years indulge in erotic play together and most boys and girls have had their first experiences long before puberty. Elder people are amused and tolerant of the sexual adventures of their children. They appear to object to any attempt to correct them. They take the line that such adventures did them little harm and that in any case youth is a time for freedom and experiment.' Verrier Elwin has noted among Baigas that 'by her wedding night each girl is already an experienced lover', while of the Mundas Sarat Chandra Roy has referred to 'the sexual liberty permitted to the unmarried of both sexes' and has described how 'bachelors and maidens often find their way to each other's dormitories'.

It is not surprising therefore that once a Santal boy has reached puberty and a girl has 'flowered', they enter a romantic period which lasts until marriage. Earlier experiments now give place to serious affairs of the heart and it becomes a point of honour for a boy to have his village girl and for a girl to have her boy. In most cases these relationships do not last for more than five years and barring certain developments they are not expected to be trial unions. The girl will normally marry another boy and the boy will be provided with a different wife. But during their currency, both boys and girls experience sex not simply as a physical routine but as a need of the heart. It is a phase in their lives which will always be connected with romantic happiness and which, even after they are happily married – to others – a few at least may sometimes be tempted to revive.

These liaisons are regarded with strange ambivalence by Santal society.

On the one hand, they are supposed to be a secret of the village youth and from the official point of view, not to exist at all. On the other hand, every villager takes their existence for granted. It is not, in fact, the affairs which seem to matter. It is the manner in which they are conducted. Provided the rules are observed – and it is this which is supremely important – Santal boys and girls may act as they wish.

2 LANGUAGE AND BEHAVIOUR

A striking aspect of Santal life is the great refinement with which sex is treated. We have already seen how small a part is played in Santal invective by physical expressions. This avoidance of sexual language extends to the whole of public life.

A party of girls from Kurum were going to see the Dibi festival at Dumka. As they went through the village of Gidni, they were singing songs when one of them who was slightly drunk suddenly cried out 'Deper, deper' ('Fuck the lot of you'). On this a man of Gidni at once caught her and only after her friends had given her some clothes and she had left her own as security was she allowed to go. Two days later there was a meeting of the two villages – the girl's village and that of the affronted parties – and the girl was fined five rupees.

In Dumarthan the men were getting ready for the annual hunt. While they were waiting, two co-wives began to quarrel and in the course of the argument the elder said, 'You are always going after him like a bitch in heat.' Everyone took offence at this breach of village conventions and the next day the woman was fined two rupees and eight annas.

The headman of Choudhury was drinking rice-beer at the Sohrae festival when he said in public to a group of boys, 'Won't you let me fuck your sisters?' All those who heard him were disgusted and the villagers fined him fifteen rupees.

This general prohibition on sexual language is slightly relaxed in the case of certain relatives. A husband, for example, can make slightly daring remarks to his wife's younger sister. So can a husband's brother to his wife's sister. The following relatives also enjoy with each other a special 'joking' relationship, known as landa sagai.

Wife's brother	Husband's sister
Grandfather	Grandson
Grandfather	Granddaughter
Grandson	Grandmother

Granddaughter	Grandmother
Grandfather	Grandson's wife
Husband	Wife's grandmother
Son	Father's sister's husband
Daughter	Father's sister's husband

Even these persons, however, must be careful what words they use and must also avoid too frank a reference in public.

There is a similar control of public behaviour. In village dancing, gestures by the drummers are often frenzied but they are never sexual. In the village itself, there are no sexual pantomimes and the wearing of mock genitalia is permitted only at the annual hunt and at bitlahas. Similarly, neither men nor women may appear naked in public and a breach of this rule may lead to a heavy fine and considerable social censure.

A girl of Bodacapar took off her clothes and dragged a boy down the village street. The villagers intervened and fined her seven rupees.

Kuar Kisku, the pargana of Chandna, was returning home from market a little drunk. He decided to undress and go on his way with nothing on. Many others were also going home and on the way he stopped an old woman and asked her to salute him. The headmen of five villages met and he was fined twenty-five rupees.

Ronjon Tudu of Bhatka was drinking with some friends one afternoon when he decided to go off to the tank and have a bathe. He came out of his house, took off all his clothes, tied them round his head like a turban and went strolling down the street. Next morning the village held a meeting and punished him.

3 CONVENTIONS OF MEETING

Provided these conventions are observed, social intercourse in a Santal village is free and unrestrained and boys and girls, men and women can talk to each other without embarrassment. Talk, however, is always a potential means to greater intimacy and there are three rules that circumscribe the general freedom.

So long as girls are unmarried or divorced they can talk and joke with boys from other villages but such boys must always be Santals and the conversation must take place in the boys' village and not in that of the girls.

Secondly, within their own village, Santal girls can laugh and joke with Santal boys but only with those who are of the same village.

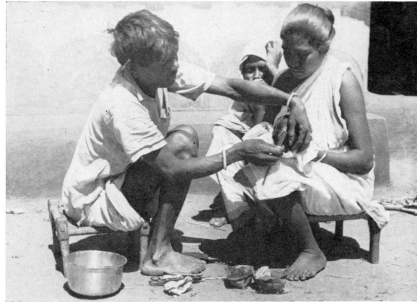

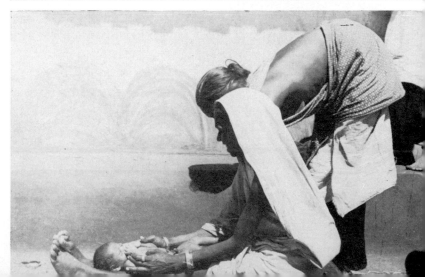

antal boy with umbrella
irth: shaving the child's
ead
1idwife with new-born
antal child

16 Santal chil○—l
'sitting, sta▮▮▮▮
17 Santal chil○ ·l·
'goat's ble▮▮▮▮
18 Santal chil○ ·l·
'caki dar'

ata festival: Santal
hogta swinging
antal girl weeding maize
inding paddy sheaves

22 Carrying paddy she
23 Lifting paddy sheav
24 Santal women retur
   from the spring

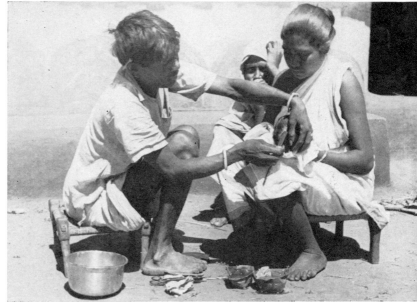

Santal boy with umbrella
Birth: shaving the child's
head
Midwife with new-born
Santal child

16 Santal children playi
    'sitting, standing'
17 Santal children playi
    'goat's bleat'
18 Santal children playi
    'caki dar'

In Susni, a Hansdak' girl was washing clothes in the village pond. A boy from Majdiha was passing and began to talk to her. The girl's father saw them, called his son and the two caught the boy and took him to their house. Two men of Majdiha were called and the boy paid a fine of five rupees.

One day in Manjhla Sarwa, Jasmi Soren went to the forest and began to talk to a boy of Boro Sarwa. They were standing by a stream and the boy was urging her to let him take her. Suddenly the girl's brother chanced upon them. The boy was dragged off to the headman and although the incident had taken place in the forest, the fact that the spot lay within the village boundaries weighed heavily against them. Both boy and girl were punished with a fine.

For the purpose of this rule, the fact that the stranger has come in a wedding party makes no difference and in this respect there is a striking difference between boys and girls. A girl for example who goes in a wedding party to another village is regarded as fair game for the boys of that village. She is no longer 'at home' and can therefore be safely approached. But a boy who enters a strange village must avoid all the girls he meets and a wedding song describes the penalty which awaits too boisterous a gesture.

47

Two drummers
Play your drums
Two dancers
Dance your will
But do not come too close
Or they will fine you ten rupees.

Finally, when a girl is married, she can still talk to men and boys but except in the public circumstances of a dance, a wedding or a festival, she is not expected to 'laugh' or 'joke' with them. If she is found flirting with a boy, her husband can divorce her.

4 BAHONHAREA AND AJHNAREA

But besides these conventions which surround ordinary talk and conduct, certain relatives are bound by special rules. These relatives are known as

Bahonharea   A man and the wife of his younger brother.
              A man and the wife of his wife's younger brother.

Ajhnarea   A woman and the husband of her younger sister.
A woman and the wife of her younger brother.

The terms 'younger brother' and 'younger sister' include also 'younger cousins' – their mutual ages deciding the family position and not the fact that they are children of older or younger brothers.

All these relations must honour each other by never using each other's names while a woman in the presence of her male counterpart must observe a number of intricate conventions.

She must not, for example, sit on a cot in his presence and though she may sit on something else, she must not expose her person. During the night, if the male relative is in the room, she may lie on anything except a bed. She must not touch his cot or clothes belonging to him. She cannot sit on the same mat or by his side. She must not touch his shadow neither may she eat or drink anything left or touched by him or his wife. Equally, she must not loosen her hair nor allow anybody to free her of lice in the presence of this relative. If she is unmarried, she must keep her breasts covered in his presence and must neither climb a tree nor mount a ladder lest he should chance to see her thighs or sex. If she should unawares sit on his bed or touch anything belonging to him, she must at once wash or pour water on herself, as well as on whatever she has touched belonging to him.

The male relative, for his part, may sit or lie on a bedstead in her presence but he must not touch her or her shadow, her bedstead or her clothes or anybody carrying anything which she has worn. He must not tread a rice pounder for her, sit by her side or squat on the same mat. If he should accidentally touch her, the two must take water in a cup, pour it over each other and do johar.

So great is the need for avoiding even accidental encounters that both parties are always on the qui vive and the matter is even referred to in two songs.

48

From the right and the left
Come my husband's elder brothers
Do not stumble on this big thorn
Do not tread on the little thorn.

49

Dodging into the shed
You came, boy

Take care of your feet
Or you will kick me
Take care of your clothes
Or you will cover me with dust.

On the part of women who stand in this special relation, i.e. a woman and the wife of her younger brother, the restrictions are much fewer and in fact there are no prohibitions concerning lying down, sitting, avoiding shadows or touching clothes. The younger, however, must on no account touch the elder on her body though the latter may massage the former or extract a thorn from her foot.

These rules are of great importance for they protect a junior member of a family from exploitation by his elders and if they are broken at all the offender is liable to exemplary punishment.

In Surjudih, Saman Hansdak' had been drinking in his house when he went into the street. As he did so, he chanced to knock against his younger brother's wife. The girl exclaimed when she saw him coming but it was too late and he blundered into her body. His relations saw the collision and next morning they called a village meeting. As Saman had not intended any liberty, the two washed each other's feet and Saman paid a rupee and four annas as the cost of the meeting.

In Hororaidih the jogmanjhi touched his younger brother's wife. The villagers fined him fifteen rupees and when he did not pay it, they semi-outcasted him and removed him from his post.

A much more serious contact occurred at Kusma in 1935 when a woman was kicked by her husband's elder brother. The Santal who told me of the occurrence said, 'A kick by anyone else would not have mattered. She would have said, "What is he up to? Does he want to make love to me?"' But the special relationship made the kick intolerable. The matter went to the village and when the man did not pay the fine, he was completely out-casted and bitlaha was also done.

5 RULES FOR EATING

The feeling that intimacy between certain parties and relatives must at all costs be avoided accounts for a number of rules concerning food. The first is that no Santal may on any account eat with non-Santals, while a Santal woman may not eat any food cooked by someone not a Santal. For men the latter convention is not quite so strict but even men may not eat food cooked by a Jolaha, a Muhammadan, a Paharia, a Dom, a Chamar, a

Muchi, a Hadi, a Bauri, or a Mahali and when the food is cooked by someone not of these communities they may not eat it from the same plate.

This rule is so widely understood and approved that no one would normally think of breaking it. If, however, a Santal girl were caught eating food with a non-Santal, a 'Diku', or even consuming some Diku's food she would be punished as if she had had intercourse itself.

The second rule concerns eating from the same plate. This is forbidden to the following relations:

Mamo bhagna	Maternal uncle and nephews and nieces
Mami bhagna	Maternal aunt and nephews and nieces
Bahonharea	A girl's husband and her elder brother
	A younger brother's wife and her husband's elder brother
Ajhnarea	A girl's husband and her elder sister
Honharea jawae gomke	Son-in-law and father-in-law
	Son-in-law and mother-in-law
Honharea (kumin)	Daughter-in-law and father-in-law
Bochamisera	Married younger sister and her elder brother and elder sister
Balaya	Girl's father and her husband's father
	Girl's mother and girl's husband's mother
Balakora, balakuri	Girl's mother and girl's husband's father
Haram budhi	Husband and wife

If any Santal breaks this rule, he is liable to fine and semi-outcasting while in the case of husband and wife the act disqualifies the man for life from making sacrifices to the bongas. 'He has become a woman.'

There are similar restrictions on eating food that has been left over. Bahonharea, ajhnarea, balaya, balakora, balakuri and husband and wife cannot consume each other's leavings, but in all other cases the younger relative can take the leavings of the older. A niece or nephew for example can take the leavings of an uncle. A married younger sister can eat the leavings of her elder brother or sister.

In Dundua the elder brother of a girl's husband was taking his night meal in the dark when he noticed that he was eating some left-over food. A light was brought and the girl confessed that she had given him her leavings. The family was disgusted at her conduct and at a village meeting her husband divorced her.

6 INCEST AND INTEGRITY

If these conventions set the tone for sex, a variety of rules determine the scope of intercourse itself. These rules are by far the most important in the whole of tribal life. They define what Santals understand by tribal integrity and there is scarcely anything that Santals will not do in order to maintain them.

The first law is that no Santal may have relations with anyone who is not a Santal, and amongst the tribesmen intimacy is forbidden between the following relations:

I

Son	Mother
Father	Daughter
Son-in-law	Mother-in-law (wife's mother)

II

Brother	Sister
Nephew	Aunt (father's sister)
	Aunt (mother's sister)
Uncle	Niece (brother's daughter)
	Niece (sister's daughter)
	Niece (daughter of paternal uncle's son)
	Niece (paternal uncle's daughter)
Cousin	Cousin (father's brother's daughter)
	Cousin (mother's brother's daughter)
Step-son	Step-mother (father's co-wife)
Brother-in-law	Younger sister-in-law (younger brother's wife)
Father-in-law	Daughter-in-law (son's wife)
Nephew-in-law	Aunt-in-law (father's brother's wife)
	Aunt-in-law (mother's brother's wife)
Cousin-in-law	Wife of younger cousin, i.e. son of father's brother or son of mother's brother if the man himself is younger
Son-in-law	Sister of mother-in-law
Uncle-in-law	Niece-in-law (wife of brother's son)
Step-father	Step-daughter

III

Step-brother	Step-sister
Cousin	Cousin (father's sister's daughter)
	Cousin (mother's sister's daughter)

Grandson	Grandmother (father's mother)
	Grandmother (mother's mother)
Grand nephew	Grand aunt (father's father's sister)
	Grand aunt (father's mother's sister)
	Grand aunt (mother's father's sister)
	Grand aunt (mother's mother's sister)
Father-in-law	Sister of daughter-in-law (sister of son's wife)
Grandfather-in-law	Granddaughter-in-law (grandson's wife)
Brother-in-law	Wife of brother-in-law (wife's brother's wife)
	Sister of brother-in-law's wife (sister of wife's brother's wife)
	Sister-in-law (mother of son's wife)
	Sister-in-law (mother of daughter's husband)
Father-in-law	Sister of son-in-law (sister of daughter's husband)
Uncle-in-law	Niece-in-law (wife's brother's daughter)
	Niece-in-law (wife's sister's daughter)

In addition to these kinsmen, all relations who possess the same kinship by comparative analogy are also banned. For example, a Santal is debarred from marrying his grandfather's brother's granddaughter for she stands on the same level to him as an uncle's daughter. A Santal cannot marry his father's brother's granddaughter for her relationship to him is that of a niece. Equally, a boy cannot have relations with the wife of his father's brother's grandson for she, too, ranks as the wife of a brother's son. All relatives therefore who come within these prohibited degrees or stand on a parallel footing are debarred from sexual intimacy.

There is one last group within which sex is totally forbidden. No Santal may have intercourse with a girl of his own clan. A Tudu boy, for example, cannot go with a Tudu girl, a Murmu girl may not sleep with a Murmu boy. If they do so the act is incest and the direst penalty may be imposed.

7 'FLOWER' FRIENDSHIPS

There remains one further type of relationship that, while strictly nonsexual, has responsibilities and obligations. Boys, for example, can have a friendship termed 'phul' or 'flower' and an alliance known as Karmu Dharmu.

To start the former two boys attend a Shivratri fair. Each takes a brass plate with some sweets, a garland of flowers, and a cloth. When the fair is over, each garlands the other and gives him all he has brought. Their friends then ratify the pact by sharing the sweets.

The tie of Karmu Dharmu is somewhat rarer but is equally significant. At the Dangua Karam festival, which is celebrated only once in five years, the jogmanjhi tells two unmarried boys of the same clan to erect the Karam branch. These two boys are called Karmu and Dharmu and continue in this role until they are married. When the festival is over, they take the branch away, report themselves to the headman and are given a meal of cold rice. This meal ratifies their partnership and inaugurates a tie of permanent friendship.

Both these youthful alliances have important consequences. They are primarily pacts of mutual assistance and are thus forms of insurance against crisis. If the occasion demands it the friends share each other's wedding expenses, help each other in cultivation and lend each other plough cattle. They rally to each other's aid at birth, sickness or death and assist each other with loans that carry no interest.

Similar institutions exist for girls and as with boys the two main types of friendship are 'flower' and Karamdar. Two girls become 'flowers' by exchanging presents, sweets and garlands at a fair in the presence of their friends, while the two girls who do the circling ceremony of the Karam branch put leaves from the branch in each other's hair, are given cold rice by the headman and are then recognised as life-long 'Karam twigs'.

These girls' alliances are important both as emotional supports and as a means to domestic aid. The friends give each other presents such as little rings or bangles, put flowers in each other's hair and sometimes exchange clothes. At weddings the bride gives her 'flower' or 'Karam twig' a necklace of flowers or beads. After marriage the two visit each other, attend weddings together or go to each other with presents at Sohrae. The alliance is in no way lesbian, but rather represents an intimacy of the heart, a means of comfort.

But besides linking two friends, the alliance gives each of the parties a set of new relations. The ritual converts the boys into brothers and the girls into sisters. A boy who is 'flower' or 'Karmu Dharmu' to another boy is therefore debarred from sexual intimacy with his friend's sister, mother, stepmother, mother-in-law and so on and is exposed to the same penalties for a breach of this law as if his friend were a true brother. Equally a girl who is the 'flower' or 'Karam twig' of another girl must avoid intimacy with the friend's brother, father, step-father or with any of a true sister's prohibited kinsmen. This new relationship does not extend beyond the parties themselves and does not act as a bar to the inter-marriage of their children; but in ordinary life its significance is profound. It creates in effect a supplementary code of exogamy.

8 SEX AND PRIVACY

If a Santal avoids the above partners, he is free to 'take whatever girl he wills'. But even here his conduct is hedged with certain rules. He must always, for example, observe the strictest privacy.

50

They are crackling the raher bushes
Where you went to have me
O Mirza boy, let me go
My bangles and anklets are tinkling
And all the traders will hear us.

In Dumarghati the daughter of Lodga Hembrom 'showed her thumb' to seven village boys and defied them to take her. The seven accepted the challenge and one day they dragged her to the forest and attempted to have their way. The girl repulsed five but succumbed to the last two. The matter came to the village and all the eight were fined two rupees and eight annas each – the girl for inciting the boys to have her in public and the boys for accepting the challenge.

In Basdume, Khara Murmu induced a girl of another village to go with him. The villagers caught them in each other's arms and the meeting punished Khara with a fine of fifteen rupees.

In certain cases even though the boy and girl are merely anticipating marriage, they are liable to be punished if they are caught engaging publicly together.

In Siakhuri, Nandhna Murmu was caught with his village girl in actual intercourse. The villagers gave them a beating and although the boy's father paid a bride-price and the girl was then and there accepted as a wife, the boy was fined five rupees and the girl two rupees and eight annas.

The same principles apply to attempts and preparations.

In Bodacapar, Chundka Murmu was caught with his village girl. They were about to start intercourse when the girl's brother reached the scene. Chundka was dragged to the headman and was fined five rupees.

Even more important is the rule that intercourse must always be with the girl's consent. If a boy cannot win a girl by words or presents, he is not entitled to have his way by force. If, in spite of this, he takes her, the girl is entitled to five rupees as damages and the boy can also be fined. Finally, if after marriage a girl admits a lover, the adulterer must compensate the husband.

9 SANCTIONS: PANTE BEGAR

These conventions are expected to be observed by all Santals. What, however, is current practice? Do Santals actually obey the rules of sex or do they observe them only as it suits them? The answer is that in the great majority of cases the rules have become so ingrained in their minds that obedience is automatic. From early childhood their parents and other children have so impressed the rules on them that they have become, as it were, second nature to them. No rules, however, could survive without sanctions and it is probably because all breaches carry with them strict penalties that they are hardly ever broken. The rules are observed primarily because they constitute a valued code of Santal behaviour, but if a rule is broken, Santals see to it that whoever breaks it is broken also.

When a breach of rule occurs, the offender is either seized and brought before the local headman or a complaint is lodged before him. The headman summons the villagers to a kulhi durup' – 'a sitting in the street' – the matter is then talked out, each side putting its case, and finally agreement is reached. If the matter is either fairly unimportant or is capable of being adjusted, the offender is required to pay a fine and in certain cases damages. But whatever is imposed must be paid at once. If it is not, the guilty party is exposed to a form of limited excommunication – pante begar – 'exclusion from the line'. When the village gathers for a festival and is eating in a row, the offender will not be debarred from joining the feast but the villagers will keep him from the line. When a bullock dies and the whole village shares its flesh, the offender will have no part. If another Santal is punished with a fine, he is deprived of any share. If there is a birth, wedding or death in the offender's house, no one will assist at the ceremonies. Similarly if there is a birth or wedding elsewhere in the village, the offender will not be invited and if there is a festival his house will be ignored. He will also be excluded from communal drinking and dancing. These disabilities do not gravely disturb his general routine. He can still eat and drink with the villagers though in a private manner. He is not deprived of fire. He can take water from the common wells and springs. It is rather that the restrictions convey the village sense of disapproval. They induce a vague disquiet and sooner or later the sense of being 'under a cloud' compels him to submit.

In Sibtala the mother of Mundri Soren refused to pay a fine. The Sohrae festival was at hand so on the day for garlanding the cows, the villagers treated her cattle as if they did not exist. Similarly on the begging day, they sang in all the other houses but left out Mundri's mother. This brought her to her senses and she paid a little extra money and came back into line.

In Telni, Champai Tudu was pante begar-ed for failing to pay a fine. At first he was defiant but a little later he noticed that the village boys were always stopping his sons from playing on their flutes and were continually running off with their drums. His daughters went down to join the other girls in a lagre dance but the line declined to open and the women drove them back. This broke Champai's spirit and at the Sohrae festival he went to the headman with rice and a fowl and begged to be taken back.

When the fine is paid, the matter ends and the offender is again as much a member of the line as he was before he left it.

10 SANCTIONS: BITLAHA

If fine and pante begar effectively dispose of 'minor' breaches, different methods are reserved for all the graver infringements. Clan and kin incest, intercourse with Dikus, eating with forbidden relatives, contact with tabooed kinsmen – such actions provoke intense and angry disapproval. The village bongas are deemed to be polluted and in many cases the offenders are liable to full and immediate outcasting followed by the ceremony known as bitlaha. If in certain cases the offence is punished with a fine, that is because Santals are often capable of pity and even when insisting that 'all are fingers of one hand' are yet prepared to grade offences in order of enormity. Kin incest, for example, of the kind which I have placed in group I, is more abhorrent than incest in group II, and it is therefore almost always visited with the supreme penalty.

Dewan Tudu was married as a ghardi jawae in the house of a widow of Pokharia. One night Dewan's wife discovered him in congress with her mother. She complained to the headman and although Dewan and his mother-in-law both pleaded to be fined, the villagers called the neighbouring headmen, completely excommunicated them and did bitlaha. In Patsara, the wife and son-in-law of Jolha Murmu were similarly caught together and were punished by being driven from the village. In Beldiha, Chundu Soren married a widow with a daughter. The girl lived in his house and after some time became pregnant. She named her step-father and here also bitlaha was done.

Kin incest in group II, on the other hand, is sometimes punished with a large fine. When Barka Kisku of Kesa had relations with his sister as a result of which the girl became pregnant, the villagers imposed a fine of fifteen rupees and Barka was made to purchase a husband for her by giving two bullocks, twelve maunds of rice and twelve rupees. In Kitajore, Kanha Murmu had relations with his brother's daughter, Jasmi and was fined twenty-five rupees. Sukol Murmu of Jorbhitha was caught with the widow of his younger brother and fined one hundred and forty rupees.

Incest of the kind covered by group III is regarded as considerably less serious and while bitlaha can also be inflicted for even this offence, it is more usual to close the incident with a smallish fine. In Supaidih, Sundar Marandi seduced the daughter of his father's sister as a result of which the girl became pregnant. Sundar was fined twenty-five rupees and made to buy the girl a husband but there was no suggestion of performing bitlaha.

Cases of clan incest as well as of misbehaviour with Dikus are on a somewhat different footing. Both are flagrant breaches of the code and bitlaha is regarded as the only proper punishment. But here also much depends on the attitude of the offenders and the mood of the village and while bitlahas have often been done for these offences, large fines have also in certain cases been accepted.

When a major crime is brought to their notice, the villagers hold a meeting and if the matter is still in its infancy or is known only to themselves, they at times dispose of it on the spot. 'Why should we bring in others' said the headman of Khajuria 'when we can settle this ourselves?' In such cases, they question the parties and come to a finding. Often the offenders admit their guilt. 'It began in Bengal' a boy from Borowar told a meeting. 'The girl and her father were there. We were of the same clans. We were sleeping apart. One night the girl took my penis and made it stand. I went and lay above her. After that I went to her each night. When we came to the village, we went on meeting. We slept in our houses in separate rooms. I used to go to sleep and the girl would come to my house and poke me with a pole. In the winter when the paddy was heaped and I slept at the threshing floor, she would pull me out and make me have her in the field. I told my master that we had ended it last year and paid a fine but the girl was making me go on. One day she said she would tie a string to her toe and sleep near the door. She put the end of the string outside and told me to come and pull it. For three nights she went to sleep with the string on her foot but I never went. Then she came to my house and forced me to have her.'

If the crime is admitted or proved, the villagers consider all the circumstances and sometimes impose a small fine. In certain rare cases of clan incest, they may even resort to 'false' adoption. In Talwa, Dhorba Soren eloped with Khendle, a girl of the same clan. When they returned the boy was fined twenty rupees and the girl ten. They were so much in love, however, that they found it impossible to part. The villagers again considered the position and the village jogmanjhi then performed a 'false' adoption. He bongatala-ed the girl (or in other words, brought her into his own set of bongas), gave her his own clan of Tudu but accepted no other responsibilities. When the girl had changed her clan, the lovers married. Similarly in Bordoha when Mansingh Soren fell in love with the daughter of Durga Soren, the villagers tried to part them but the two 'insisted' on being married. When the people saw that there was no alternative, a Murmu man was paid to act as a 'false' adopting father. He took the girl into his bongas, named her Hisi Murmu and later the boy and girl were married.

Such leniency however is distinctly rare and even though the parties plead for mercy, the villagers may decide to inflict a heavy fine.

When, in such cases, a fine is inflicted, the offenders usually pay the sum at once. If they cannot pay immediately and their attitude is not defiant, they are sometimes given a date by which to collect the money. Delay, however, is always avoided for until the money is paid, the village bongas remain polluted and not only the offenders themselves but all those who share their kitchens are completely outcasted. They can no longer borrow fire. They lose access to all wells dug by the village and to all other people's houses. No one will accept tobacco from them or allow them to use a rice pounder. No one will eat or drink with them. They are not invited to village councils and if they bring any complaints, no notice is taken of them. They are not allowed to join a hunting or fishing expedition. They cannot attend a dance, a wedding, a birth or a funeral and if there is any ceremony in their house, no one will go to it. None of their family members will be accepted as a servant and if one of them falls ill, no medicine-man may attend him. They are disqualified from getting settlement of waste lands. No one will help them in cultivation and the village women will lose no opportunity of taunting and abusing them. It is not surprising that in the great majority of cases, they promptly pay up.

If, however, the date for payment expires and still the fine is undeposited or if the infringement is so serious that a fine is obviously inappropriate, the villagers often purify the bongas by themselves offering a goat and then take steps to perform bitlaha. This ceremony is one of the most impressive in the whole of Santal life. It is performed by an enormous crowd. It is done to the thunder and roll of drums. The crowd advances on the culprit's house in long surging lines. Finally a ceremony of symbolic defilement is performed in the heart of the courtyard. In its disciplined expression of revolted disgust, its intense assertion of tribal values, its vindication of the rules of sex, the ceremony is unique in tribal India.

The first step for holding a bitlaha is to obtain regional approval. The village headman must first inform the local pargana, tell him of the village decision and ask him to consult the headmen from the five nearest villages. These act as a reviewing authority and until they have confirmed the village decision, no bitlaha can correctly take place. Once they have confirmed it, they approve a date and the headman then sends out an emissary to all the local markets to show a dharwak' and announce the performance. The dharwak' is a twig or branch of sal wood, with its leaves stripped to indicate the number of days in which the bitlaha will be held. One of the leaves is folded into a cone to represent the penis and another is pinned into a groove to represent the vagina. As the herald shows the branch, he tells the people what has happened and invites them to attend. Only males can come and on the night previous to the ceremony, men and boys from all over the countryside troop in, headed by their respective headmen. They carry sticks, drums, flutes and buffalo horns and settle down for the night in small groups. Some of them light fires, some doze while others gather into circles for discussion or entertainment. Two or more nude jokers appear on the scene and the customs of the annual hunt are re-enacted. In the course of the night the dihri or local hunt-master arrives and under his chairmanship the assembly discusses local matters of tribal concern. The next morning a messenger is sent to call the offenders. These hardly ever come so, after hearing the facts, the assembly formally ratifies the decision, the hunt-master takes a branch, goes to the head of the throng and the crowd then starts its thunderous descent upon the village.

It will illustrate the course of events if I describe in detail a bitlaha which I attended at Khajuria in 1944. During my time in the Santal Parganas, I attended over twenty of these ceremonies. The Khajuria bitlaha arose out of intercourse between a Santal girl, Khari Murmu, and a non-Santal, a Sauria Paharia, but as the procedure at the Santal's house was the same as if both parties had been Santals, it will serve as a typical example.

The village is two miles south of Dumka with a pleasant sandy street, shaded by large jack-fruit trees. The meeting place was a field five or six hundred yards from the houses with airy views across the uplands to wooded hills on the horizon. When I reached the scene, five hundred men had gathered and there was a great din of drums. Six rows of men were dancing naked. A dozen drummers were racing to and fro and boys with flutes and horns were dancing in the crowd. As the lines went backwards and forwards the dancers sang lewd songs and as each song finished there was a shout of 'Der, der' and 'Deper, deper' ('Fuck them, fuck them').

93

As the dancers swung to and fro they thrust out their buttocks and jerked their penises.

A little later the recital of the facts began. The headman and villagers of Khajuria squatted round and a headman of another village expounded the law.

'Why have you summoned so many?' he said.

'One is now two. The girl is a Santal. The boy is a Paharia. We caught them copulating. There were two and they were one.'

'Do Santal girls go with Paharias?'

'Never. From the seven ages, from the time of the earliest ancestors, Santals and Paharias have never come together. Santals with Santals, Dikus with Dikus, Bhuiyas with Bhuiyas, Kamars with Kamars, Paharias with Paharias, Sahibs with Sahibs. That is the law.'

'For how long were they one? Did you catch them?'

'They were caught at night. For three years we have tried to separate them. They never listened. They never did what we said. They have not given each other up. So we have sent out the wedding knots. Even if they give one hundred rupees now we will not take it. Today we will marry them. They are no more with us. They cannot eat and drink with us. They cannot join in any village talks. There can be no wedding with them. We have put them apart. We will not have them at any death or any trouble or any festival. We will not link anything to them. We will not take their girls or give them our boys. Today all the countryside will know of them. If anyone joins himself to them he will go the same way. We will not mix with them. They will live alone like mongrels, Doms and sweepers. Until they come back by giving a feast of a hundred plates, they will have no peace with anyone. Hear what we have said. And listen men of the country-side. Whatever is the custom we will now do. But we will do no damage, spoil nothing, harm nothing. But according to custom we will dance before the house and piss in the courtyard.'

The headman of Khajuria then brought a bowl of water and five rupees, begged pardon for the crime in his village and besought the assembly to spare his house. Five headmen from nearby villages then took the money and exempted his house from entry and defilement.

More dancing and drumming then started and for half an hour, the lines jerked backwards and forwards. Two nude jokers began to dart like snakes among the crowd. One of them had a string of cream coloured flowers around his neck and head while a great red apron of hibiscus flowers flapped to and fro about his sex. As the jokers ran they jerked their organs, grappled with on-lookers and dashed at the dancers. Gusts of mirth swept through the crowd while the clear sound of flutes rippled in the air.

The headman of Khajuria then brought out a sal tree branch with the leaves sewn to represent a penis and vagina, and a soiled leafplate stuck on the tip. He held the branch aloft and with the dancers moving slowly behind him, the crowd went up the slopes to the village. Forest songs broke out. There was a great thunder of drums and again the cries went up of 'Der, der' and 'Deper, deper'.

When they reached the village they went to the girl's house. This was locked and deserted and the crowd went down the street. At the end, they turned, came back and finally swept into the courtyard. The headman stuck the branch into the roof, the dancers jerked to and fro and twenty of them went inside the verandah and made water on the walls. Again they did the thrusting jerking dance up and down the courtyard shouting 'der' and 'deper' with laughing fury. Then they left the reeking walls and the crowd streamed out of the village and back to the field.

Before the crowd dispersed the headman of Mortanga who was acting as hunt-master stripped himself naked and offered three fowls at the end of the village. Two were to Manjhi Haram and to Maran Buru on behalf of the whole assembly, while the third was to the Ronga Ruji bonga on behalf of the nude jokers. As he made the offerings he said, 'Manjhi Haram, today the people of your village and the men of the countryside were gathered. We danced your village through and through. We were forced to do it. We did no harm or sin. We are giving you your due. Accept it in your pleasure.'

For the Ronga Ruji bonga he marked a circle with his loin cloth, took a pinch of charcoal, touched it with his organ and put it in the circle. Then he took some vermilion and sun-dried rice, touched his organ with them and put them in the circle. Finally he took up a fowl, pressed it to his penis and cut its neck on the axe. Then he said, 'Ronga Ruji bonga, today we pulled our foreskins back and before the people we exposed our penises. We did it well. Let them no longer stay exposed. Let each penis return to its sheath. In gratitude we offer you this fowl. Accept it in your pleasure.' When the sacrifices were over, the jokers resumed their clothes, the dance and songs ended and the crowd went quietly away.

This bitlaha which was typical of many such ceremonies differed in only two respects from the standard ritual. Since only one of the offenders, the girl, was a member of the village, and the other – a Paharia – came from a remote part of the district, the ceremony was done in only one of the houses. Had the two houses been in the vicinity, both would have been bitlahaed and the Paharia would have suffered equally with the Santal. In the second place, somewhat fewer symbols were employed than is sometimes the case. When Ratu Rai, a Bhuiya of Ganduparta was bitlahaed, a piece of half-burnt firewood and a worn broom in addition to the soiled leaf-plate were hung up on the roof. An earthen hearth was cracked and beside pissing in his courtyard, the crowd excreted in the house. When the ceremony was done to a Brahmin of Sijua in 1922, there was no urination or defaecation but a bullock's hoof was hung up on the roof. In 1935 when Bhagua Kahar of Ganga Rampur was bitlahaed, a bullock's skull was thrown in his house. In 1938 when Isri Sahu, another Diku, was similarly punished, some pigs' legs as well as bullock's hoofs were suspended to his roof and the crowd urinated and defaecated on his verandah as well as at the entrance to his house. At Khajuria the worn broom and the piece of half-burnt firewood were omitted and since only a Santal house was involved there was no recourse to a pig's foot or a bullock's skull. Apart from this, however, the ceremony was identical with others and might have happened anywhere.

II THE SIGNIFICANCE OF BITLAHA

It will be obvious that much of the effect of this ritual is due to the hugeness of the crowd whose presence dwarfs the village and infuses it with awe and terror. Just as the effect of sculpture is inseparable from its size, a bitlaha would be nothing if only a dozen men took part. It is because it mobilises a whole area and focuses in one place the resentment of a region that it reinforces powerfully the tribal code.

But numbers alone are far from fully explaining its significance and there are five aspects of the ritual that contribute to its force.

A bitlaha is in the first place a hunt in which the offenders are the quarry. 'They are like beasts. They must be tracked and hunted down.' For this reason the men carry the sticks of hunters, a hunt-master presides, and the dancing, the drumming and the flutes all parallel the activities of the annual hunt.

Secondly, a bitlaha demonstrates the beast-like behaviour of the culprits. 'We have made them cattle,' said a headman. 'They have acted like the early ancestors whose conduct ruined the world. They have rutted like buffaloes.' For this reason also the songs dwell constantly on bestiality.

51
Father, what is that yelping
In the hole in the ridge?

Grandfather, hush
He is coupling with a bitch.

52

In the plantain garden
What is that noise
Of phen phen ?
A deaf old man
Is going with a bitch
Ban ban *it sounds*
Kae kae *it whimpers*
As he goes to it.

53

Across the river, Barsa
You are always at a sheep
I shall tell your father
But my father goes to girls.

It is these songs which give the offence its setting. They reduce it to its ritual level. They show it for what it is – a coupling with a beast.

In the third place, a bitlaha is an ato bapla 'a wedding by the village'. The bitlaha crowd is 'a wedding party'. 'The family did not marry them', Santals say, 'But the people did.' The village puts the two offenders together, exposes their secret relationship and broadcasts it over the area. For this reason, leaf emblems of a penis and vagina are made to dangle on a branch and impromptu songs bandy about the names of the guilty lovers.

At a bitlaha in Haripur, the original offenders were Mongol Tudu and Sonodi Tudu and the men sang:

54

Mongol, you pressed my body to you
And now you are smiling
But what a wrong you did me
For the courtyard is filling
With village relations.

55

The street is filling
With men from the country
What a wrong you did me
But you flirted, Sonodi
You flirted with me
And we are both to blame.

56
Mongol, from the spring below the pond
Pick the blossom for me
Like bel fruits are my breasts
And you may take them
My cunt
Is like a lamp
And I will give it to you
Utterly.

These mocking songs enlarge the offenders like shadows on a screen. They toss their names from lip to lip. They degrade their intimacy and rob it of all its feeling and romance.

But besides portraying the act by song and choreography, a bitlaha is also a form of tribal punishment. In Santal society the sole wish of individuals is to remain anonymous, to lead their lives quietly, not to attract attention, to remain merged in their tribal setting like crustacea in a pool. Bitlaha reverses all this. It invests the offender with all the publicity that he most dislikes. It pulls him out of his obscure setting and dangles him before the whole region.

57
In shining clothes
Come the men of the country
In clothes to their ankles
Swagger the chiefs
Girl, it was you
Who brought me to this shame
Father, when they come
The harm will be ended
The world is big
To east and west
To north and south
Hide us in a corner.

It is the exposure to collective shame that is the essence of the ritual and which makes it far more dreaded than physical torture or confinement in a jail.

Above all, bitlaha expresses the tribe's sense of defilement. Besides a soiled leaf-plate, other objects – a worn-out broom and a burnt piece of wood – are often tied to the branch. A broom is an almost universal female symbol, and Margaret M. Murray in *The God of the Witches* offers the following comment. 'The connection in the popular mind between a woman and a broom probably took its rise in very early times, the explanation being that the broom is essentially an indoor implement, belonging therefore to the woman; the equivalent implement for a man is the pitch fork, which is for out-door work only. This is the reason why in medieval representations of witch dances, the women or witches often hold brooms, while the men or devils carry pitch forks. The broom being so definitely a feminine tool came to be regarded as the symbol of a woman. Until within very recent times cottage women in Surrey, when going out and leaving the house empty, put a broom up the chimney so that it was visible from the outside, in order to indicate to the neighbours that the woman of the house was away from home. In other parts of England until the last century a broom standing outside a door showed that the wife was absent and the husband at liberty to entertain his male friends.'

Similarly, fire is a sexual symbol and in a contemporary poem by David Gascoyne the same imagery is used.

> '*Supposing the sex*
> *A cruelty and dread in the thighs*
> *A gaping and blackness – a charred*
> *Trace of feverish flames.*'

Just as the worn-out character of the broom implies the degradation of the act, the burnt piece of wood suggests the sexual ruin which the wilful breach of rule has caused.

In the same way the overriding sense of defilement is stressed by the urination in the courtyard and this is often reinforced by defaecation and by the pounding of excrement in a rice pounder. 'At certain stages of early culture,' says Havelock Ellis, 'when all the emanations of the body are liable to possess mysterious magic properties and become apt for secret uses, the excretions, and specially the urine, are found to form part of religious ritual and ceremonial functions. Even among savages the excreta are frequently regarded as disgusting, but under the influence of these conceptions such disgust is inhibited, and these emanations of the body which are usually least honoured become religious symbols. Urine has been regarded as the original holy water, and many customs which still survive in Italy and various parts of Europe, involving the use of a fluid which must often be yellow and sometimes salt, possibly indicate the earlier use of urine. Among the Hottentots, the medicine man urinated alternately on bride and bridegroom, and a successful young warrior was sprinkled in the same way. Mungo Park mentions that in Africa on one occasion a bride sent a bowl of her urine which was thrown over him as a special mark of honour to a distinguished guest. Pennant remarked that the Highlanders sprinkled their cattle with urine, as a kind of holy water on the first Monday in every quarter. Even the excreta of animals have sometimes been counted sacred. This is notably so in the case of a cow, of all animals the most venerated by primitive peoples, and specially in India.

'Moreover,' he continues, 'in the folk-lore of modern Europe we everywhere find plentiful evidence of the earlier prevalence of legends and practices of a scatalogical character. It is significant that in the majority of cases it is easy to see a sexual reference in these stories and customs. The legends have lost their earlier and often mythical significance, and frequently take on a suggestion of obscenity, while the scatological practices have become the magical devices of love-lorn maidens or forsaken wives practised in secrecy. . . . Among many primitive peoples throughout the world and among the lower social classes of civilised peoples, urine possesses magic properties, more especially it would seem, urine of women and that of people who stand or wish to stand in a sexual relationship to each other. In a legend of the Indians of the northwest coast of America, recorded by Boas, a woman gives her lover some of her urine and says 'you can wake the dead if you drop some of my urine in their ears and nose. . . . Among both Christians and Muslims a wife can attach an unfaithful husband by privately putting some of her urine in his drink. This practice is worldwide: thus among the aborigines of Brazil, according to Martius, the urine and other excretions and secretions are potent for aphrodisiacal objects.'

In the Santal ceremony of bitlaha, urination is partly a symbol of the act of the two lovers, but it is even more a symbol of the tribe's pollution. Just as the house is defiled by the urine or the faeces, the tribe has been defiled by the conduct of the offenders. The action is a forceful expression in symbolism of all that Santals feel.

What then is the attitude of Santal culprits to the ceremony? When they have been sentenced their attitude is almost always one of resignation or sullen despair. In many cases they suffer bitlaha because they cannot pay the fine and it is after days of patient effort that the expenses of a penalty feast are finally got together. But in a few cases the offenders prefer the ceremony of bitlaha to the alternative of abandoning their guilty relationship.

Dewan Tudu of Pokharia was bitlahaed for sleeping with his mother-in-law. The bitlaha took place in January 1945 but in July they were still sharing a cot while his wife slept in another room.

In rare cases the offenders show active defiance and bitlahas have occurred in which instead of following the usual practice and going quietly from the scene the offenders have remained to face the crowd.

In a sensational case in the Dumka subdivision an old woman got ready some pots of boiling water. When the party arrived, she went to face them and threw the water at the leaders. Then when the pots were finished, she turned away. But the crowd was so angry that they stripped her naked and marched her through the village touching her private parts with their penises.

At Dhamni in 1933, a newly married girl of seventeen was going to her parents' house without her husband's consent. Her father-in-law went after her, forced her down and had intercourse. The girl complained to the manjhi and bitlaha was ordered. She herself was polluted and was therefore subjected to the ceremonies. Since however she herself was the complainant and was also the victim of force, she attended the ritual and carried the branch of sal leaves. The party observed the usual uproarious dancing, uttered cries of 'der, der' and 'deper, deper' and sang lewd songs while the girl moved calmly ahead as if insulated from the scene. As they neared the house, her father-in-law rushed out and aimed a blow at her with an axe. The blow missed and the party swooped upon him and gave him a severe beating.

In a third case, resistance led to death. A middle-aged widow Fulu Tudu of Taldih fell in love with Bulai, the husband of her younger cousin. The matter leaked out, several village councils were held and the two were duly fined. They did not pay the money and it was decided to perform bitlaha. On 27 May 1940 the people assembled and the headman of Taldih led them first to Bulai's house and then to Fulu's. At Bulai's a branch was planted and the ceremony went off without incident. When, however, they reached the second house, Udru Murmu, a relation, resisted entry. A fight took place. The headman was struck on the head, first with a stick and then with a heavy pestle. Others hit back at Udru. Finally the crowd swept in, broke two pitchers and urinated in the courtyard. The headman was dragged away unconscious and died the next day.

These cases are the only ones I know of in which Santals have resisted bitlahas and the normal attitude is far more usually one of despairing submission. Indeed in the bitlaha songs which portray the reactions of the guilty lovers it is anxiety and dread that dominate their minds. The songs

show the boy and girl awaiting the results of the first meeting and viewing
with sick suspense the impending ceremony.

58

Boy, the door
Do not open it too quickly
They have written it on paper
They have played it on the flutes
At the hunt on the big mountain
They will take our matter up.

They describe the approach of the great crowd and the revulsion of the
lovers.

59

The singing of the bulbul
A boy's words
And with my grown body
I did not feel ashamed
The land has gone dim
The raiders are upon us
Girl, do not call me elder brother.

Above all, the songs emphasise the sense of overwhelming shame at
ostracism by the tribe.

60

By day the meeting
Is at the stony hill
At night they are meeting
At the pool by the kadam tree
Girl, the meeting
Is never going to end
Girl, the money for the goat
The money for the baskets of rice
Girl, the meeting
Is never going to end.

61

You, elder brother
Smiled when you had loved me

I, elder brother
Was shamed before the country.

These songs do not necessarily portray the feelings of actual offenders, but their significance is obvious. It is because bitlahas are believed to induce these feelings that they remain the most dreaded sanction in Santal life.

CHAPTER VI

The Village Lover

I THE VILLAGE SCENE

'To the average normal person,' Malinowski has said, 'attraction by the other sex and the passionate and sentimental episodes which follow are the most significant events in his existence, those most deeply associated with his intimate happiness and with the zest and meaning of life.' We have already seen that within the village itself boys and girls can go about together and enjoy each other's company. We have also seen that provided they avoid prohibited relationships and are not detected in an act of sex, there is no specific ban on pre-marital affairs. It is natural therefore that as a Santal boy matures, he becomes increasingly engrossed with village girls.

62

Why are jack fruits rough
And mangoes smooth?
Why have boys moustaches
And girls smooth lips?

63

How does juice
Ooze from the mahua flowers?
How does oil
Spring from the mahua fruit?
The son of one
The daughter of another
How do their hearts join?

64

O my friend
Find for us where the girls sleep
O my friend
I will search and look
The door is made of cotton wood

The bolt is of baru
O my friend, how will you break in?

65

The local chiefs
Are fighting over frontiers
In the village the boys
Are fighting for the girls.

66

What is this bickering
Of girls in a big village?
The girls are too many
The boys are too few.

The boy enters in fact a period of awkward quest in which his sole concern is to gain a village love.

This state of affairs is described in a number of songs – some of them sung ostensibly by outsiders, at weddings, festivals or at annual hunts, others by the boys and girls themselves, when they meet in the forest, away from older people, singing to each other, flirting or making love.

67

O you two boys
Playing on your flute
You look for my heart
On the shelf for the water pots
You can see a flower
In the flower is my heart.

In another song, a girl refers to a lurking boy

68

Mother,
A snake from the river
A snake from the river
Wriggles in the palm tree.

Or again

69

In a new place
We dug a tank for water

And the lotus flowers came out
With a pot I went for water
And a black snake slid by.

Sometimes a boy describes a girl either as an oriole who is still evading capture or as a cotton tree spreading out its red flowers.

70

Oriole, at the spring or tank
You see me and you hide
If once I catch you, oriole
I shall carry you
Away and away.

71

At the end of the village
Is a cotton tree
And its flowers are red, my love
People say it is meat
It is not meat
It is a flower
It is a flower, my love.

72

By the bushes with the white flowers
You are grazing buffaloes, my love.
Pick me a white flower.
Picking, I will pick it
I will put it in your hair
Then what will you give me?

Occasionally boys are seen through the eyes of a more successful suitor.

73

O my love
The land is dark
Do not go out for water
Two handsome young coots
Are straying down.

At the same time the need for prudence is gently stressed.

74

O you two boys on the mountain
Do not split faggots with your axes
O you two girls
Do not make bundles of leaves
On the lower hill
For the tears will fall
Will fall from the eyes.

75

You are walking in the village street
You are strolling up and down
To right and left of you are marigolds
But do not take them in your eyes.

76

The spider of the small hill
Went up the big mountain
Go from branch to branch, spider
But do not make the flowers fall.

77

The spider of the big mountain
Came down to the lower hill
Spider, spider
Walk slowly
Or you will break your thread.

In these songs the marigolds are girls and the spider is a boy.
But if these songs describe the boy's pursuit, others are content to hint at the situation, or to show village girls as waiting to be approached.

78

On the mountain
The drums sound
In the village the two deer
Browse on the cotton.

In this case, the two deer are girls who are heedless of the boys' approach.

79

In a pool of the river the fish
On the hill

The white rabbit
The white peacock.

80

On the big mountain the fat rabbit
On the small hill the peacock with its tail
Scamper away, fat rabbit
Fly off, peacock with your tail.

Here the rabbit and peacock are girls whom boys have begun to notice.

81

In the upper village
The tiger eats
In the lower village
The oriole sings.

The meaning is that both boy and girl are ready for adult adventures. The girl is lovely as an oriole, the boy ravenous as a tiger.

Finally in a number of songs it is as if the quest is nearing conclusion and the boy has at last decided on a girl.

82

Below the field
Is a young parrot
In the creeper on the tree
Shoot it for me, brother
Its tail points at us.

83

On the big mountain
The deer graze
In a dried-up stream
Are feathered peacocks
Bring a gun
Load it with shot
The feathered peacocks
Are far too tired to fly.

With the winning of a girl, a Santal boy is on the road to young romantic joy.

2 STANDARDS OF CHARM

Among the tribes of Middle and Eastern India, two types of beauty compete in general esteem. The first is represented by the slim 'tubular' girl whose charm consists in a straight erect figure and perfectly moulded breasts. This ideal exists among the Ao and Lhota Nagas and is also favoured by the Murias. A Muria girl, Verrier Elwin has stated, 'should have a slim waist so that when she ties her cloth round it, buttocks and waist will be level.' The loveliest girl, in fact, should be trim and slender as a pole.

The second ideal is more rotund and buxom. Among the Konyak Nagas, a girl should be short, well-covered and with firmly rounded buttocks. Her narrow cloth which is often only four inches wide should slip and slide on them as she walks revealing the median line and firmly stressing their round shape. The Bondos of Orissa give equal stress to the girl with firm belly, slim waist and large posterior. 'Bondos,' Verrier Elwin has said, 'are apt to be plump, rather sleek and smooth, big-lipped, bagpipe-breasted with ample buttocks, large thighs, thick calves. Boys describe a girl's body as 'beautiful as a white cloud', her arms and legs as 'round and shapely as a bamboo', her breasts 'sparkling as two fishes', her shadow 'broad and healthy as a buffalo'. Similarly, among Hos, Kharias and Mundas, it is the robust and rounded girl who is generally admired.

Among Santals, it is this second type that evokes constant approval. A girl must be solid and supple, with small hips and hardly any waist. 'She must be neither too tall nor too short, neither over large nor too slim.' The line of her back should dip at the waist and then swell out in a firm magnificent curve. Her buttocks – deke – should be samtao – round, compact and smooth. Yet rotundity in itself is of little worth unless it is accompanied by a certain sleek smartness. A girl who has an over-flabby bottom – who is dhamir gom – is not approved of. Similarly, a girl with cutun lindhi, an over-large posterior, is considered clumsy and awkward. If a girl has a large bottom and then over-stresses it by bunching her clothes up like a bustle, her movements are slightingly referred to as laskae loskoe or lidgoe lodgoe – a wobble. The most lovely girl is bondkol, dhakerae or dhamela – with buttocks firm and soft, round and strong. 'They should jut out – neither fat nor big but rotund, sleek and smooth. As she walks they should swing and jerk a little. You should be able to admire their roundness.' A girl who strides along – lehec' lehec' – with a soft easy smoothness, her buttocks swinging gently, is considered very charming. So also is a girl whose walk is chalka chalki – neat and brisk – whose clothes rustle on her figure.

84

Boy, little boy
What kind of wife did you bring?
A girl with a lovely body
That sways as she dances.

85

By the river
A white goat grazes.
Jackal,
Do not eat it
Let it go
There is a black goat
Far plumper.

It is the plump goat, the buxom girl, who arouses a Santal's love and admiration.

Besides having a robust and round figure, a girl should be full-bosomed and from this angle Santals employ a conventional classification. Potkel are breasts that are just appearing, kortal cunci when they are a little bigger 'like the raised portion of a pair of cymbals', sosor deren 'when the nipples get black', hapa mu 'when they are ripe for boys'. All these are in process of formation and are valued more for their promise than their actual shape. It is a little later that they achieve their fullest charm.

86

Darling
It was with you only
That I slept at the door
Like the budding horns of a calf
Were your little breasts
And they are round as bowls now.

The most lovely are sinjo towa, 'round and firm like the fruit of a bel' or tengo towa, 'breasts that stand up firmly'.

87

O my love, your body is a mango
And your breasts
Are the half-ripe fruits of a bel

O my love
Let me take them for the first time
And kiss them with my mouth.

88

Where are you from, boy?
Where are you going?
What is your village?
My body is a mango
My breasts are golden marrows
Lift and take them in your hands.

89

Boy, I am now a mother
And you are still untried
What is it roused your love?
Your thighs
Are mangoes
Your breasts
Are the half-ripe fruits of a bel
I saw them and they fired my love.

These aspects of a girl's body are of great importance but her face and features must also have appeal. Her nose should be nanka, small and straight, her hair long and neat, her eyes neither too small nor too big, her teeth straight and regular, her cheeks round and chubby. Kokor met', 'eyes as big as an owl's' or ruka data, 'teeth that are over-large' are bad to look at. Equally disfiguring is a nose that is capia or flat, a face that is dab daba or too broad, and cheeks that are miko moko, fat and puffy. Complexion, on the other hand, is not of great account. Fairness is preferable but darkness also has its beauty. 'A dark girl with lovely breasts – she also is beautiful' and a number of songs express a Santal's rapture at the loveliness of a 'black' skin.

90

Father,
The wives of others
Are tall and fair
My wife is dark and black
But she nods and sways
Like a flower.

91

Glossy as a berry
Is that black girl by the river
My heart burns
My heart goes to her
O how shall I win
That black and glossy girl?

92

Grit on the ground
And the sky glares
O my love
Earth and sky are aflame
O you black berry
Do not cry, my love.

If these points contribute to a girl's beauty, it is her dress and ornaments that give her the final dash of style. Except in Pakaur, where blue and sometimes greenish cloth is favoured, a Santal girl in the Santal Parganas invariably dresses in simple staring white. The cloth is first wound round the legs to form a long, freely-moving skirt and is worn almost six inches lower than is usual with Mundas, Kharias and Uraons – the long flowing line often giving its wearer a supple stately elegance. The cloth is then taken up over the left shoulder, brought down to the right hip, passed round in front of the belly and finally tucked in at the small of the back. In this way both breasts are covered while the two arms are left entirely free. Ornaments are equally simple – the commonest being a long silver chain which dangles on the chest and some silver bangles and anklets which adorn the arms and legs. It is the way she wears this simple dress which marks out one girl from another.

93

O my love
Tie the cloth tightly round your thighs
And look to your body.

The girl whose smart white cloth sets off to perfection the glossy brown of her skin, whose body shines with a clean freshness, whose skirt stresses the roundness of her figure, whose black hair is trimly set with a white flower – it is this type of girl who most inflames a Santal's love. Above all,

25 Santal young women

26 Golwari 'vulture' da
27 Santal young wome
28 Golwari 'vulture' da

Kolwari 'greeting' dance
Kolwari dance: 'putting
flowers in the hair'
Kolwari 'greeting' dance

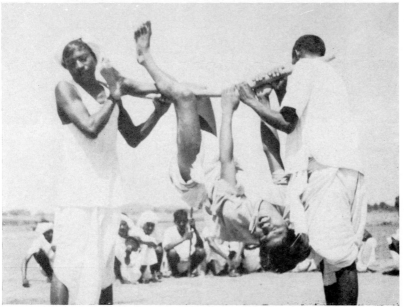

32 Dasae dancers
33 Dasae: the spider 'b
34 Dasae: the tiger 'bo

a girl who is strongly sexed, who is jolly and bouncing, may excite where others fail. 'A girl who smiles, a girl who is full of fun,' said Dhunu, 'she too is good to look at.' It is the personality linked to a strong robust physique that is often the final factor in determining a girl's appeal.

In contrast to what is beautiful in girls, masculine charm is somewhat more diffused. A boy should have a smart and springing walk. He should be jolly by temperament, a skilful drummer, a good flute-player. His broad shoulders should taper slightly to the waist. He should exude a natural vitality. If his hair curls or his features are regular, his cheeks slightly chubby, that is an additional charm but it is more his manner, 'his way with girls', that singles out one boy from another.

94

I am poor
You are rich
What made you like me?
It was the parting in your hair
And your long dhoti
That made me wild with love.

95

Boy, on your left arm
You wear a silver bangle
On your right arm
Is a golden clasp
Do not put on
Your golden armlet
For the girls
Will fight each other
For it.

96

On the drum
My former friend is playing
And like a plantain shoot
He sways and bends
On the flute
My present friend is playing
And his body swings
Like trim bamboos.

97

My former friend
Is playing on the drum
Like the twittering of quails
My present friend
Is playing on the flute
Like the dangling of a plantain.

98

'Bhuktu bedo bhuktu bedo'
O brother beat the drum
And only you shall have me.

It is the mixture of all these qualities that constitutes a boy's appeal.

3   THE WINNING OF A LOVER

Once a boy has fallen in love, he has only one wish – to possess his girl as fully as possible. This desire is sometimes the result of a slowly deepening friendship, and a forest tale, which is sometimes related at annual hunts, describes how the change is finally accomplished.

'There was a girl who was my sister-in-law by village relation. We used to graze the buffaloes together from the time that we were children. Then the girl grew bigger and whenever I saw her smooth uncovered thighs like a ripe mango, my sex reared like a plantain stem. One day we were with the cattle and while we were sitting, her thighs became uncovered and I saw up to their end. I could check myself no longer and I pushed her down with my hand. The girl was a virgin and I had to hurt her. Her sex was very tight and I was full of joy. After that we grazed cattle together and I took her every day.'

The same crisis in a youthful friendship is described in several forest songs. They show the girl protesting.

99

Phudan, my sex
Is a little bamboo shoot
And my waist
Is the bud of a plantain
Phudan, let me go
I am not yet ripe for love.

100

My breasts are mangoes, Sitaram
And my body is a young cucumber
Not this year, Sitaram
But next year
You may toss it up and down.

101

O my love,
Like a mango is your body
And like marrows your long breasts.
All the body at the waist,
O my love,
I will give you
And you may do with it as you will
But my breasts
I will not let you have.

102

We wandered into every jungle
Through a whole forest we went
But not a single shameful word you uttered
Now I am drawing water at the spring
Why are you tugging at my clothes?
No, no, I will not let you do it here.

But the boy does not always listen and the girl must then suffer his first attack.

103

O my love
You are young
And I am still younger
Let me go.
O my young darling
You may cry and cry
But today, my love
I will not let you go.

104

Your body is full grown
And I am still too young

You will harm my young body
Do not catch at me
Do not force me
If you force me, I shall weep.
With your young body
O my love
You may cry and cry
But I've seen your breasts
Poking from your dress
And I've caught them in my hands.

While active love is sometimes the culmination of an early acquaint-anceship, it may also result from a single sharp encounter. The boy and girl may not have known each other from before and love may suddenly flare from a chance meeting. When this happens, courtship is rapid and direct.

105

It was seeing you
That made me love
My love was not short
I cry when I think of you
I think of you and my eyes
Brim with tears.

Sometimes a mere smile is enough.

106

In the plaintain garden, boy
You are smiling at me
If you will only
Fill my mind
I will give you any girl you want.
I will keep you, girl
For ever.

107

I came from the house
And sat at the back
My lover saw me and waved his hand
He looked at me and smiled.

108

I am on this side
You are over the river
You flutter your eyebrows at me
Had there been words between us
I might have smiled at you.

Sometimes the boy sees a girl from a distance, whistles to her and in this way 'overcomes her mind'.

109

Boy, from the mountain
You are whistling to me
If you want to take me, hurry down
If you want to keep me
Catch me by the hand.

110

I am going
To a lower field
If your heart
Goes with me
Whistle on a finger
Wave your arm in a ring
And I will come to you
In a lower field.

Or the girl herself may take the initiative.

111

Below the garden plot
You are going, boy
With a book under your arm
I asked you, boy, but you wept
I am going after you
You look so handsome.

112

Below the headman's pond
Which is that boy

With a turban like a basket?
Shall I whistle to him
Or wave my hand?
O who is that boy
With a turban like a basket?

Occasionally boys and girls meet on their way to market or when going to the forest and a dialogue then ensues. A boy says to another, 'Some peacocks are passing. Let us go with them.' Sometimes they say to the girls, 'Where are you going?' 'To the market.' 'Come and buy some sweets with us.' Or a boy simply says, 'Girl, I am very thirsty.' In the late hot weather, when the mahua fruits are forming, a girl herself sometimes says, 'The mahua fruit is falling. I will eat some with you.' When she says this, a boy knows what she means and they fix a spot and meet.

But of all the aids to love, nothing is more compelling than the flute.

113

Do not play your flute
By the bank of the river
If I do not, what shall I do?
How shall I show
My heart is not a child's?

114

On the mountain of fiddles
A fiddle plays
On the hill of flutes
A flute is sounding
Listen, Sumi, Samia
Listen, you two girls
On the mountain of fiddles
A fiddle sounds
On the hill of flutes
A flute is playing.

115

Over the five mountains
Are five pairs of flutes
O does it matter
If I have five children
For I feel my youth has come.

116

I went to the cowshed
But there were no cows
I went to the buffalo shed
But there were no buffaloes
I stood at the back door
And from the dried-up stream on the mountain
I heard the flute come down.

117

On the banks of the river
O my life
You are grazing your buffaloes
As the buffaloes pace gently down
You keep time with your flute.

118

Under the sal tree by the river
A flute is sounding
To be whirled away is all my wish
'Chio chio', you naughty thing
'Chio chio', you little flirt
Your elder brother's flute is sounding.

If a boy cannot win these first exchanges, he is sometimes so inflamed by a girl that he decides to break the tribal rule and possess her by force.

119

Elder brother, I called you
But you did not listen
I did not want him
But he dragged me with him
And he had me as he liked.

Such a course however defeats its own ends for it does not endear the boy to the girl and often leads to punishment. There is in fact only one circumstance in which force is successful – when it is used as an act of discipline by the village boys as a whole. Santal boys feel very strongly that the village girls are their 'property' and while a girl may choose whichever boy she likes, she has no business to refuse to have a boy at all. If her parents try to keep her segregated, this only has the effect of making her a special object of attack and sooner or later the boys combine to bring her to her senses.

120

In the field by the spring
Who loved you so well
That the ants have all come up?
My father and brothers
Had stretched the rope
And spread the grass
And shut me in a rice bale.

The same situation is vividly illustrated by a forest tale which in spite of its droll absurdity is a valuable index to Santal sentiment.

'In olden times, people say, a certain paranik had a most lovely daughter. She was so beautiful that when a man saw her he could not say whether she was a human being or a bonga. Her parents and relatives said to each other, "If we marry this girl, her body will be spoilt and all her beauty will vanish." So they decided not to find a husband for her. They forbad her to talk to village boys and to keep her safe they provided two dogs. One was called Chaora and the other Bhaora. Whenever the girl went out, the two dogs went with her and sprang on any boy who ventured near her.

'In the village the headman had a cowherd boy. The boy had set his heart on having her. One day a buffalo died and the boy set aside a leg. That day the girl went to the forest for collecting leaves. The boy saw her and followed with the meat. When they neared the forest, the two dogs rushed on him but he threw the meat away and the dogs went after it. As they ate the meat, the girl left their minds and the boy overcame her. In her trouble the girl sang:

121

O Chaora, Bhaora
For only a little meat
You went astray
O Chaora, Bhaora
You have put me from your minds
O mountain bonga
Father and brothers
If only you are true
Stop him at my clitoris.

And the boy sang:

122

Bongas, bongas
If only you are true
Let it point only a little
And quickly go within.

When the other boys of the village heard of it they were all delighted and in their joy they started up this song:

123

The headman's cowherd
The paranik's daughter
By the grove's boulders
They made the wallow of a pig
Beat the drums
Sound the trumpets
By the boulders in the grove
He has tied her like a moth.

When the boy had finished with her, the girl went home and said to her grandmother:

124

Mother, to the grove I went for leaves
And there, a snake
A snake, mother, touched me
A snake's poison
A bonga's poison
By charms they come down
But a boy's venom, mother
Mounts up to the chest.

It is unnecessary to take this story very seriously or to assume that such occurrences are common. But the assumptions behind it are very clear. It is necessary that a boy should have a girl and sooner or later each girl must have her boy.

4 ASSIGNATIONS

When 'the minds of a boy and girl are tied', they have only one desire –

to possess each other as fully as possible. Continual association is not of course possible and secrecy must govern all their movements. None the less they are always meeting. 'Most boys,' said Sibu, 'try to meet their girls twice a day. If they cannot meet twice, they meet once. But once at least they must meet – whether in the night or in the day.'

The safest and most obvious place is in the forest and a number of songs describe these secret encounters.

125

On the big mountain, a jackal
Comes ambling down
On the small hill, a peacock
Slips quietly through the leaves.

126

Two boys
Ploughing, ploughing
Two girls
Drawing water
Water on the lower hill
Did you see my father
O you two boys
Ploughing on the hillside?
Did you see my mother
O you two girls
Drawing water on the hill?
We saw your father
High up on the mountain
We saw your mother
Far away below.

127

To the rice field in the jungle
To the field by the plum tree
We will go and fish, my love
The fish we will kill
The fish we will clean
And gazing we will have each other.

128

Through forest after forest we went
Through a whole forest we wandered

And in the trees you caught me to you
I am not old that I should cry
I am not a child that I should tell
Today we were a boy and girl
And had our love.

129

Daughter, you are grown
Girls of your age are married
Go to the forest
For the white flowers are faded
Your time has passed its noon.

130

Under a tree by the rock
We spread a cloth and had each other
Boy, it may only be for now
It may only be today.

131

Jungle after jungle was fired, my love
And a whole forest was burnt
But the jungle where we go, my love
They have not yet fired it.

132

You in the upper village
I in the lower
O my sweet love, what dried-up stream shall we meet in?
Over there is a gully with a plantain
And there are the garni bushes
In the gully with the plantain
I will meet and wrestle with you.

133

Through forest after forest we went
Through a whole jungle we wandered
But, my love
Where did you tell me anything?
The birds in the jungle
Are singing from tree to tree
But, my love, where shall we do it?
In among the bushes
We will go, my love

Into the bushes
Where not a bird will see.

134
Under the bushes
Which two are struggling?
The girl has caught his chest
The boy is holding her breasts
Boy and girl, they rock together.

135
Under a bush they are struggling
For a bun of hair
The girl is saying
'I will hold your belt
And never leave it'
The boy is saying
'I will live
Holding your breasts.'

Besides the forest, a favourite trysting-place is kudam sec – 'the back of the house'. This romantic phrase includes all the fields behind the village where a boy and girl can meet unobserved and in fact to 'go to the back of the house' is often a euphemism for intercourse itself.

136
Cutting thatch on the big mountain
Sister-in-law, I am thirsty for water
Come to the hollow by the plantain
In the hollow with the plantain, boy
There are many men
Take me to the spring with the tamarind
To the spring with the tamarind, sister-in-law
The elder brother went
Come to the cow-shed at the back of the house.

137
Lark and wagtail
At the back of the house
What are you seeking?
For a tree with thick leaves
A tree with many twigs
Where we can roost.

138

The rain is drizzling down
Take me, boy, to the back of the house
If you care for me only a little, girl
We need not wait as long.

139

While the mother
And the father lived
My love was in the house
When the mother
And the father died
My love went
To the back of the house.

Most of these meetings are by a previous arrangement and wherever possible are linked to a part of the day's routine. If the girl is going to the forest for leaves, the boy will go there for a stick. Another day she will go to the river for washing clothes and the boy will go there to wash his buffaloes. Or the boy will graze his cattle in a certain field and the girl will go to gather cowdung.

140

My love, we will go out
To the burnt jungle for picking mushrooms
To the free forest for grazing cows.

141

In the upper land
They dammed the river
Listen, third girl
In the last village
There will be snails
In the dry sand.

142

In the upper land it rained
And the river filled below
Girl, we will make a net
And catch the green fishes.

On such occasions they try to meet by pre-arranged signals.

143

You by the big rock
I at the end of the village
How shall I know if you are there?
With the little finger of your left hand
Give me a loud whistle
And I shall know that you are there.

144

You in the house
And I by the river
How shall I know you, my love?
Stand on the bank of the river
And sound your flute
And I shall hurry when I hear, my love.

145

Darling
Play your flute on the mountain
I will hear you at the spring
If I leave my pot, the men will see me
If I stay away, my love will scold me.

Not every encounter however is decided from before and certain songs describe the sight of a lover at a distance and the girl hurrying to her boy.

146

The dahu tree has fruited
And the tamarinds are showing
You leave your pot of water, friend
You see a friend going for water
And you leave your pot of water, friend.

147

Cutting grass on the big mountain
O my love, I am thirsty for water
O my love, take me
To the spring by the tamarind
In the spring by the tamarind

Are many leeches
O my love, take me
To the spring by the mango
At the spring by the mango, O my love
There are many cowherd boys
Let us go to Maenamati
And strain some water from the pool.

If for any reason a boy and girl fail to meet in the day, they try to meet at night. In the evening after the night meal, the girl comes out to wash the cooking vessels and if her boy is waiting, they saunter off to a field.

148

In the river is a snake, a snake.
Come to me in the night, the night.

These meetings do not usually last long but there are several songs which suggest a whole night spent in love.

149

When the moon comes up
He goes among the plantains
As the sun rises
The red flowers
Droop their heads.

150

The moon has risen up
The moon has sunk away
O let me go
We had no food at midday
I must husk some rice now.

151

On the higher land were cows
By the river there were buffaloes
We were threading green flowers
We did not notice it was midnight.

Although these meetings are taken for granted by the villagers – they know that something of the sort is going on – the lovers must on no account be caught. A long absence from home may have to be explained and the songs jokingly record the symbolic subterfuges to which a boy and girl may sometimes be compelled to resort in order to allay suspicion.

152

At the spring we met
By the spring we had each other
Let me go, my love
Or they will scold me at my home.

153

Girl, you went for water in the morning
But the noon came
The afternoon dragged on.
Below the pond
Under the leaves of lotus,
Milk tree,
I was resting and forgot.

154

As I was tying leaves, mother
How the string kept breaking
I climbed to the fork of a tree
And it was midnight when I came down.

155

The day was hot and dry
Where were you, boy?
Under the white tank
Were two white pigeons
And I lingered as I looked.

As the time for the girl's marriage draws nearer, the risks of meeting grow bigger. Until then, her parents do not greatly concern themselves with what she does and provided she is not surprised with her village boy and does not neglect her household duties, she can meet him as she likes. After she has reached the age of sixteen, however, her parents are less inclined to acquiesce.

156

Girl, comb your hair and smarten your body
But do not cross the borders

Of your mother and father
Boy, put on a dhoti and turban
But do not pick the milk-flower
That the mother grew.

157

Friend, friends
We were friends too greatly
We lived too near each other
I made you itch with love
What are they saying in your house?

158

Because of you
They nag at me in the house
I should give up talking to you
O the creeper on the tree
Like a tree's creeper
My mind is tied to you, my love.

An attitude of hostility begins to make itself evident and both boy and girl have sometimes to abandon their meetings if their families are over-suspicious.

159

Come, girl
To the middle of the line
I will not come
The milk-tree, my mother
Will scold me
The father tree, my father
Will chide me
The oleander, my brother
Will beat me.

160

My love, his shoes squeak
And his stick tinkles on the ground
Little brother, be careful
Or big brother will catch us.

161

The flutes sound
And the drums beat

O why have you not come?
At the door of the house
My brothers were standing
And I did not dare to come.

162

Elder brother
In the fallow rice land
We said that we would meet
Why are you returning?
Why are you going back?
Why should I not return?
Why should I not go back?
Your father and mother
Are standing like spears.

163

Yesterday we said
We will go out when the moon is up
The moon had gone half way
But, O my love, I could not see you
It was the love of the milk-tree
O my love
It was the love of the flowering tree
But still I was to come
When the moon had gone half way.

The need for circumspection may even result in a tryst being broken and the songs show a lover impatiently waiting as the moments drag on and still his girl does not come.

164

Black dog, stop barking
It is only my friend
Like a hungry tiger or a leopard
He is slinking around.

165

Yesterday you said
We will go out
When the morning star has come
Today the sun is up

And still you do not come
In the garden
I have leant against a mango
And shut my eyes.

166

The time has come
The time to have each other
My friend is going to the plantain grove
For my friend is tired of waiting.

Yet if the risks of meeting are now much greater, parental vigilance may merely give the boy and girl a reckless daring.

167

At noon we said
But you come at midnight
You are knocking the legs of the bed
O my love, move very slowly
The father and brothers
Have their axes and arrows ready
They will wake and seize us.

168

O my love
With an axe like a fan
And arrows like thatch
Is my brother coming
O my love
Let my life go
And my head fall
But never will I leave your love.

169

You in the upper village
I in the lower
O my love
My heart is tied to you
Your father and brothers
Are standing with axes and arrows
But, my love

You do not make my heart sad
With thick creepers
The tree is hidden
You have glued me to you
Like a bird trapped in lime.

When a Santal boy and girl feel like this, there is nothing that they will not do.

CHAPTER VII

Beyond the Village

1 INTRODUCTION

Although a girl expects her boy to remain constant to her, there are various ways in which an over-rigid fidelity is qualified. During the seven days of Sohrae, boys sometimes exchange their village girls by mutual consent. On visits to fairs, jaunts to the hook-swinging and umbrella festivals and trips for seeing the idol at Kali and Durga puja, the whole Santal youth is on the move. Boys and girls feel themselves free to flirt with other Santals and if necessary spend the night with them. They must not, however, do it too openly or in the face of their permanent lovers. If a girl gains another boy and her own lover fails to get a girl, she does not brag about it to him. Both keep their adventures private but provided these conventions are observed, each is not averse to exploring a new physique. If a boy and girl are not already attached, these adventures sometimes end in marriage and if a boy likes a stranger, he sometimes asks his parents to negotiate their wedding. In fact it is the chance that this may happen which lends a thrill to a fair and gives an air of refreshing novelty to a festival.

2 THE HOOK-SWINGING FESTIVAL

The first spectacle that sometimes leads to extra-village romances is the pata or hook-swinging. This festival which is Hindu in origin occurs only in certain villages and takes place either in mid-April or when a Santal bhogta or devotee discovers a new 'Mahadev' stone. If a man is fishing and stumbles on a smooth 'bonga-like' stone and if he then scratches it and it shows white, he cries out that it is Shiva and that the stone is giving milk. He then puts the stone in a new pot containing sun-dried rice and hangs it in the cattle shed. Each evening for seven days he goes down to a pool or stream, takes a bath and offers frangipani flowers, milk and sweets. He takes a thin cane with him for driving away evil spirits. Then on the seventh day a gathering of other bhogtas is held and swinging is performed.

When the swinging is done as a festival, crowds from all the neighbouring villages come in. Lines of girls and women perform lagre dances throughout the night. Pet quails are brought in their cages. Little stalls are set up. Rallying poles poke up above the heads and the celebration has all the excitement of a fair. The devotees who are chosen, one or two from each village, must not have eaten oil or salt for three days or taken any of the new season's leaves or fruits. If they have swung for three years, they must not swing for another three. The ritual begins with offerings of flowers, leaves and milk at the Mahadev shrine in the early part of the night. The bhogtas then dance together in a line striding backwards and forwards and swinging their arms. Then in the morning they go down to a tank for washing. At Karhabel where I saw the festival in 1943 it is customary for the bhogtas to take with them a wooden stump representing Shiva's consort Parvati. The image has five nails like breasts, a cotton thread is wound round them and a cane is pushed beneath the cotton. After they have washed, the devotees take the image in their hands, swing it to and fro in the water, dance together and at last immerse it. After this they bring it ashore, return to the shrine, bow and kneel before the stones, scatter leaves and flowers and pour milk. All the time a drum beats and a cymbal clashes. They now go over to the swing. This is a thick mast with a long pole on the top which is pulled round by ropes below. The wives of the bhogtas wait at the mast with their hands folded and bowls of water on their heads. The chief bhogta kneels down, rubs vermilion on the mast and pours milk. He then climbs the mast with a ladder and puts vermilion on the axle. Finally he ascends the mounting platform, anoints the pole with vermilion and is strapped onto the end with rope and cloth.

In earlier days, it was usual to employ hooks and Man has described the ritual as follows:

'At the ceremony observed in honor of Pata Bonga and which is performed before the raised mound and stone outside the village, the same ordeal is gone through as when the Jatra Bonga is celebrated, but at the finish the Sonthals formerly used to have the Churruck Pooja, or swinging festival; the hooks for suspending the devotee being inserted in the muscles of his back, who was generally an inebriated oracle. He was then suspended in mid-air and swung round, apparently hanging by the hooks. I have, however, seen a good many of these revolving martyrs, and although to a casual observer it appears very dreadful to behold a man thus pendant, it is not quite so bad as it seems, for his friends take the precaution to tie a girth of strong cloth round the victim's body, in such a manner that his weight rests upon the cloth rather than on his muscles. The perforation of the flesh may cost him a few drops of blood, but that is all; perhaps he may feel a very little more pain than is felt by a schoolboy when he inserts a pin up to its head in his thigh, and yet I fancy there are very few English schoolboys that have not tried the latter tricks.'

In the Santal Parganas, hooks are now dispensed with and after the bhogta has again poured milk on the mast, he takes his basket in one hand and goes out into the air. He sails round three times, first in one direction and then three times in the other, scattering frangipani flowers and sinjo leaves as he goes. He then comes slowly to rest and his place is taken by another. As the bhogtas swing solemnly and gently round, the crowd cries 'Mahadev, Mahadev,' the drums beat and lagre dancers go circling round the field. The actual swinging is done only by bhogtas and the number is limited to one, three, five or seven. Each bhogta swings not only for himself but for his village and the object is to secure increase and ward away disease. This ritual is of great importance for the bhogtas but to Santals generally it has merely the entertainment value of a spectacle. It acts as a rallying point for the neighbourhood. It attracts a crowd of new faces. Above all, it provides an excuse for that scrutiny of jolly forms which may later end in brief encounters under the trees.

3 THE UMBRELLA FESTIVAL

Since chata rhymes with pata, the chata or umbrella festival is similarly associated by Santals with annual romance. The festival occurs in the late rains and is often spoilt by bad weather. If, however, the night is fine, similar crowds assemble; and there is the same excited dancing as girls explore new boys. During the last one hundred years the festival has widened its scope and somewhat changed its ritual. Man, for example, recorded in 1867, 'The chata bonga festival takes place during the rains, and is only observed by one tribe, the Hansdah, and by their Kewars or blacksmiths, who are naturalised Hindoos. In almost every village one of these knights of the forge is to be found, and as they are always wanted to repair the plough-share or other agricultural implements, they drive a fair trade. The village communities pay them in kind, and each village is yearly compelled to contribute a certain share towards their supports.

'The preliminary proceedings at this festival resemble those of all the others, but at the end of the offering a ceremony takes place, the significance of which it is difficult to discover. At a given signal a pole, some twelve cubits long, is erected and made to turn a half circle, perpendicularly and horizontally; the pole is fastened on a loose but strong iron pivot, which rests in the holes made in two upright pieces of wood about a man's height from the ground. On the top of this revolving pole is tied a small ornamented umbrella, and as this is caused to jerk first one way and then the other, a peculiar style of worship is offered to it. Upon the erection of the pole, which is hailed with shouts and other noisy demonstrations of delight, the people gather handfuls of dust and dirt and forthwith begin to pelt the umbrella. This novel mode of veneration is at the same time accompanied with war dances by the men, the women also performing the usual Sonthali marriage dance. Refreshments and drink are dealt out from sheds erected for the purpose and the whole assembled population regale themselves in the open air. The sacrifices in this festival are always eaten at home, and not consumed on the spot.'

At the present time, Santals of every clan flock to see the 'umbrella'. A pigeon, fowl or goat is offered to the chata bonga and when I saw the festival in 1945 three small paper umbrellas had been fixed above each other to form a flimsy towering parasol. As the pole was swung up into position, lagre dancers swung to and fro and Dasae boys in white skirts came striding out and joined the crowd. The object of the festival, I was told, was to avert illness and special umbrella festivals are therefore held in order to redeem pledges made at times of sickness. 'The umbrella is the man's head,' a Santal told me, 'and the pole going up is the man rising from his cot.'

4 KALI AND DURGA PUJA

If the hook-swinging and umbrella festivals fascinate Santals because of their apparatus and the strange gymnastics of their ritual, the Kali and Durga pujas arouse excitement by the blazing colour of the idols and the pomp with which they are surrounded. In the Dumka area, for example, Kali puja or worship is celebrated for two days though it is less in honour of Kali than as a holiday from field work. Santals assemble near the shrine, they buy sweets from stalls and paper flowers to put in the hair, lines of dancers go round and round and a long queue files slowly past the idol gazing at the ferocious face till, late at night, the crowds go dancing home. The next day there is dancing in the village and the older men and women sit calmly around and quietly carouse.

The same procedure characterises the Durga puja and wherever an idol is taken out, Santals flock 'to see the Dibi'. In Dumka itself on the closing day the whole town is given up to Santals and all the roads adjoining the shrine are packed with boys and girls. Some of them go hand in hand. Others have their arms round each other while in the centre drums beat and little circles of women dance the lagre. A great blond moon looks down on the huge throng and late in the night, the lines of men and women go ambling home.

With the brilliant moonlight, the mild night air and the thrill of the crowds, it is not surprising if boys and girls sometimes go off together.

5 FAIRS AND MARKETS

A similar function in Santal life is served by the melas or fairs which are held each year in various parts of the district. The largest is at Hijla, two miles out of Dumka where small hills slope down to the Maur river. Other important fairs are at Kasikund and Pakaur. At each of these fairs, booths are set up, sweets, utensils, and cloth are sold and amusements ranging from revolving wheels to games of skill are dangled before the crowd.

On all these occasions, it is the Santals themselves who most excite the Santals. A village goes in a body – the boys with flutes, the girls and women with flowers in their hair. At the outskirts, they often change their clothes – the girls emerging in shining white cloths which flap jauntily on their buttocks. As they enter the crowd, they form long lines holding each other's shoulders or hips. A village boy holds aloft a rallying stick to which the village emblem has been tied. This consists of anything they can pick up on the way and at one Hijla fair, a dead crow, a bow, a bunch of tamarind pods, some arrows, bar tree leaves, castor fruits, a dead mouse, a broom, a fox's tail, sugar cane, a silk cocoon and a sprig of oleander moved slowly over the heads. If a boy (or girl) gets separated from his village, he looks for the emblem and at last regains his friends. As the lines shuffle slowly through the crowd, excited talk mingles with the flutes, boys scan the girls, girls glance back at boys and new friendships sometimes follow. As the sun sinks, visitors from the more distant villages begin the long walk home but others linger and go singing back beneath the moon.

Finally, the weekly visit to a market is often an occasion for making new acquaintances. The village does not usually go in a body but men, women, boys and girls set out in little groups. As the afternoon wears on, lines of villagers converge like ribbons on the market site and as the sun goes down, the lines stream back across the fields. It is possible that a Santal family could buy a month's supply in a single trip and thus avoid the weekly expedition. But not a single Santal family would ever do this. The visit is important less for what the family buys than for whom it meets. Relatives mix at a market, weddings are often arranged, brides and bridegrooms are subjected to scrutiny, and occasionally boys secure new girls. The market is a Santal 'club' and its very essence is the opportunity it provides for intermingling.

CHAPTER VIII

Conflict with the Parents

I THE END OF ROMANCE

The Santal attitude to marriage is practical and realistic. Any arrangement by which a boy and girl live openly together as man and wife and are not subjected to tribal boycott, is a valid union. For legitimising children and inheriting property, it matters little how this union is brought about. It is the public character of the arrangement and its acceptance by the village that gives it legal status. But between a wedding properly solemnised by the village and a union patched up or only grudgingly accepted, there is the greatest possible difference. A marriage is only respectable when various conditions have been fulfilled. The girl should be publicly 'lifted in a basket'. Her forehead should be formally smeared with vermilion so that her own bongas are replaced by those of her husband and she can henceforth assist him in their worship. The full ceremonial of a dol bapla – a wedding 'with parties' – should be followed so that the union may be loudly acclaimed, evil bongas scared away and the marriage made truly auspicious. The elaborate round of family visiting, the exchange of clothes and presents, the mock battles dissolving into amiable truces and the constant tying of the couple with threads of cotton – these must be observed in order to demonstrate the strength of the union and to make it permanent. Even the sexual symbols of the 'water marriage' – a crucial part of the ritual in which arrows are first stuck in a little hole, pots of water are poured over them and the tips of a bow and a sword are then plunged into their midst – should not be disregarded. Like the jerking dances in which the women of both sides indulge, these actions simulate intercourse and thus promote fertility. To be married but to have missed out on all these basic rites is like opting for a registry office marriage when a church service with full ritual is available.

Yet, important as all such actions are, they are as nothing compared to the way in which the union is arranged. To achieve respectability a marriage must be negotiated by the parents of the boy and girl, a match-maker must be employed and the villagers must be fully consulted. Anything else is furtive and disreputable – a 'jungle' or a 'copse' wedding. Marriage, in fact, is as much a union of two families and two villages as it is of two persons, and for this reason compatibility in breeding and manners, a common level of living and acceptance by the neighbours must all be taken into account. While therefore the boy and girl are not entirely ignored, they are expected to trust the judgment of their parents and the question of mutual liking is not regarded as of first importance. The Santal view of marriage is, in fact, markedly similar to the view expressed by Bertrand Russell. 'Marriage,' they would agree, 'is something more serious than the pleasure of two people in each other's company. It is an institution which through the fact that it gives rise to children, forms part of the intimate texture of society and has an importance extending far beyond the personal feelings of the husband and wife. It may be good that romantic love should form the motive for a marriage but it should be understood that the kind of love which will enable a marriage to remain happy and to fulfil its social purpose is not romantic but is something more intimate, affectionate and realistic. There is something to be said for Mrs Mala-prop's principle that love and aversion both wear off in matrimony so that it is better to begin with a little aversion.' If the girl actively dislikes the boy, she can usually persuade her parents to abandon the match but otherwise the correct attitude for the prospective partners is to resign themselves to each other's company and willingly accept the family decision. This does not mean, of course, that a negotiated marriage never reflects the wishes of the boy and girl. In many cases, a boy takes his parents into his confidence, secures their agreement and uses them to secure a girl of his choice. But such a course is on the whole exceptional and the majority of Santal parents aim rather at persuading their children to respect their wishes than at surrendering their own judgment to the fancies of their offspring.

Accordingly, as a boy and girl reach the ages of eighteen and sixteen years respectively, their parents begin to negotiate their weddings. The boy's family usually commences the talks (though initiative by the girl's parents is not debarred) and their first effort is to secure a bride in another village. This convention is favoured for several reasons. 'Parents-in-law in the same village,' Santals say, 'are like broken pipes. The fire falls out. They hear each other's quarrels.' Moreover if a boy weds a girl of his own village, he may sometimes have to endure the presence of her previous lovers. The boy may have been only her latest flame and behind their marriage may lie a history of romantic experiments. In this view it is wiser to wed a daughter in another village where she can join a new family and be free of earlier entanglements.

It is this convention – wise and business-like but to the boy and girl, coldly callous – which strikes at the roots of village romance. From the days when they commence their love, they know that family sentiment will oppose their ultimate union and that their love must therefore be 'only for a day'. But it is one thing to know this in the abstract, and another to accept it as a fact. As a boy and girl get ripe for marriage, they watch their parents discussing their fate and the approach of the ceremony fills them with sick aversion. It is now that each of them must take a decision – to flout their parents or bow to their will.

In the great majority of cases, the lovers take a 'sensible' view and when the girl's wedding is decided, they suspend their relations altogether. It is wise to do this for if intimacy is detected after the betrothal, it damages the family honour and is liable to result in a breaking-off of the match. Equally, if a girl is pregnant at her wedding and the fact has been suppressed, its sudden discovery may cause the wedding to end in confusion. For this reason certain songs advise the boy to practise a cautious prudence.

170

By the banks of the river
Do not play your flute
Flute, the date is near
The rice-beer has been made
Do not make muddy
The water of the spring.

171

In the mountain stream
The water trickles
In the hot days
Love flows away
Drink the water, oriole
Do not make it dirty
For love trickles
And flows away.

172

On the big mountain
The flower is red at noon

As you pick the flower
Do not break the branches
For the body sways
Like a red flower.

Yet if prudence dictates separation, the prospect of the final parting is often so painful that it is as if everything which ever made life happy is over.

173

I called you
But you did not answer
O my heart
You have gone
Strolling away.

174

Lovers we were lovers
Lovers like pigeons
Look below the banyan
For I must leave you now, my love.

175

Leaning by the eaves
Why do you weep?
Our love has altered
O do not cry
Saying my name
Again and again.

176

Like a creeper falling
Or water swilling from a cup
My friend went quickly away.

177

What shall we do
Do with the love of friends?
A gust of wind
Tears the leaves of the plantain
And the love of friends
Is split in two.

It is not surprising, therefore, that while certain boys and girls contrive to accept this rupture, others view the break-up of their love with angry grief.

178

You have no wife
I have no husband
We have tied our lives together
If you leave my love now
I shall drift away
Like a leaf
Tossed in a whirlwind.

179

Below the garden
You are grazing buffaloes
And you laugh at me and smile
O my life
Do not twist the stem of the bush
If you had given me your word
I would have gone with you
Anywhere.

At times the girl attempts to get a love-pledge – an article of clothing, an ornament, a necklace or a ring by which she can hold her boy to his word.

180

I by the river
You on the far side
Put down your cloth
And throw across your beads
Will your beads talk?
Will your ring speak out?
Give me your armlet
And I will keep my life.

But words and pledges are often of no avail.

181

From the stream on the mountain
I heard the words of lovers

Lovers' words
Are lovers' words
They sound like empty brass.

Sometimes a boy promises to marry his girl only to discover when the time comes that his parents are too much for him. In such circumstances he is forced to go back on his promise and the songs record the bitter feelings of a jilted girl.

182

In the plantain grove
You promised you would keep me
By the spring you say
My wedding day has come
Say no more, my love
I shall scold you so bitterly
A fire will scorch your heart.

183

You are clashing the cymbals
I am playing on the drum
Speak to me in your heart
Think of me.
But I am angry with you
In my heart.

184

On the banks of the river
Why are you strolling
In your Government clothes
And the shoes of the English?
Why is it
You are not keeping me?

185

The first time you said
Do as I say
And I will keep you in my care
I heard you and I did it
O why are you not keeping me?

186

My former lover took me on his thighs
My new lover seats me on a stool

144

O my old love
Speak to me again
Our love was like a flower
But you left it.

187

Once you said
Though our lives go
And our heads fall
We will never leave our love
Now I see
That what you said was false
You are leaving me with a heart
Smouldering like a fire.

Yet if at times a boy decides to leave his girl, in other cases he may find the prospect quite unbearable. There is now a tussle between loyalty to the parents, the shame of defying the village, the discomfort of acting dependently and on the other hand, the agony of losing a girl whose charm of person has overwhelmed his mind.

188

My heart burns with grief
How can I give up
The love in my heart?

189

Muni, my heart is in you
And in me is your heart
Like the web of a spider
Our hearts are tied together
From half way up
The cotton tree
A spider's web is shining
From the cotton tree
To the palm tree
The spider's web is stretched
Like the threads of a spider
Our hearts are tied together.

190

Your life in me,
My life in you,

Our lives are tied.
A spider's web
Is knitting the cotton tree
And O my life
Our lives are tied.

In such circumstances the boy may decide to put the girl above his parents. He summons all his resources and the lovers proceed so to stage matters that both the family and the village are forced to agree.

2 ELOPEMENT

When a boy and girl decide to flout the village, the first and most drastic of their remedies is elopement. This is attempted when neither of the two families is in favour of the match and the boy and girl are therefore compelled to look for sympathy elsewhere. If they know of another place to go to, there is a certain thrill in suddenly leaving the village with its stale hostility and setting up for themselves in a new area.

191

Midnight
And the headman's servant
The paranik's maid
Have run away together
Sound the drums and blow the trumpets
Like a silk-worm moth in a thicket
They have linked their lives together.

192

O two white doves of the big mountain
Was it dew or care
That made you fly away
In the day the heat
In the night the dew
You went away in secret.

193

O my love
The dust rises on the land
The sky is hot and red
Take me to another land

With shoes for the hot earth
And for the sky an umbrella
Take me to another land
On a bullock with a long and tufted tail
O my love
Load up some rice
Take me to another land.

More usually however the couple leave the village with the intention of shortly returning. They argue that the elopement will sufficiently compromise them and that after the first outburst of anger has subsided, their parents will welcome them back.

In a case from Dholpathar, Kandan Soren had a village girl, Manjhan Marandi. Both of them wanted to marry but neither of their parents approved. The boy's side objected because the girl was older while the girl's parents were against a marriage in the same village. When the boy and girl failed to persuade their parents, they decided to elope. They went away for three months and when they returned the boy's father paid a bride-price and a wedding was celebrated.

In another case from Baratanr, the parents began by approving of the match but later when the girl's party were paying a ceremonial visit, they saw some earth being dug on the way. They considered this a bad omen and the wedding was broken off. But the boy and girl were very much in love and when the girl's parents had arranged her marriage elsewhere and the wedding booth had almost been erected, she mustered her courage and ran away with her lover. They lived together for a month and when they returned, her parents demurred no longer and the two were formally wedded.

In yet another instance, Dudun Murmu fell in love with Talamani Hembrom and used to meet her in the fields. He was doubtful if his parents would approve of the union so he took the girl with him and eloped to his brother-in-law's. The two stayed there for a week and when they returned, the village accepted them as married.

3 MARRIAGE BY DISCOVERY

A similar principle is exploited in another type of marriage called kundal napam. We have already seen that in all pre-nuptial matters, the boy and girl are expected to keep their intimacy a secret. If their friendship is detected, the girl's status is immediately lowered. She is made to look 'cheap', her parents 'lose face' and her marriage prospects are worsened. If therefore the boy and girl abandon precautions and court detection, they will undoubtedly annoy their parents but at least the girl's family will now be in favour of the union.

This development is vividly illustrated by a forest story, which is sometimes told at annual hunts.

'Ratu and Ratni used to play as children in the dust of the village. Then Ratu would lift up Ratni's legs and the two would go to each other. Later when they grew up, the villagers learnt of their congress and their parents said that they must give up being friends. They found it hard to meet. Then Ratu said "If ever I meet Ratni, I will certainly have her" and Ratni said "If I can meet Ratu, we shall certainly go to each other". One day when all the people of Ratni's house were drunk, Ratu brought Ratni into the courtyard. Then Ratni sang:

194

You brought me from my house
You stood me in the courtyard
But how much longer must I wait?

Then the boy went from the courtyard to the door by the street. And Ratni sang again:

195

You brought me from the courtyard
You stood me in the door
But how much longer must I wait?

From the door they went to the bushes below the garden field. And Ratni sang once more:

196

You brought me from the door
You brought me to the bushes
But how much longer must I wait?

Then they lay in the bushes and commenced to copulate. For hours on end they had each other again and again. When it was almost dawn they made a little shed beside the spring and again set to. When it was morning a servant girl of the headman came down to draw water and saw them both. When she returned she sang out to her master:

197
O father headman, by the spring
A sow has had a litter
Father, come and see them.

The headman said, "How can I go alone? There are the paranik and the messenger to be thought of. I must take them with me too." Then he called them as well as others of the village and they all went down together. In the shed they found Ratu and Ratni and saw signs of intercourse. Then the headman said, "Who are you to have gone into this hut together?" Ratu replied, "It is only us." "What have you been doing?" Ratu said, "We have done nothing." Then they brought the pair of them out, talked the matter over, made them one, and Ratu took Ratni to his house.'

This very strategy was employed in the village of Babupatojoria. Bhagmat Tudu was in love with a village girl named Mukhi Soren. He wanted to marry her so, in order to force a decision, they slept together in the open during a Sohrae festival. As they hoped and expected, they were duly caught and after a village meeting, it was decided to accept their union as a marriage.

Sometimes the circumstances in which a boy and girl are living leave no doubt of their relationship. This is particularly true of boy and girl servants who sometimes sleep together in their master's house or even engage in nocturnal love with a member of the family. When the relationship becomes obvious, it is sometimes accepted as a properly arranged marriage, a goat is killed by way of fine and the two continue to live openly together as husband and wife.

In Churipathar, Munshi Kisku was taken as a servant. He fell in love with the daughter of the house and the two slept together. The girl gave birth to two children and Munshi was accepted as her husband. Similarly in Bagjori, Hopni Kisku worked as a maid-servant in the house of a widow, Sumi Marandi. The widow's son fell in love with her and when Hopni became pregnant, their union was recognised as a marriage.

4 MARRIAGE BY CAPTURE

While it sometimes happens that both families are obdurate, it is more usual for only one of them to be hostile. Santal parents do not like to drive their children to extremes and when they see that a boy's heart is completely set on a girl and that all their efforts at persuasion have failed, they sometimes agree to let him have his way rather than invite the miseries of domestic friction. The same is true of girls and the result is often a lop-sided tussle between the boy, his family and the girl on the one side and the girl's parents on the other. When this happens, the lovers sometimes decide to force a decision by resorting to 'capture'.

Dundo Baske of Mendip met a girl of Ronchura at a wedding in his village. He fell in love with her and some months later he met her in Borio market and went to her village. The girl was willing to marry him but her parents disapproved. Dundo accordingly 'captured' her and took her to his house.

In Kalipathar, Hapai Marandi wanted to marry Mokhadi Murmu. A matchmaker was appointed but the girl's father refused to agree. A month later, Hapai met the girl at Dalahi market and persuaded her to be his wife. He took her to his house and although her father still opposed the match, the girl remained with the boy and their union was recognised as a marriage.

In Semra, Ram Soren was in love with Thurgi Murmu. Since the boy and girl were of the same village, the girl's parents did not approve of the marriage. With the girl's connivance, therefore, the boy 'captured' her, took her to his house and they have since had four children. In this case, there was no other celebration and their union has all along remained a marriage 'by capture'.

When the root opposition is the boy's family, 'capture' is sometimes resorted to by the girl.

Maiya Tudu of Jaraki 'captured' Jhago Hembrom, a boy of her village, and after she had 'dragged' him into her house, his parents agreed to accept her as his wife.

In Tarajuri, Mandri Soren, a divorced girl, fell in love with Mandal Murmu, a boy who was still unmarried. As she knew that his parents would not relish a wedding with a girl who had been divorced, she 'captured' him and kept him in her house for two weeks. When the villagers asked him why he was living there, the boy said that he could not help it as the girl would not let him leave. The marriage was then approved by the villagers.

When the lovers come from the same village, the act of taking the girl from one house to another brings their relationship into the open and unless they subsequently change their minds, there is very little that the ag-grieved family can do. If, however, the girl is of a different village, the matter is not so straightforward and a complicated procedure often ensues. The girl's family first informs the jogmanjhi that the girl is missing and this official with a few villagers then goes ahead to scout. He asks cowherds if they know where the girl has gone and in due course he learns the village to which she has been taken. He now meets the headman and the following typical dialogue ensues. 'Where do you come from? You are strangers to this village.' 'We come from such and such a village.' 'You never came before. What has brought you?' 'Nothing much. Two days ago a weak and thin goat was left by the herd and is missing from the fields. A leopard carried her to your forest. The tracks point this way.' 'I will call the jogmanjhi,' the headman replies, 'and ask him to look for it. Perhaps the leopard has dragged it somewhere near. These days leopards are getting very bold and snatch their prey from under one's very eye.' The jogmanjhi of the boy's village now arrives and the headman says, 'Jogmanjhi, our friends say that a leopard has brought one of their goats into our forest. Is this so?' The jogmanjhi answers, 'Yes, I heard yesterday that somewhere in the lower part of the village a leopard brought a goat. I will ask about it. Wait till I return.' The jogmanjhi then tells the boy's family that a party has come in search of the girl and a date is then fixed three or five days later for a joint meeting of the villages to adjust the matter. If the girl has been taken forcibly, the jogmanjhi of the village brings her back. Otherwise she is left with the boy and the party returns.

On the day fixed, the two villages hold a joint meeting. The boy and girl are asked to state how it happened and whether any compulsion was used. When the interrogation is over, the headman or the jogmanjhi asks the villagers to decide the matter, and if the girl decides to stay, her parents bow to the inevitable and merely ask for the usual costs.

5 MARRIAGE BY INTRUSION

If marriage by 'capture' is often resorted to by boys, nir bolok' or intrusion is a common expedient of girls. 'This marriage,' says Campbell, 'consists in a young unmarried woman intruding herself into the house of the parents of a young man upon whom she has set her affections, or with whom there may have been love passages and he has ceased showing her attentions. Being hurt at the treatment she has been subjected to, she resolves to venture on the intrusion marriage and thus assert what she regards as her right. It is always Leap Year in Santalia and a Santal maiden need never pine away in single blessedness or sigh her heart out for the man she loves.' Such cases presuppose a certain unwillingness on the part of the boy. But in other instances the boy himself may be far from unwilling and intrusion may occur if his parents are opposed, have arranged his marriage elsewhere or are merely indifferent. The girl then resorts to intrusion not in order to coerce the boy but with the object of inducing his parents to accept their union.

When Chotu Ramu Murmu of Amtala was a young man he met Gungi Hembrom of Choudhuri during the Dasae celebrations at Katikund. They met from time to time and three months later Gungi intruded into his house. His parents said, 'Have you come as a guest? What is your work?' She brought an extra cloth with her but no rice-beer or leaves. The girl said, 'I have come to live with him.' On this, some villagers were called and Chotu Ramu was asked if he had given her his word. Chotu Ramu said, 'I told her she could come.' After that the two villages sat together and the girl was accepted as a wife.

In Beldiha, Dhunu Tudu was in love with the daughter of Pitho Marandi of Hathipur. Neither parents approved of their union so in order to win them round the girl forced herself into Dhunu's house. The parents were then obliged to accept the marriage and in the end a wedding was celebrated.

But besides intrusion by a girl, nir bolok' is also resorted to by boys, and a common circumstance is when the parents of the girl approve the union but the boy's parents oppose. In such cases the girl may invite the boy to intrude into her own house in the expectation that after some time the boy's parents will allow them to go to his house.

Kubraj Murmu of Dumdumi was in love with Sorno Hembrom of his village. His parents were opposed to the marriage so the boy intruded on the girl. The girl had no brothers and her parents were glad to have him with them. At the village meeting, the union was accepted as a marriage and after some time the boy returned to his parents taking the girl with him.

Finally, intrusion is sometimes made by a boy if the girl has either been once married to a ghar jawae or serving son-in-law and then divorced or widowed, or her father is proposing to bring a ghar jawae as her husband.

Bangi Murmu of Amtala was the eldest of three sisters and had once been married to such a husband. The boy had deserted her and while she was gathering mahua, she met Sam Marandi of Salaipahari and began an affair with him. The only other member of Sam's family was a brother who had gone to Assam while he himself was a casual servant. As their love affair was progressing, Sam heard that the girl's father had started negotiations for another ghar jawae. That night he went to Bangi's house. Bangi's father said, 'Why have you come?' 'To work as your servant.' As the father needed a servant, he let him stay and a few days later he found the boy sleeping with his daughter. After that there was a meeting and the boy said, 'I have come to live with her.' The girl said, 'I told him he could come.' Then the boy was accepted as her husband and the two lived openly together.

In Parba also, a girl had once been married to a ghar jawae but her husband had deserted her. One night a wedding was going on and the girls and boys were dancing in the village lane. A boy of the village had set his heart on the girl and fearing that others might take her, he decided to intrude. He went to her house, called to the girl and went inside. The two slept together and the next morning the villagers found them in her house. They asked the girl, 'Will you keep him?' The girl said, 'I will take him as my ghar jawae.' The boy's parents agreed and the boy stayed on.

When a girl decides to intrude, she makes her preparations and these are described by Campbell as follows: 'A young woman having decided upon a nir bolok' marriage takes a few of her companions into her confidence and informs them of her design, and looks to them for their countenance and assistance. She prepares a large pot of rice-beer and carrying it poised on her head goes straight into the inmost apartment and having disposed of her pot of liquor sits down to await events. She has, of course, chosen her time so that there is no one to oppose her entering. The action has been performed in daylight before witnesses and it soon spreads that such a woman has gone into such a man's house. The man's mother, when she hears of it, is greatly incensed, but by the unwritten law governing such cases is precluded from ejecting her from her house by force. If she can by hook or by crook prevail upon her to come out herself she is at liberty to do so. Of course, a small crowd soon assembles in the courtyard, some of whom sympathise with the intruder, and others take the part of the man against her. The mother, however, sets to work resolutely to do her level best to drive her out. She carefully closes up all apertures by which air can enter and then flings a large handful of pepper into the fire, and shutting the door anxiously awaits the result of her strategy. A Santal house is generally divided into two apartments by a partition wall about five feet high, so that there is no obstruction to the fumes of the burning pepper, pervading every corner of it. The crowd in the courtyard are speculating as to whether she will be able to hold out or not, and the mother is scolding in her shrillest tones. When a considerable time has elapsed the spectators begin to urge the irate dame to open the door, as the fumes of the burning pepper must have in a large measure become innocuous. She, thus counselled, opens the door and the girl is brought out into the fresh air, where she rapidly throws off the effects of the burning pepper. By the time she has recovered her breath her mother-in-law – for now they stand in the relation to each other of mother-in-law and daughter-in-law – appears with a quantity of millet, with which she has mixed some oil. This she puts in the dhinki or large mortar and orders her daughter-in-law to pound it into flour. This of course owing to the presence of the oil is impossible, but a brave attempt is made and continued till the bystanders begin to indulge in uncomplimentary remarks directed against the older woman, and she feeling the force of them, or being ashamed to longer indulge her spite brings the exhibition to a close. She accepts the position and, as the story books say, all live happily together.'

During my own time the battle of pepper rarely occurred, and the impossible tasks were also not inflicted. The girl merely goes to the boy's house, sits in the courtyard or on his verandah and finally explains her presence to the boy's parents.

If the parents do not relish the intrusion and the girl is of the same village, they call the villagers and try to coax her out.

While Bale Marandi, a divorced girl of Majdiha, was living in Amtala with her father's sister, she had a love affair with Maidan Murmu and decided to marry him. During the Sohrae festival she went and sat on his verandah. Maidan's parents asked her what she was doing and she said, 'I have come to live with Maidan.' The villagers intervened and said that as Maidan was still unmarried she had better go away. 'Even if he keeps you.' they said, 'he will take a fresh unmarried girl later.' In the end they coaxed Bale away and she returned to her village.

If, on the other hand, the parents do not strongly object and the boy himself is anxious to keep her, the girl is allowed to stay in the house. If she comes from another village the jogmanjhi arrives with a party and tells the boy's headman, 'A she-goat has run off with a he-goat from the grazing ground. It went towards your village. We have come to look for it.' The headman then takes similar action as in a case of capture and the two villages hold a joint meeting three or five days later. At this meeting, the whole position is reviewed and while the boy's parents are often won round and are finally induced to accept the intruder, they sometimes flatly refuse to acquiesce.

In Hathi Hariri, the daughter of Dunbai Marandi intruded in the house of Matal Soren. At the meeting Matal said that he would marry her but his parents refused to have her in the house and in the end she was returned to her parents.

The daughter of Nunku Hansdak' 'intruded' at the house of Ceda Soren of Dhundli. The boy and girl were both divorcees. After the girl had stayed in the house for some days the boy and his parents did not want to keep her and at the village meeting their union was not accepted and the boy was fined five rupees.

Similarly, if a boy 'intrudes', a meeting also adjusts the matter. If there is no objection on the girl's side, the intrusion is accepted as a marriage. If his presence is unacceptable, he is asked to leave the house and may also be punished with a fine – both parties paying the costs of the meeting.

Phudan Besra of Kelabari fell in love with a daughter of Jiban Murmu of Ghangrabandh and intruded in her house. The girl refused to marry him and her parents also did not accept him. Phudan was therefore driven out and the villagers fined him five rupees.

If a boy 'intrudes' at the instance of the girl, and is later on rejected, the boy himself is awarded damages.

Keota Hansdak' of Baromasia was due to be taken as a ghar jawae by a girl of Borband. The girl invited him to intrude so he went to her house and stayed a night with her. The next night the girl went out with a different boy. When Keota complained to the village, he was paid five rupees and sent home.

6 THE FORCED WEDDING

If elopement, capture and intrusion are ways of securing public acceptance, there is a further expedient which is sometimes employed to obtain village acquiescence. This is known as iputut' and is a more or less illicit exploitation of the vermilion which is put on a bride's forehead at a formal wedding. If the two families are opposed to the union and a 'jungle' marriage seems impracticable, the boy sometimes takes a little vermilion or if none is readily obtainable, some mud, earth, sand or grit and smears it on the girl's head. He does this in front of witnesses and if the girl's head has never been previously marked, the act has the same effect as if he had smeared her forehead at a full-dress wedding. The vermilion immediately changes her bongas and makes her his wife in the world to come. This abrupt alteration in her status usually causes the girl's parents to change their attitude. They realise that it will now be difficult to negotiate a marriage for her in a good family and if the girl herself desires the boy, the act usually unites them in marriage.

Tibu Tudu of Baskia was due to marry a girl of Duaria. Suddenly his father died and the girl's party said, 'There is a bonga in his house. We will not marry her.' The matter dragged on. Tibu used to meet the girl when she went to gather mahua flowers. Both of them wished to marry but the girl's parents continued to refuse. At last the boys of Baskia told Tibu to do iputut'. They made their plans and at the Gamra hook-swinging the boys of Baskia all surrounded the girl, shut her in a ring of arms and Tibu rubbed vermilion on her head. After that, they rushed away. When the two villages met, there was no more delay, all the details were settled and a public wedding was celebrated.

Similarly in Sanarghati, Sital Marandi desired to marry a Soren girl but the boy's parents objected as the girl was older. Sital did not listen so one day, during Sohrae, the two went inside the jogmanjhi's house and Sital put vermilion on her. They told the headman's wife and after that Sital took her home. A little later a formal wedding was performed.

In another case of Simaljore, the brother of Singrai Murmu was married as a ghar jawae in Dhamna. Singrai was in love with his sister-in-law's younger sister, Gondo, but the girl's mother was objecting to their marriage. Singrai went to Dhamna on the morning of the Baha festival. That evening the girls were throwing water on the boys but because Singrai was of another village, they did not throw any at him. Then on the spur of the moment, Singrai picked up some mud and rubbed it on Gondo's head. Two of the villagers pounced on him, saying, 'Why have you done it on her head? Why did you not do it on her body?' Then they gave him a thrashing and took him to the headman. Next morning Singrai was sent to his own village and the matter was reported to his headman. A day was fixed for a joint meeting and early in the afternoon, the villagers of Dhamna went to Simaljore with axes, arrows and drums. When the headman said, 'Why have you come?', they replied, 'A leopard of your village has scratched one of our calves.' After that, they all sat round and Singrai was asked, 'Did you do it?' He answered, 'I picked up a little mud and put it on her head.' This was held to be iputut' and two goats were then killed. Singrai was told to settle the marriage accounts, give the headman five rupees 'for saving his head' and pay a fine of five rupees 'for doing it by force'. Then the villagers went back and Singrai gave a goat in Dhamna 'to clean the axe'. A date was settled for a formal wedding and a matchmaker was appointed. The matter, however, did not end there for a little later Gondo's mother changed her mind. The wedding, in her view, meant a second marriage in the same family and she believed that as a result one of the two girls would shortly die. So, in spite of the occurrence, she at last said, 'I will not give her'. She did not press for payment and the matter dropped. Some time later, Gondo was married in Jobalda as a divorcee and there was neither a public wedding nor any smearing of her head with vermilion.

In all these cases the act was resorted to in order to bring pressure on the parents. But occasionally one at least of the two families is privy to the plan and, if more than one suitor is in the field, iputut' may even be done with the full connivance of the parents. In a case of 1944, talks had started for a girl in Paharpur. The boy's parents had inspected her at a market and a proposal had been made through a matchmaker. Meanwhile a boy from a well-to-do family of Dundua met the girl at a market, took a fancy to her, decided to marry her and the matter was broached through various friends. The girl and her parents thought this latter boy would be a better match but as they had not expressly declined the first proposal they felt some embarrassment in breaking off the negotiations. Finally they suggested that the boy from Dundua should settle matters by doing iputut'. He agreed and after the vermilion had been put on her, the two were wedded.

Finally, it may happen that a boy is wildly in love with a girl but the girl and her parents are hesitating. In such circumstances, iputut' forces the issues. It is done not entirely against the girl's will nor entirely with her consent. It is a way of precipitating a decision and usually it succeeds.

None of these cases were regarded by Santals as 'good' marriages. Everyone suffered a loss of dignity. It was thought vulgar for a boy and girl to force their views on the village and acceptance of the position was regarded merely as the lesser of two evils. Even the young Santals concerned were not over-joyed at getting married in this way. Some of them even had the matter improved by getting their parents to employ a matchmaker and subsequently arrange a respectable wedding. But the fact that, none the less, the marriages were recognised is a singular tribute to tribal commonsense. Santals consider that even if it were desirable it would be quite impossible to prevent pre-nuptial love, however unsuitable this may prove as a basis for matrimony. Public opinion is therefore directed towards two objectives – the maintenance of love affairs but on a secret 'underground' basis and the insistence that these must end at marriage. In most cases, as we have seen, these objectives are secured. The lovers part and go to their respective spouses. When however human nature proves too strong, the situation is retrieved by Santal kindliness. Lovers who take matters into their own hands are neither admired nor encouraged, but they get their way.

CHAPTER IX

Accidents

I THEORIES OF CONCEPTION

If the plans of Santal parents are sometimes thwarted by the wilful actions of their children, they may also be foiled by unwanted pregnancies. Until the age of fifteen, this contingency is rare – so rare that through all their years of early love, Santal boys and girls behave as if it were unthinkable. They take no precautions. They observe no controls. They practise no restraints. After fifteen, however, the phase of care-free irresponsibility ends and from then onwards the girl is careful when to have or not to have a boy.

Santals do not doubt that semen is responsible for the making of a child but instead of assigning the sole role to men they credit women with semen also. They believe that a man's seed is made in the following manner. 'Blood has juice which is the bones' marrow. Marrow also has its own juice. It trickles down a vein to the testes. There it is made into semen and gathers in a little bag. When the bag is full, the whole body overflows with strength.'

'A man,' said Sibu, 'goes to his girl every day but his semen never ends. You can dig a hole by a river and the water fills it. You bale the water out but still it returns. Only when you give up taking does it stop.'

A girl's semen is made in much the same way. 'The juice from her marrow seeps into her womb. There it turns to semen. It mounts in a little bag. When the bag is full, the girl cannot contain herself. She seeks a boy. She has no peace until he has exhausted her.'

If semen, however, is necessary for making a child, it must enter through the vagina and reach the womb.

'A woman,' said Sibu, 'cannot get a child by drinking semen. One road goes to Suri and one to Rampurhat. You cannot reach Rampurhat by the Suri road.'

'The day her flower ends,' said Dhunu, 'the man's seed enters. It finds the flower's root from which her blood comes. It mingles with it. Then the blood gathers, and the next month the flower fades.'

'Women have semen like men. A woman's seed comes before the man's. It smoothes the way and then his seed glides in.'

Sibu, on the other hand, said, 'A girl's semen issues from the womb. It comes from one side and the boy's semen goes to meet it. They mix and go inside together. Until her semen comes, the boy's seed is blocked. When the girl is ready it dashes on its way.'

'The girl's womb has a mouth. When it is hungry no matter how big is her vagina, her mouth will suck the semen in.'

At Sundarpahari, the headmen told me, 'A girl has a vein in her vagina from which her semen comes. There are two kinds of semen. The first is like water. It warms the penis and makes the boy's seed rise. Behind it comes the girl's true semen. This is like the boy's and mixes with it. When a girl is excited a second vein peeps from the womb's mouth, grips the seed and sucks it in.'

When conception occurs, the two semens change into blood. 'They get bigger. The outer blood forms a bag. The ends make a cord and the bag rests in the belly. The soul or jivi is swimming in the blood. In four months a child forms and the jivi settles in it. The head comes first and after it, the arms, chest and legs.' 'The blood,' said Dhunu, 'grows from the flower's root. It grows long and round. A shell forms on it like an egg. Then the head sprouts and the eyes come. After that the body forms and there are arms and legs. In four months the jivi enters from the root. As the child grows, the girl's semen feeds it.' The last two days of a woman's menses and the first five that follow it are believed to be a 'danger' period. 'The first day,' said Dhunu, 'the blood begins. The second day it flows like a stream. The third day it slackens. On the fourth it stops. If a boy has a girl on the first two days, his semen does not remain. If he goes to her on the third day, his semen enters and the blood stops. For five days from the end of her flower, the boy must wait.' Sibu was equally emphatic on the risks of early connection. 'For three days from the flowering,' he said, 'the mouth is open. After that it shuts.'

A boy of Katyuria, Sibu told me, encountered a girl by a tank in Sitasal. It was noon and no one was about. The boy could not restrain himself and though he had never seen the girl before he said, 'Let me do it.' The girl's period had only just ended and no one else had been with her. The girl said, 'If I have a child, will you keep me?' The boy agreed and then the girl yielded. When it was over they parted and the boy went to Assam. The girl did not go to any other boy but the next month 'her flower withered' and a child began to come. The jogmanjhi said, 'Where did you find it?' 'It was that boy.' 'How many times?' 'Only once.' A year later the boy returned and they were married.

Pregnancy, however, does not always follow intercourse within the 'danger period' for while it is necessary to copulate in order to get a child, the grant of life rests ultimately with the Bidhi Bidhanta. These are aspects of Thakur Jiu and it is they alone who mix a man and woman's seeds. 'A woman,' said Sibu, 'may hunger for a child each day but only when Bidhan wills it do their semens mix. If the Bidhi Bidhanta will a girl, Bidhi gives the two sets of semen a jivi, and if a boy, then Bidhan does. A child then comes.' At the same time, it is only in this week that conception is usual and provided the girl avoids this period, intercourse is thought to be safe.

Apart therefore from the 'danger period', Santal boys and girls have few anxieties and the idea of contraception in any of its Western forms fills them with undiluted glee. Coitus interruptus, for example, is never even considered. 'All joy would go.' 'Once the rice is in the mouth, you must eat it.' 'Once a boy has started, he will never stop until his seed has come.' As for douching, 'What is the use of water? If the semen enters, it goes where water cannot reach.'

Occasionally, long after marriage, steps are taken to avert additional conceptions. If the placenta is buried in the corner of the house with the lid of a pot over it or if it is buried with the cord side downwards, further children will be unlikely. Permanent sterilisation can also be attempted and when Dhunu had had two children by the latest of his wives, he gave her a brew made by powdering the root of a betel nut with a pinch of gunpowder and mixing it with the strongest brand of mahua liquor. His wife drank it and they have had no further children.

2 ABORTION

If, in spite of caution, an unmarried girl conceives she is immediately faced with a difficult decision – whether, on the one hand, to have the baby or, on the other, to procure an abortion. If she is certain that her boy will marry her, she usually does nothing and allows events to take their course. If, however, she is doubtful of the outcome or fearful of her parents' rage, she sometimes prefers to have the child expelled. Such a course is so normal that certain forest songs, sung at annual hunts, bluntly refer to it:

198

In a lucky month
The child was born
And so, my love
It did not live.

199

Like a bone
Was the first child born
And the white ants have eaten it
O my love, do not weep
Do not mourn
We two are here
And the white ants have eaten it.

200

In the unploughed field, elder brother
The vultures hover
O elder brother
It is a dead cow or a buffalo
At midnight the headman's second daughter
Has rid herself of a child.

If the girl decides to take this step, she confides in an old woman and is taught one of the customary methods. She is advised, for example, to take a little jormohol root 'no bigger than a pice' or a similar quantity of oleander and drink it on a night with no moon. Opium or asafoetida can also be drunk and abortion may result. In the alternative she can introduce a root as a chemical expulsive. The root of the bir kitauri, a plant a little like sugar cane but with red flowers, is sometimes used. The root must be six fingers long and must be pushed into the vagina until it touches the uterus. It must stay in place for six hours 'from morning to noon' and a thread is tied to it to prevent it from working upwards. 'If it enters the womb, the girl dies.' The root of the caulia bush can also be employed. This is pushed into the womb 'until it touches the bag. The bag bursts and blood and a half-formed child come out.' This can be tried only in the first five months. A third variant is the root of the catom arak'. Of the two plants which bear this name only the thicker variety known as tandi can be used. A final method is to tie a thread to the leg of a ghugri or mole cricket. The cricket is put in the vagina. 'It crawls to the womb and tears the skin. Blood comes and after the blood, the child.' This method is possible only in the first three months and 'if the thread snaps and the cricket burrows into the womb, the girl dies.'

3 THE PREGNANT BRIDE

Abortion, however, is not invariably successful and in certain cases it is not even tried. If the girl decides against it, exposure must sooner or later follow and her parents must then abruptly abandon any preconceived ideas about her marriage. Their sole aim is now quite different – to discover the boy responsible and to induce his parents to agree to an early marriage. As soon, therefore, as a girl is visibly pregnant, the news spreads through the village, the jogmanjhi is told about it and a meeting is called to discuss and settle the matter.

201

In the upper village
A banyan formed her garland
In the lower village a pipal made her necklace
Alas, my love, that when your form was swelling
You went and left me.

If the boy acknowledges the paternity and agrees to marriage, the solution is fairly simple. He pays a fine of two goats to the villagers and the bride-price to the father, and the girl becomes his wife by being 'captured' and entering his house. In many cases this arrangement is merely a prelude to a public wedding. While the child is in the womb such a celebration is banned but once the baby has been born the ceremony can proceed and the girl can be lifted in the bridal basket and receive vermilion. There is only one qualification. The baby itself cannot enter the basket with its mother and must not be present at the wedding. In such cases, the fact that the child is suckled in marriage nullifies the fact that conception occurred outside it. The child is no different from a baby conceived and born in wedlock. Similarly, although its origins are not entirely decorous, the marriage itself relieves the girl's parents from much of their embarrassment. The boy may not be all that they had expected in a son-in-law but his ready acceptance of their daughter averts the shame of having an unmarried mother in the family. If they receive the original news with angry annoyance, it is with feelings more akin to relief that the parents view the outcome.

4 THE UNMARRIED MOTHER AND THE KNOWN FATHER

While acknowledging his paternity, however, a boy may refuse to marry the girl.

Prem Kumar Murmu of Kusma admitted to the villagers that he had made Kapra Tudu pregnant but as his father disliked the family, he refused to marry her.

Similarly the boy may deny his paternity but the villagers may fasten it on him.

In Bodaha, Bale Hembrom fell in love with a girl of his village. He first met her in the forest and then came to her almost every night and slept in her house. After a few months, the girl became pregnant and Bale hurriedly married another girl. The matter was referred to the jogmanjhi and although the boy denied responsibility, he was adjudged to be the father.

In such circumstances, the girl's parents are faced with a difficult and embarrassing task. Since responsibility has been fixed, there can be no question of hurriedly arranging another marriage for the girl and thus leaving her to rear the baby. Her parents have, therefore, for the time being, to accept the somewhat delicate situation and press instead for a full discharge of his obligations by the boy at fault.

This settlement is both expensive and complicated. When the boy's role is either admitted or known, the villagers require him to maintain the girl during the later stages of the pregnancy – from the date the village meets to the time the child is born. He must also compensate the girl for suckling the baby. After that he has either to take the child into his house or go on maintaining it. He must also pay the girl's father a correct bride-price and must meet the expenses of the naming ceremony. At this ceremony he must give the child his clan – either in person or by proxy – and admit it to his bongas. He must, in other words, become the legal father of the child and treat it as if it were in every way the offspring of a valid union.

Such a course relieves the girl's parents of their grand-child but the problem of their daughter is still, to some extent, unsolved. So long as she is suckling the baby, there is little hope of arranging a satisfactory marriage. After the child has gone to its father, however, and the incident has ceased to be uppermost in people's minds, her parents can begin to discuss her future. Since the boy was obliged to pay a bride-price, even though he declined to keep her, the girl has now the technical status of a divorcee. Her brow has not, however, been marked with vermilion and she can therefore enjoy the privilege of a public wedding and become the permanent wife of her husband – for his lifetime as well as in the realm of the dead. Her prospects in fact are by no means hopeless and although her wedding is delayed for one or two years and the parents can hardly hope to obtain the type of family which they might otherwise have liked, some sort of marriage is at last arranged. The girl and her parents endure a period of nervous anxiety but they win through in the end.

5 THE UNKNOWN FATHER AND THE BOUGHT HUSBAND

In certain cases, however, paternity is denied and the village holds that the matter is not proved.

202
O my love, come inside
Like yours the hands and feet
Like yours the eyes and face
O my love, a child has come.

But other evidence may be lacking. The girl's friends may know of her friendship but no one may have actually seen the boy and girl together. Or the boy may have promised the girl everything but given her nothing to prove his association with her. At the same time, her unexpected pregnancy may bring a sudden revulsion or even arouse his suspicions.

203
While you were keen to have me
'You were always about
Now I am having a baby
You keep away.

The boy may wildly deny any kind of intimacy and if they have been careful lovers, it is only the girl's word against the boy's. Occasionally the circumstances may be such that even the girl does not know which boy is to blame.

The girl's parents have now an even more unhappy task. They know that even if they postpone all action until the child is born, the birth itself will bring the crisis abruptly to a head. The birth will pollute their household and defile the village bongas. This pollution, they realise, can only be removed by holding a naming ceremony and this in turn can take place only when the child is provided with a father. If they postpone the ceremony indefinitely, the household will be 'driven from the line' and semi-outcasted. It becomes therefore a matter of extreme urgency to obtain a father for the child. All hope of recovering expenses is abandoned and the parents anxiously explore the only two alternatives.

Their first effort is to secure a 'false' father – a boy who will marry the girl and accept the child as his own. A poor family with little land is sometimes not averse to supplying one of its boys for this purpose. In such cases, the girl's parents forego the bride-price and the various marriage dues. They sometimes offer to take him as a ghar jawae or resident son-in-law or, if no boy is forthcoming on lesser terms, they purchase a husband by paying him cash, giving him cattle or even securing the villagers' approval and giving him some land.

Dulhan Tudu of Dhanbad did not know who was the father of her child so her father bought a husband for her by exempting him from payment of a bride-price. The husband accepted the child as his own and the boy has now inherited his land.

In Majdiha a girl became pregnant 'by gathering it at a dance'. The father was unknown so Phoce Tudu was brought from Lukhipur. He was purchased for ten rupees and exempted from the bride-price.

In Damakol a girl became pregnant but here also the boy could not be proved. Her father, therefore, bought Dukhia Hansdak' of Belpahari. He gave him ten maunds of paddy and a pair of bullocks and exempted him from the bride-price and all the other dues. Dukhia lived in the girl's house until the child was born. He then went back to his home taking his wife and 'false' child with him.

In Bara the daughter of Sankho Kisku became pregnant and Dhano Tudu of Ulatari was purchased as a husband. With village approval, he was given eight bighas of land and the child has since been named as if it were his own.

When the terms of purchase are discussed, it is also settled who will pay the costs of the naming ceremony. These are often met by the girl's father and when Rengta Kisku of Dumdumi was purchased for a girl of Garduara, he was given ten maunds of paddy, a dhoti and a pair of bullocks, was exempted from all other payments and had all the costs of the naming ceremony borne for him.

In Kajikend, on the other hand, the father of Sugda Hansdak' purchased a husband more cheaply. He gave him a pair of bullocks and exempted him from the bride-price and other payments but when the child was born, he was required to pay the costs of the naming.

In all these cases, the boy became the girl's husband, took over full responsibility for the child, named it as if he were the true father and the child acquired all the rights of a true son or a daughter.

6 THE BOUGHT FATHER

Not all families, however, can arrange a bought husband. Moreover, if the child should prove to be a boy, a 'false' father may not always want him to inherit his property. Another method is therefore explored. Instead of linking the 'false' father to the girl by marriage, a man or boy is produced who becomes the child's father but without any civil responsibilities. At the naming ceremony, he is the last to be shaved, to receive the marks of flour upon his chest and to drink the rice gruel and nim water. He acquiesces in the midwife's announcement. He gives the child his clan and admits him to his bongas. But he does not marry its mother. He becomes a 'god-father' rather than a father and his obligations are neither civil nor economic.

In Baramasia, the daughter of Odga Tudu became pregnant by a boy of the Tudu clan. Her father did not purchase a husband but paid another Santal twenty-five rupees for naming the child.

In Malipara, the daughter of Phudan Marandi gave birth to a child and Charan Hansdak' of her village was induced to give the child his clan on payment of twelve rupees.

In such circumstances, the girl's parents maintain their position in society. They escape the ignominy of going out of caste, of being 'driven from the line', and of enduring the boycott of their neighbours. But their daughter remains a source of permanent anxiety. No respectable family is likely to want her and the most her parents can do is to secure a young widower or someone who has been once or twice divorced. This is not an enviable outcome but it is all that the circumstances allow.

7 THE MULTIPLE LOVER

If the father is sometimes unknown because the actual lover is in doubt, instances have been known when several boys admit a joint connection. Such cases are not at all common since a Santal girl almost always prefers to have a single 'permanent' lover. But occasionally the case occurs and in that event, the true father remains unknown but responsibility can, none the less, be fixed. When a situation of this sort arises, the boys are fined and with the money either a Santal is paid to give the child his clan or a husband is purchased for the girl. Part of the money goes to the girl and some of it is kept by the villagers.

The daughter of Dharma Hembrom of Ladapathar became pregnant and proved before the village that three boys had had relations with her. The boys admitted the connection and were fined seven rupees each. In this case, the village did not take any of the money but gave it all to the girl's father. The girl's elder sister's husband was then purchased and the girl became a co-wife.

When the daughter of Matru Tudu of Kundli became pregnant, four boys admitted responsibility. In this case all the boys and the girl herself were each fined ten rupees. The money was taken by the villagers who then purchased a father for the child while the girl's parents took him as a resident son-in-law.

If a girl has had relations with several boys but one is more involved than the others, the latter is sometimes required to pay a larger fine. In Mohulpahari the daughter of Sukri Marandi had intercourse with three boys and became pregnant. All three admitted responsibility but one of them had been with the girl more frequently than the others. He was there-fore fined ten rupees and each of the others five rupees each. In addition, the three boys and the girl had each to give the villagers a goat. When the child was born it was given the clan of the boy who was fined ten rupees but he did not become the girl's husband.

In a final case which vividly expresses the Santal attitude, the daughter of Dalu Marandi of Guhiajuri became pregnant and on being questioned by the villagers declared that Lodo Hembrom was responsible. Lodo denied all relations with her but the villagers forced the paternity upon him. Twenty days later, labour pains began but for two days the child was not delivered. When the midwife saw the obstruction, she told the girl that the baby seemed to be of several fathers and she must know their names so that a vermilion mark might be applied for each of them and the delivery of the child secured. By now the girl was at the point of exhaustion. She therefore gave out the names of fourteen boys. The midwife made fourteen vermilion marks on her pelvis and shortly afterwards a baby girl was born. When Lodo heard that the girl had admitted relationships with fourteen boys, he obstinately refused to have anything to do with the child or its mother and the villagers also could obviously not abide by their former decision. There was deadlock for a month during which no naming ceremony was performed and finally the girl and her parents left caste and became Christians.

8 INFANTICIDE

If the child is the offspring of a non-Santal – a Diku – the outlook for the girl's parents is even graver. There is no longer any hope of obtaining either a bought husband or a bought father while intimacy of this kind is so abhorred that the local Santals will almost certainly impose the dreaded punishment of bitlaha. In such circumstances, resort is sometimes had to infanticide. This is nowadays very rarely practised but at the beginning of the century, Bompas recorded the Santal opinion that 'often if a father will not acknowledge a child the mother will strangle it at birth and bury the body.' and as recently as 1944, a case of infanticide led to two Santal women hanging themselves in jail. A young Santal girl, Mundu Marandi, was working as a servant in the house of a Muslim of Gopalpur and after some time, became pregnant by him. At the village meeting she declined to say who was the father and matters hung fire until the time of birth. One rainy day she gave birth to a girl and the same night her mother took the baby, smothered it and buried it in a hillock behind the house. The girl's aunt had advised her to do this and when the matter was reported to the police, both the old women were arrested and lodged in jail. A few days later, they hanged themselves by taking off their clothes and tying them to the bars of the cell. In this case, the shame arising out of their daughter's misconduct with a Muslim proved too much for the women and after disposing of the baby they killed themselves rather than endure any further agony.

9 THE VILLAGE FATHER

If the girl's parents seem unable to meet the situation, the villagers are sometimes constrained to intervene. We have already seen that until the naming ceremony is performed, the village bongas remain defiled and although pollution can sometimes be removed by the independent offering of a goat, this is not always thought to be wise. At the same time, the spectacle of a child condemned to live without bongas, to remain a bidhua or permanent bastard, to be utterly and permanently out of the tribe, arouses their compassion. Accordingly if the family fails to obtain a father, the villagers have, in certain rare instances been known to intervene. 'To save the child's head' they have either fined the family or subscribed for re-admitting the household into caste and at the same time, they have compelled the jogmanjhi or another villager to act as the father.

In Manglapara a widow, Lukhi Soren, had a baby girl. No one agreed to be purchased so in the end the villagers intervened. They chose an old man and against his will they made him give the child his clan and admit it to his bongas.

In Mahuadangal, a widow had a child. The alleged father absconded so the family was semi-outcasted. As the father was not proved, one way or the other, the naming ceremony was not performed and the bongas remained impure for seven months. At last, the alleged father appeared, admitted his connection and named the child. This purified the bongas but because of the delay, the widow was fined a large goat.

Finally, if no one in the village is constrained to give the child his clan and all efforts by the village fail, the girl's father is made to give a goat, and his daughter and the baby are expelled from the village. The goat is then sacrificed at the manjhithan and the bongas are deemed to be purified. This is the last resort, when all else fails; but I do not know of any case in which this has been done.

CHAPTER X

Marriage
and the Family

I BETROTHAL

For Santal parents, the marriage of a boy or girl is a major crisis in the family. It is not only that a suitable partner must be carefully chosen and the boy or girl coaxed into willing acceptance. Each stage in the intricate business of betrothal must be done with customary hospitality and with due regard for the feelings of the village. The family is, as it were, on trial. If the boy and girl are submissive, if the entertainment is generous, if everything is done with calm efficiency, the parents will win general esteem. If for any reason they cannot implement their words, they must immediately offer compensation. A betrothal is not merely the bringing together of a boy and girl in a more or less arbitrary manner. It is a business transaction, a test of values, an exercise in tribal manners.

The first step is the appointment of a matchmaker. This envoy is usually an old and respected friend, who represents either of the two families. During the course of the negotiations it is necessary for a number of dates to be fixed and on all these occasions the boy's father must bring the match-maker and the village officials together and give them rice-beer. Similarly, when dates are considered by the girl's family, the officials of her village are consulted and they and the matchmaker are given rice-beer in the girl's house. At the end of the wedding when all has been successfully accomplished the matchmaker is rewarded with a small present.

When the matchmaker has been chosen, his (or her) first task is to scour the neighbourhood for a suitable girl. She need not be particularly good-looking. In fact, the very qualities which excite youthful passion are often disqualifications for the drabber duties of the home. The dashing lively girl, the girl with a bouncing rounded body, who is popular with boys – such a girl, it is feared, may prove a somewhat risky wife. It is regarded as much safer to choose a quieter kind of girl, one who is known to be strong and healthy, a good cook and a thrifty house-keeper. All these virtues are implied when, using the traditional symbols, the parents instruct the match-maker to embark upon his task. 'Can you find us a new pot?' they say. 'For whom is it wanted?' 'For our eldest boy.' 'There is possibly a spare one.' 'But it must be from the shed of a good potter, with a good form and burnt to a turn.' 'Would I offer you a bad one?' asks the matchmaker. 'Then how long will you take?' reply the parents. 'I will come back in five days' time.'

When he has been briefed, the matchmaker selects a family and first secures their agreement to consider the proposal. After that a date is settled for a first inspection by the families. This is usually arranged at a market, a fair or under a tree between the two families. In some cases it takes place at the jogmanjhi's house and almost all the families of the two villages attend the inspection. Each person is saluted by the boy and girl and the villagers subject them both to critical scrutiny.

If the meeting is held at the jogmanjhi's, a further symbolic dialogue ensues. 'Jogmanjhi,' says the matchmaker, 'Are you at home?' 'Yes. Come inside. Where are they from? Let all of them come inside and sit down.' 'They are strangers from another village.' 'Let them tell us all their news.' 'By the grace of Cando Baba, we are all well these days. And you?' 'By the grace of Cando Baba, we also are well. But to whose house have you come?' 'There is nothing to fear,' replies the matchmaker. 'We have come for a good reason to the house of one of your men. We are searching for a new pot. Please show us one.' 'Is it a new pot or a used one that you are looking for?' the jogmanjhi asks. 'A new pot in beautiful condition is what we want and we have already seen one in a house. If there is no other applicant, please show us this pot first.' 'Wait while I ask about it,' replies the jogmanjhi. 'There are quite a lot of pots here and we shall certainly be able to fix you up.'

At this meeting neither side commits itself to more than a polite neutral-ity but on the journey home, the boy's parents discuss their impressions with the envoy. If they are well disposed, the talk proceeds on the follow-ing lines. 'We saw a pot and looked it over carefully. How did it strike us? The pot was quite a good one. I would not call it bad.' 'What sort of pot do you want?' asks the matchmaker. 'We have to see if it is withered or crippled and how it walks, speaks and laughs.' 'I sounded and tapped the pot,' says the boy's mother. 'It talked and laughed very nicely. Its girlish nature was all it should be. But what are the mother and father like?' 'Both of them are good people,' replies the matchmaker. 'Then we shall make them our relatives. The pot is good to look at, its shape is pleasant and it has a lovely ring. Envoy, you showed us a good pot from a good potter.' 'Then what is one to say?' the matchmaker answers. 'It is not for one day or half a day. It is for a whole lifetime that we are getting this pot. We shall look at it and test it and if it is not good, why should we take it? If the potter is not good, can the pot be good?' 'You are speaking truly,' say the boy's parents. 'We shall hasten to have it in our family.'

A day or two later, the matchmaker sounds the parents of the girl. If either side is unimpressed, they regret that they did not find a good omen and the negotiations go no further. If both sides are willing, they accord provisional approval and the matchmaker then arranges for a fuller view.

This full inspection is called 'the viewing of the household' and is sometimes held at the boy's house and at the girl's, sometimes first at one or first at the other and sometimes only at the boy's house or only at the girl's. When it is done at the boy's, the matchmaker brings the girl's father, her uncles and aunts and the headman and paranik of her village and the whole party is shown the boy's house and conducted round the family lands. If a visit is made to the girl's house, similar formalities are followed but the lands are not inspected.

When the visit is over, the parties again consider the proposal and inform the matchmaker. If they are unimpressed, they politely withdraw their provisional approval but otherwise, they confirm the original agreement.

Once the 'viewing of the household' has been completed, the families decide whether to perform the wedding quickly or allow some time to elapse. If they do not want the ceremony immediately, they arrange for a formal betrothal to 'block the way'. This usually takes place at the girl's house and is then followed by a visit to the boy's but in certain cases the boy's house is visited first and the girl's later. If an early wedding is desired, the visit to the boy's house is all that occurs.

Each of these visits is known as 'a recognition by clothes' and the subject of the first is to give a cloth to the bride. The boy's party consisting of most of his male relatives but not the boy himself goes to the girl's village. They take with them the headman, the paranik and a few villagers. In the girl's house they are given a small feast, the girl's father seats them in the courtyard and the girl is taken up by each of them in turn. The boy's father gives her a piece of cloth and the other members of the party make small gifts.

The purpose of the visit to the boy's house is to give a cloth to the bridegroom. The girl's party goes and is given similar entertainment. They take the boy on their knees, kiss his right ear and give him small presents. The girl's father gives him a cloth and the other members of the party present him with either a bangle, armlet, necklace or a few annas. On this visit also the principal person, the girl, is almost invariably absent.

These two visits constitute the formal betrothal and if the boy and girl already like each other, there is now no bar to their paying each other visits and also sleeping together. Explorations of this kind, in fact, are encouraged rather than frowned upon since the wedding itself is likely to go more smoothly if the partners are already friends.

All is now clear for the wedding but before this is solemnised there is one last stage to be passed – the payment of the bride-price. For this purpose, the boy's parents with the village officials, their wives and a few others go to the girl's house. Rice-beer is drunk, the bride-price or most of it is paid, the remaining wedding dues are settled and at last the way is clear for the wedding itself.

During all these days the strain on both the parties is very great for at any moment a tiny incident may wreck all chances of agreement. While paying the different visits, for example, omens are carefully taken. A man carrying an axe or a mattock is ominous. So is a man cutting wood, a branch falling from a tree or ashes being carried. All of these actions are in various ways connected with death – the axe because it is used for cutting wood at a funeral, the mattock because it is used for digging a grave, the branch because it may swell a pyre, and ashes because this is what the dead become. Other bad omens are a fox, a jackal or a snake going to the left, an empty pot or a call from behind. Good omens on the other hand include a pot full of water, a herd of cattle, a corpse, some washed clothes, an oriole calling on the right, a piyo bird on the left and an empty pot about to be filled. A full pot is good because it shows that the journey's purpose is about to be fulfilled. A corpse is also good since death is temporarily appeased and the man's destiny is accomplished. Clean clothes are auspicious 'because all the dirt has been washed away'. These omens do not necessarily make or mar a proposal but they are not without importance. Often they seem subconsciously to affect the decision while occasionally they are even 'staged' in order to deter a party from proceeding with its plans.

204
For only a little girl
The friends have come
How shall we say no?
Girl, sweep the courtyard
Take out the ashes
So that the omens are not good.

Even therefore when everything appears to be going without a hitch a sudden unforeseen happening or an unpredictable encounter may blight the prospects.

Moreover even though the sudden breach of an agreement enables the other side to recover all its costs, the greatest care is necessary to avoid this troublesome development. In Amtala, Chotu Ramu Murmu had negotiated the marriage of his son in Jamni. After 'recognition by clothes' had been done in his house, he went with a party to Jamni. There the girl's father refused to give them a meal, there was a tremendous quarrel and they went back in a huff. After that, Chotu Ramu broke the marriage off. When he told me about this, he said that he could have claimed the cost of the previous ceremony. He did not do so, however, and in view of his rather explosive temperament my own feeling is that he himself was partly to blame.

Mandal Baske of Patardih had arranged his son's marriage in Haldidih and the bridegroom's cloth had been duly given in his house. Then the girl learnt that the boy had six toes on each of his feet and refused to go on with the marriage.

In another case from Kusumba a marriage failed, also after the boy had received a cloth, because it then transpired that the brother of the girl was a leper.

In a case from Durga, a marriage had been arranged between Hopna Murmu and Hendi Soren. The bride's cloth had already been given and a few weeks later a party from the girl's side went to the boy's house for giving the bridegroom his dhoti. A good deal of merry-making took place and the women of both parties smeared each other with oil and turmeric. Presently the mother of the girl got excited, stripped off all her clothes and started dancing naked. This conduct disgusted the boy's mother and a few days later, the matchmaker was instructed to suspend the negotiations. The girl's mother was very angry and her husband attempted to recover the cost of entertaining the party. Since, however, they themselves were at fault, the boy's father declined to pay and in the end they got nothing.

2 THE WEDDING CEREMONY

Once the wedding day has been chosen, the first important task is to erect the marriage booth. This is a shed consisting of a canopy of sal and mango branches covering a central altar. The altar is made of two branches – one of sal and one of mahua – planted together with a little mound of earth heaped up at their base.

When a booth is erected it is put up one, three, five or seven days before the wedding and the boy and the girl are rubbed with oil and turmeric from the day of its erection. For making the booth the services of the village boys are impressed and in return for their work they are given a meal of rice each and a pot of rice-beer to share. A wedding booth sacrifice must also be made in the sacred grove. The priest takes three fowls – one brown and two white – two pais or handfulls of rice and a pot of rice-beer. At the grove he says, 'Jaher era, in the name of the wedding booth I am offering you a fowl. Look on it with favour. When we go to the girl's village as the bridegroom's party, may there be no trouble or danger on the road or in the forest. May there be no stumbling or fumbling. Let nothing be broken. Let no one be bewitched. Let every trouble be removed to the left and right of our path. When we eat and drink, let no one have an ache of belly or head. Let the two families be of one mind. May there be no quarrel, no accusations, no checks or hindrances. May this wedding come to its end in calm and peace.' He then offers the brown fowl to Jaher Era and with similar invocations sacrifices the remaining chickens to Maran Buru and the Five-Six.

During each day that the booth is standing, three maids-of-all-work attend the bride or bridegroom, assist in the annointing and are given their meals each day. The jogmanjhi also supervises the ritual and is given food and drink for every day the booth stands.

But besides these incidental charges, the erection of the booth is of great importance for it commits the family to a village feast. In the girl's village, her family must entertain the whole village with rice-beer and a meal of rice and also provide the bridegroom's party with a similar meal. In the boy's village his family must give the villagers a feast on the return of the party with the girl and her friends. On the side of the villagers, it assumes co-operation in a 'circling ceremony' and the giving of small presents to the boy and the girl.

If, for any reason, these expenses cannot be incurred, a much simpler shed is put up instead. No sal or mahua branches are erected in the court-yard and there is no earthen mound. The boy and the girl are not given turmeric in its shade and at the circling ceremony only the family intimates attend and the present-giving takes place in the privacy of an inside room. No sacrifices are necessary and the village boys can claim no feast. Rice-beer, however, is brewed and the village drinks and dances.

It will illustrate the later stages of a Santal wedding if I now describe a ceremony which I attended in the Dumka Damin in May 1940, when I was touring the district as Provincial Census Superintendent. This wedding was between Jarpa Tudu of Katikund and Maika Hembrom of

Dhakodih. Jarpa was accompanied by his little cousin, Somla, who acted as best man. The proceedings fell into two parts – those at Jarpa's house in Katikund and those at Maika's in Dhakodih.

In Katikund, the rites were almost over when I reached the village at dawn, and I could only learn at second hand what had happened. The ceremony had begun the day before when the marriage booth had been erected. This was a booth 'of only one day'. If Jarpa's father had been well-to-do the booth would have gone up earlier but as his means were meagre, it was delayed as long as possible. The booth consisted of a framework of sal poles while under a roof of branches, strings of mango leaves were inter-crossed.

On the completion of the shed the planting of the trees had taken place. For this, a little rice, turmeric and dub grass had been buried in a hole in the centre and over them the boy's sisters had made a small mud pillar. Into this pillar, the branches of sal and mahua had been thrust.

There had then followed a massage of the village. Each married couple had squatted down before the pillar on some thatching grass and been carefully rubbed with oil. In this way the village priest and his wife, the headman and his wife, the other village officials, the villagers, the boy's relatives and Jarpa himself had all been anointed.

The next morning at cock-crow a 'water marriage' was performed and this led on to a ceremony in Jarpa's house. For this a small trench was scooped out in the courtyard and a pair of ploughing yokes put down on either side. Jarpa's mother squatted at one end while his father stooped at the other with a sword pointing down his back. Jarpa sat in the middle. Water was poured down the sword, and he calmly drank it.

A packet made of mango leaves with some rice, a little dub grass and some turmeric was then fixed to his right wrist and he was given a little iron utensil like a fish containing oil for blackening the eyes. When I arrived, the bridegroom and best man were standing in their marriage garments by the manjhithan and the blessing ceremony of the village founder had just ended. Jarpa was clad in a yellow-stained cloth with long streamers of red, green, yellow and violet paper flowers dangling from his head while his hat was a tinsel paper crown with a little paper bird on the top. His best man wore a conical cloth cap like the hat of a Sherwood Forester.

As we stood about, a dom dance started. The drums thundered and six men holding sticks jumped and capered down the village street lightly bouncing up and down with legs astride, kicking their heels, and whirling about, as if parrying foes. A little later it shrank to a paik don dance in which a pair of dancers ran round a circle, fencing with their sticks, and hurling their bodies around with smiling ferocity.

As they danced, the matchmaker, an old lady with a calm natural dignity, began to get restive and presently she took up a big bamboo basket containing the bridegroom's presents – a turmeric-coloured sari with yellow tassels, oil, turmeric, a comb, a mirror, a little rice and some dub grass. Then, glancing round to see that the others were ready, she put the basket on her head, took up her umbrella and set out firmly down the village street. As she started, Jarpa's cousin, a strapping girl in her twenties, picked him up while another girl picked up her cousin Somla; and with the boys astride their hips, they hurried down the street. A small band of Dom drummers went along with them and from the last house, I watched them go rapidly away across the fields. About an hour later, the rest of the village left for the ten miles' march to Dhakodih.

When we arrived, the bridegroom's party were already there and were resting under a huge mango tree. It was a cloudy afternoon and a cool wind was blowing across the uplands. At the girl's house all was noise and bustle. A line of women were dancing. The girl with her little bridesmaid was seated on a mat inside the wedding booth. Both were being rubbed with oil and turmeric. In front of them was a brass plate with leaf-cups, oil, paddy, grass and turmeric, and almost immediately a circling ceremony took place.

Five of Maika's relatives – her mother, her two aunts and her two elder sisters – came up and each in turn performed the following ritual. First the brass plate was picked up and passed over the heads of Maika and her bridesmaid. Then a pinch of rice was taken and passed over their heads. Finally they were saluted either with the hands or by pressing the head. When this was over, Maika got up and one of her elder sisters led her round the pillar three times, sprinkling the ground with water as she went. Another sister followed with the mat. They then brought bowls of water and welcomed us to the house with bending johars.

All this time the women were dancing in the courtyard – three of them with chains of pink flowers, clashing cymbals, while the others sang wedding songs. As the space cleared, they edged into the shed and swung round and round the central pillar, their bodies undulating firmly and seriously, their haunches bobbing up and down with a sharp jerk at every step, their thighs going backwards and forwards with savage stabbing thrusts. As they went round they worked themselves up into an excited flopping rush, a pause succeeding each climax and leading in turn to yet another round of violent acceleration.

As the dance developed into a series of shouting collisions, the worship of the family ancestors went quietly on in an inner-room, each ancestor receiving a small libation of rice-beer.

The stage was then set for the 'water marriage'. Two girls with cotton pads on their heads took up two pots of parched rice and with a turmeric-stained cloth for the bridegroom wrapped round their bodies and over the pots, strolled slowly down towards a stream. As they went a crowd of women issued from the girl's house and danced down behind them in three noisy rows – shouting, singing, striking gongs, clapping hands, jumping, and floundering, while the drums thundered beside them. Leading the mob went Maika's mother and her two aunts – her mother with a bow and three arrows, one aunt with a sword and the other with a large knife. Backing and advancing, the lines gradually trooped down across the uplands to the stream while the two girls with the pots wandered sedately on. Finally as the water came into sight, there was a general scamper into the field.

A man then took a mattock and facing east made a shallow triangular hole about twenty yards from the water. Maika's mother gave the jogmanjhi the arrows and he inserted them in the hole, standing them on end in each of the three corners. The two girls made over their pots to him and he emptied the parched rice into their laps. He then gave the pots back and sent the girls to the stream to fill them with water. While they were strolling down, he wound a long cotton thread three times round the three arrows, put two copper coins inside the fence, and placed some vermilion on the coins and an arrow. The two pots of water were poured into the hole and the three women went jigging round dipping into the water the tip of the bow and the point of the sword. As they danced and plunged their weapons, the jogmanjhi went aside and made a libation of rice-beer to Maran Buru, and the first Santal couple, Pilcu Haram and Pilcu Budhi.

When this was over, he came back, untied the threads, uprooted the arrows, washed off the vermilion, and put back some of the water into the pots. The two girls then lifted the pots back onto their heads, were again draped in a single yellow wrap and with the mob of women gaily surging and dancing before them, they began the slow walk back to the village.

As we went up the wide and airy slopes, the dance became a general scamper and frolic – girls chasing boys and boys chasing after girls, girls in pairs tossing and flopping, a few of the older women keeping a ragged line, the gong beating quickly, the drums dinning loudly in the afternoon sun, while the three magnificent old women slowly bore their weapons back.

When the procession reached the bride's house, it went slowly round the central pole three times and at last dispersed.

I then went over to the boy's party and sat around waiting for the girl's party to emerge. The jogmanjhi had preceded me with a pot of water which he formally made over to them as a gesture of welcome.

After we had waited an hour, a new note was heard on the drums and at about 4 p.m. we saw the men of the girl's party gradually come down the upland fields, and straggle into the village. A little later the women came slowly down while the drum beat solemnly and lightly.

The dancers in Jarpa's party were now getting ready, putting on their gear of coloured cloth leggings and red and white turbans, while a boy wound some cloth snakes up and over his shoulders. They then sallied out, making a detour of the village so as to approach it from the west.

The men of the girl's party had meanwhile formed themselves into a platoon with three ranks and were carrying out some war-like exercises, their staves held aloft, pacing forwards, turning about, kicking their feet, brandishing their weapons while the drummers with green and white turbans and yellow dhotis incited them to attack. As they gradually moved westwards the men of the boy's party came down towards them, with a forest of staves and a round of menacing gestures. The rival drums beat up against each other. Gradually they got nearer and nearer until the staves were on the point of clashing. Each surged towards the other and then recoiled and again came up and once again went back. Then suddenly all the sticks were put down in a line and the two platoons faced each other without their weapons. They then backed and advanced and from time to time made as if to pick up the sticks till, suddenly as one man, they jumped at each other, each man seizing a partner and careering round with him in a violent embrace. With this the two groups fused and then a little later, formed a ring within which individuals danced and sparred.

While this was proceeding Jarpa and Somla had been taken to one side and their legs had been washed by Maika's mother. When she had done this, she took Jarpa gently aside, put him on a mat and fed him with country sugar. After that Somla was also quietly led off and fed with sugar by her. All the time a row of girls sedately danced as if they were alone with nature instead of in the noisy bustling throng.

After Jarpa and his best man had been attended to by Maika's mother they started on a round of the village, calling at each house and having their legs washed and some sugar and water put in their mouths. At each place they made respectful salutes.

The platoons meanwhile reformed and noisy battle exercises went merrily on as the afternoon merged in the evening. As Jarpa and his mate went from door to door, the platoons followed them, stopping for a dance outside each house as Jarpa went in. When at last the visits were over, the noise ended and the crowd dispersed while Jarpa and Somla went on and sat quietly on the edge of the booth in Maika's house.

It was now getting dark and there was an indefinite period during which we simply waited, the scene curiously empty after the earlier din. Groups from the girl's village came over and a formal dialogue took place. 'So manjhi saheb, we are now sitting down together. We are sitting on a single stool, a single chair and a cot. How are our souls and kindred, and our bodies and skins? Will it not be good if we tell each other about them?'

'Yes indeed, manjhi saheb. Since you have asked about it. Our souls have shot up like mountains. Our moustaches are like buffalo horns and our chests are broad as mats. But, it is said, the debts of relatives are big debts. The children of big people are big in wisdom and manners. The children of small people are small in wisdom and manners. None the less, we are not badly off. The two themselves (manjhi haram and manjhi budhi), the husband and wife, the infants and the children, the servant girls and servant boys, the maids, the sons and the daughters, the son-in-laws, the uncles, the brother-in-laws, the elder brothers of the father, the older relatives, the fathers, the grandsons and granddaughters all those who spring from a single head, the calf's mother, the she-goat, the calf, the he-goat, the life and the body, the crops with the tank, the life with the relatives, the comings and goings, visits to the sea, the pot of water, twenty miles in front, thirty-two behind, from below the ground the cold water, the single river, by your good wishes, the mercy of people on earth, by the grace of Cando Baba, in these days all are well.'

At last the jogmanjhi arrived and a little later the drum sounded a tattoo of welcome. The girls filed out to a spot beyond the courtyard. A mat was spread and Jarpa and his mate squatted down. They were then washed and very carefully rubbed with oil and turmeric. Three unmarried girls then combed their hair. As they combed, they pretended to find a lot of lice and amid shrieks of laughter, went through the solemn pantomime of killing them on a piece of wood. The bride's elder sister then pretended to shave Jarpa, aping the barber's antics while the older women stood by and offered ribald comments. The mat was then rolled up and Jarpa and his mate were dowsed in water. The women wrapped Jarpa round with a cloth screen and he was given a new dhoti on behalf of Maika and made to change it. As he was struggling, the women sang a taunting wedding song about his old dhoti.

It isn't coming out
The after-birth is stuck
Give the cow some medicine
And then she'll hurry up.

But at last Jarpa succeeded and emerged resplendent. Some rice, sugar and rice-beer were then produced as wages for the sham barber and the rice-beer was carefully smelt and tasted. Presently the matchmaker came with her basket and followed by three boys went into the house to give it to the girl. A little later, the bride's small brother was carried out on a man's shoulder and Jarpa was hoisted on to the shoulders of a friend. They filled their mouths with rice, and each sprinkled the other with dripping mango twigs. Jarpa now gave the little boy a cloth and each spat some rice over the other's mouth. All the time a gang of girls danced madly round the pole while four or five boys stood bouncing their bodies, with their legs astride, shaking their buttocks with shivering frenzy.

When this rite was over, the boys got down and there was now another lull. The village got darker and fires commenced to glimmer in the houses. I began to think the pause would never end when suddenly the booth filled again and rows of women went surging round the altar. This time Maika herself and her maids-of-all-work were escorted into the middle. The jogmanjhi appeared and soon he was knotting and tying the spool of cotton used at the water marriage into a series of elaborate designs. He first passed a loop over the little toe of Maika's left foot. Then he drew the strands up her body over her left ear and round her neck. Finally he linked the same cotton to the little fingers of the three attendants and bound them firmly to the central pole. Some paddy was now put in their left hands. They husked it with their nails. The new rice was put in three mango leaves. Three pinches of dub grass and a piece of turmeric were added. The cotton strands were unwound. The leaves were made up into a packet and using the same cotton, were tied to the girl's wrist. When it was over, Maika was led away.

A little later, she again came out. A small trench was dug, two yokes were laid across it and water was made to trickle down a sword and wet her hands.

We were now on the verge of the central ceremony. Men were dancing in the village street. The drums were thundering and the women again went bobbing round the pole. Maika had at last put on the clothes which Jarpa had brought and presently three of Jarpa's party went inside the house, picked her up and put her in the huge capacious basket which the matchmaker had brought with her from Katikund. As they lifted Maika in the basket and struggled into the courtyard, the three maids-of-all-work made a sudden dart and amid shouts of laughter rubbed some turmeric on their bottoms. As the basket slowly emerged, Jarpa again climbed on to some shoulders. His mount brought him near while Maika drew a cloth tightly over her face. Then a piece of cloth was stretched between them, two bowls of water with mango twigs were brought and still clutching at the cloth, they thrice sprinkled each other with water. After that there was a mock fight while Jarpa tried to reach her face. At last he succeeded and dipping the thumb and little finger of his right hand in some vermilion which his father held up to him, he marked her brow three times. As he did it, there was a great shout of 'Haribol sindurdan', the drums crashed out and the cloth between them was whisked away. Jarpa got down. Maika was lowered and after Jarpa had picked her up, she followed shyly to the booth. Here their clothes were tied together and escorted by the bride's elder sister, they went slowly and solemnly three times round the pillar.

It was now so late that I decided to go to bed. The ceremonies however were not entirely over and I was told next morning that after I had left, Maika had rushed inside the house, shut the door behind her and Jarpa and his mate had only been admitted after paying four pice to her younger sister. They had then been washed by the maids-of-all-work and finally treated to a meal. Even later in the night a further circling ceremony was performed. The bridal mat was spread in the booth. Jarpa and Maika were again knotted together and led round the pillar three times. They were then made to sit on the mat and first the girl's mother and then her two aunts passed a brass plate with a light over them. After warming their hands at a lamp, they then touched the cheeks of the couple. The girl's party then offered some presents and after that, both parties sat down to the bridal feast.

This concludes my account of the Dhakodih wedding. The marriage ritual however has further phases and I will conclude my description by relating what happened at another wedding in May 1943. This occurred at Kadampur and begins where my other account leaves off.

As I entered this village, the feast had already ended and the bride was on the point of leaving for the boy's village. Wrapped in her stiff turmeric-coloured cloth, she stood patiently outside her house while one after another of her friends came up to salute her. As each one came the bride made an apron of part of her skirt, puffed rice and grain were emptied into it and three times she dropped it into the apron of her friend and three times received it back. At the end of each exchange the puffed rice and grain were put back in a pot while the bride and her friend bowed low in salutation. When these dignified farewells had at last dragged to an end, the bride was swallowed up in a protecting band of young girls while all her 'mothers' by village relationship were saluted by all the bridegroom's 'fathers'. The women stood in a pert line and as each man came up each woman bent down and peered at him through her hands. As she peered, the man peered back at her and soon there was a series of peering couples edging backwards and forwards and every now and then risking little gestures. Sometimes a woman made a grab at a man, sometimes the two whispered, sometimes there was a scamper and scuffle while the village stood and rocked with laughter. The only persons who preserved dignity and calm were the girl's own father and the boy's.

The male relatives of both the parties then embraced. The girl and her bridesmaid, and the boy and his best man slowly filed round all the guests, saluting each in turn. Finally the jogmanjhi sat down in a little ring with the other men and to the accompaniment of rice-beer, the farewell addresses were formally delivered.

These addresses followed a rigid pattern and I will record them as they are generally used throughout the Santal Parganas.

'Members of the bridegroom's party, before you leave for home I shall say a few words. In the hunt and the chase, in pain and in pleasure, with promise and no force, on the right side and on the left, with good omens, the one who wears a chain, the one who wears a nose ring, we have linked and tied together. Sitting with Sin Bonga, Maran Buru, and the bongas of the five hills, we have joined the chain and the ring. The bridegroom has secured the family of the bride, the bride has received the house of the bridegroom, the houses are now one. Whenever you went on a hunt or a chase, whenever you went to a market, whenever you went through a village or a field, you drank the water from the spring or the pool without our knowing. But now you have bought our house, from today you must never leave it either to the right or the left. Come into its shade for a pot of water and the shed of the cows.

'From twelve kilns you chose a single pot. You bought it after tapping and sounding it. If it should prove lazy, if it should start straying, if it should go blind, if it should get crippled, if it should go down into the ground, it will not be on us. If it should change its form to pewter or to copper, if it should become a loose girl, or a whore, if it should poison persons or become a witch, it will be through you that it has done it, for it is a man's house that moulds men as a cowshed moulds cattle.

'Now we have eaten the bride-price, and the gifts to the bride's brother, the grandmother and mother. Bone of her bones and ash of her ashes, we have sold. But the blood of her head and the blood of her ears, we have not sold and should she die, we shall follow you for her. And if on any day or half a day, she should burn the rice or spoil the curry, do not get angry with her. If you tell her what to do, if you instruct her and still she does not do it, O headman, send a man to us. If no man is free, send a crooked stick. If you have no stick, send a dog to us and we shall meet and talk.'

The jogmanjhi of the boy's village then replied, 'Manjhi, it is indeed true that what has been done has not been done by us. Sitting with Sin Bonga, Maran Buru, and the bongas of the five hills, tying them to the right and to the left, and with good omens, we joined the ring and the chain. From twelve kilns we chose one pot and after tapping and sounding it, we bought it. We have carried away your pet parrot from the perch it had with you to its perch with us. If it should turn to pewter or copper, it will still be on us. If it should be lazy, if it should stray, or if it should go down into the ground it will be our doing. If it should lose its skin, if it should turn into a loose girl or a whore, if it should poison people or become a witch, or if it should start stealing and thieving, the fault will be ours. Bone of her bones and ash of her ashes, from today we have bought. But the blood of the head and the blood of the ears, these we have not bought and should she die, you may follow us for her. And if on one day or half a day she should burn the rice or spoil the curry, shall we not instruct and teach her? And should she still not learn we shall send you word and meet.

'And if you ever come our way, never pass us either on the left or right. And if you go to a hunt or a chase, a field or a village, or a men's assembly, never pass us to the left or right. Formerly you drank water from the spring unknown to us, but from today our families are one. Come in and drink water from a gourd in the shade of the creeper's pole. The houses of this village are ours and those of our village are yours.'

There was then a slight pause while the drums beat up. The bridegroom loitered by his litter. At last the bride came and the party left on its jogging journey to his home.

When the party reaches the boy's village, the bride and bridegroom are washed and then go from house to house, paying their respects and being fed with sugar. They end up at the boy's house where his mother and his aunts wash them, rub them with turmeric and after warming their hands at a lamp, transfer the warmth to their cheeks. They are then taken in and given a meal.

When the meal is finished, the bride goes round washing the feet of the bridegroom's father, the village priest, and the bridegroom's male relatives. The bridegroom's elder brother then comes and the bride places her hand on his toes. This is the first and the last time when she will feel him. She keeps her hand on his foot until he gives her two pice.

The rites then turn to farce. Some boys come limping in with leaves or rags tied round their legs and pretending to be in acute pain. They go up to the bride and say, 'We hear a good doctor has come so we have come to show her our legs.' To this the bride replies, 'If you pay me enough money, I will make you well.' When this is over, the bride washes the bridegroom's feet.

After that, the bride and bridegroom are taken towards the little trench at the boy's house, toothbrushes are put in their hands and their marriage clothes are taken off. As her clothes are being removed the girl says that she will not let herself be washed unless she is shown some bullocks. A bull calf is brought out and given to the girl's brother. They are then washed together sitting on the trench.

A little later, the parties are given a meal with a pot of rice-beer, and a short farewell address is given by one of the elder men. 'A log of wood has now been tied to your neck,' he says, 'Now you are two. Stay together. Work together. Go to market together. Eat together. When you go hunting, always bring back something. Even if it is only the small portion of a kend fruit which a crow has left, bring it back.' The girl's party then goes home, leaving the girl behind. A few weeks later, the girl's brother comes and the couple pay a short visit to the girl's home. There the village welcomes them, the jogmanjhi says a prayer and the girl distributes some rice cakes and grain. After staying for five or six days, they go back to the boy's village.

3 WEDDING SONGS

Throughout these noisy activities the women keep up a stream of wedding songs. These are all connected in various ways with the plight of the bride. They are, as it were, 'shots' of what is happening, a documentary of the chief actors before the wedding, during the wedding and after the wedding. Yet although a number are realistic, the great majority resort to symbols and it is in the guise of birds, trees and flowers that the girl and her circle are depicted.

The songs commence with the bride in her parents' house, before the matchmaker has made his sinister approaches. The girl is ripe for marriage and the news is spreading through the villages.

206

In our courtyard
Is a sweet tamarind
Its branches are large
Its flowers are white and red
Its fruits hang in clusters.

207

Below our field
Are many coloured flowers
Come to our village, boy
And choose what flower you will.

They then review the process of betrothal.

208

In the market they choose
Vessels of brass
Mother, visit the four sides
And choose a partner for my son.

209

As we looked
For a husband
You played your flute
In the mahua field.
As we looked for a wife
You drew your cloth
Across your breasts.

210

Still you are little, girl
But the friends are choosing you
Where are your father and mother?
O 'haere haere hae'
My mother and father are not here
They have gone to the mountain
To knock the mahua down.

211

On the banks of the river
The black cow is grazing

Tie it with creepers
Hobble it with flowers
For the black cow
Has fallen to the ground.

Other songs portray the girl bitterly upbraiding her parents for their callous betrayal, or weeping as she thinks of all that marriage will involve.

212

You took the money but you did not tell me
You knotted the string and then I knew
You must give back the money
You must untie the knot
For my friend is in this village.

213

Girl, come and take your food
Your marriage time has come
From long ago I asked
Which friend was in the cowshed
And father, father,
I did not agree.

214

Under the banyan by the river
I spread a cloth and sat upon it
Sitting I grew cold
I forgot
The enemies were coming.

215

My parents are like the moon
My brothers and sisters are like stars
O my flower
Why was I not made
A flaming fire?

216

The ache of longing
For my mother and father
I shall wrap it in a leaf
And tuck it in the roof.

217

O my mother, my father
You gave me birth
In the hot days you reared me
With care you brought me up
But you did not keep me
My mother, my father.

218

Since I was little, mother
You hammered me with a stool
You spanked me with a fan
Now you are seeing the bride-price, mother
You are calling me 'parrot'.

219

Through the water, the water
They are taking me in a litter
O Karam twig
My father and mother
Are full of tears
But they are saying to me
'Go away'.

220

Parrot, in a big house you lived
With everything you wanted
Today, parrot
You are flying from the house
Kiss the milk-tree, parrot, as you go.

221

My mother on the stool
My father on the chair
They sit at ease
You are tired of rearing me, milk-tree
Stay as you are.

Yet other songs describe the young bride after she has reached the
house of her father-in-law.

222

In the garden a ringed dove
Is cooing in the darkness

Dove, I too
Am a poor man's child
And my cares begin at dawn.

223

By the bank of the river is a snake
The chicks of a poor man
Cheep with hunger
The pigeons of a rich man
Loll at ease.

224

The parrot I reared
From my hand it flew away
Five skeins of thread it took
I will follow in its track
Over the five mountains
It has gone
And it lives
Eating care.

225

Father, I cooked the rice
But they grumbled as they ate it
My father and brothers
Are in a far land
Who will tell them
So that they may know?

226

In that big house, girl
You had everything you wanted
Put out of your mind
Your teeth's powder
And the black for your eyes
Do not think
Of your bath in the morning.

227

Father, in a distant country
You settled my marriage
And you never visit me
Father come and see me

Leaning like a shrimp
Swimming
Lazy as a fish.

228

Do not settle my marriage
In a hilly country
The hills go high and low
Settle my marriage by a railway line
Where I can catch the trains.

229

My mother and father
Were too clever
They married me
To a boy in the police
Boys in the police
Spend their nights
Wandering through the country
I am tired
Of only holding boots.

But of even greater significance are the songs which advertise the girl's previous attachments and dwell on the abrupt ending of her earlier romance.

230

Friends, we were friends
And we loved each other wildly
We went to the woods of sex
And your son wedded my daughter.

231

Who is calling at the door
Flower, flower?
She is not here
She has gone to gather leaves
In the forest
Of hasty work.

232

In the wedding shed
Do not be so silent

You have had
Many boys.

233

At noon I went for water
And slipped on the salt soil
At the spring with lime trees
With eyes open I fell down.

234

O my former friend,
My new friend,
You kept me
But you left me.

235

We were friends of one stool
We were one chair lovers
But our love was only care
Take up our love
Wrap it in this letter
And float it slowly down.

236

Why do you stand
With a full pot on your head?
My lover is not married
And his flute
Is cool to the heart.

237

By the river a ringed dove
Is sobbing all the night
Dove, I have a lover
And I long the whole night.

238

Two girls
The mountain, mountain
Two girls
The mountain flower
Two girls
The slopes of the hillside
Two girls
The scarlet blossom.

Other songs describe the long departure, the hope that at even a late hour her lover will rescue her and at last the sickening realisation that there is no longer any chance at all of escape.

239

They have rubbed you with turmeric
And seated you on the mat
Little girl
Why are you holding your head?
Middle brother,
You ask and ask me
For my life stays
At the back of the house.

240

I am mounting the basket
And you stand with a sad heart
Come down
If you have any love or pity.

241

In the house are mother and father
In the courtyard are friends
Where shall I wipe my tears?
O my friend, if you have any love
Look back and wipe your tears.

242

You reared me like a pet parrot
You petted me like a tame pigeon
Father when did you give your word?
From my friend's love you parted me.

243

As the sun spread out its rays
I got up in the litter
O my love
You never gave me hope
And I must climb now
In the litter.

244

Beyond the river is a banyan
And its branches hang on the stream

O banyan, why do you droop by the river?
From a sad heart I droop by the stream.

245

With such a big pond, O lotus
Why have you come where the water flows away
Come to the spider's country, O my lotus
To the centre of the lake.

246

Elder brother, eldest brother
At midnight the mother
Is bidding me farewell
O you loving girl, I am here
I am hunting for umbrellas
I will come
Rushing after you.

247

In the shallow pool
The ringed doves are feeding
They are whispering and smiling
They are saying to me
We will take you
To a wide and open land.

248

They are taking me over the five mountains
O elder brother, come out in the hunt
I will give you a cot plaited with thread
And a stool of shining gold.

249

Girl, your time has come
You must go to your husband
Break the rope
Of your friend's love
Say goodbye
To your friend.

250

You took a step
And looking back you cried

My love
Why are the tears streaming?
O my love
The necklace and ring
Put them in your lap
With a necklace and ring
What shall I do?
Necklace and rings
I am full of them, my love.

251

While you are unmarried, girl
You laugh and smile
While you are unmarried
You have the love of a friend
When the silver ring
Will go on your finger
It will change your life.

252

Slim as the mountain grass I grew
But as I grew
I left behind my joy.

It is with the singing of these songs that the girl goes to her husband and the two must now commence their married life.

CHAPTER XI

Outlets After Marriage
the Sohrae Festival

Against this delicate and troubled background, how do Santal boys and girls regard their marriages? We have already seen that as the wedding day approaches, the great majority do in fact resign themselves to acting as their parents wish. Such couples usually end by liking and respecting each other and although the transition from 'sexual love without marriage' to 'domestic love within it' is very far from easy, it is remarkable how many Santal boys and girls seem able to achieve it. The settled happy marriage with all its implications is not, as we might expect, the enviable exception. It is the normal Santal rule.

This state of affairs is brought about by various factors. There is little doubt that by the time that they are actually wedded, most boys and girls desire the married state. No one is more pathetic than the boy who has reached manhood but has yet to gain a wife. Equally the big adult girl who has failed to get a husband is regarded with general pity. For the sake of self-respect, therefore, every boy and girl wants not merely to get married but to stay married. But even more than this, marriage is an in-dispensable preliminary to possessing a separate household, the means by which a boy or girl can have children without the shame of tribal disgrace and the only basis on which they can indulge fully and easily in sex. The act of getting married involves the adoption of new conventions, but the change is also so arranged as to seem more a gradual weaning than a sudden severance. If the girl must now adjust herself to living far from home, she is not expected to remain entirely aloof and never to visit it again. Husband and wife must conform to a tradition of conjugal fidelity, yet there is, none the less, an important qualification. At the Sohrae festival, married daughters are expected to return to their parents and a number of songs express the excitement of this visit.

253

Boy, take a stick in your hand
Tie the cloth round your waist
And go and bring your sister.

254

A leaf-cup for meat
A bowl for rice-beer
You have invited
Your daughters and sisters.

255

Wife, there is rice and curry
Give it to our daughter and grand-daughters.

256

Girl, while your mother and father live
Bring them the milk of the black cow
When your mother is no more
And your father dead
Your heart will burn
From heaven down to hell.

257

From over the mountain
The twelve mountains
We have called
The daughters, the sisters
Girl, give them enough rice
Give them plenty of curry.

258

Uncle, at Sohrae
Call us and invite us
Uncle, we are yours
Uncle, bring us
Leaves of lar
And leaves of tamarind
Uncle, we are many
Brothers and sisters
Feed us as you will
But uncle, we are yours.

196

259

In the village of my father and my brothers
The drums sound
If my mother were alive
She would have sought me ten times
If my brothers were living
They would have brought me twenty times.

260

Come, husband
Hold the horse
Come to my father's
If you want rice-beer
You will have rice-beer
If you want meat
They will give it to you
Come to my father's.

261

O husband
Tie the puffed rice in a bundle
Cover the pot of rice-beer
Come to the house of my birth.

During this visit, rice-beer is brewed, household chores are forgotten and for a single charmed week, the code of sexual conduct is deliberately relaxed. It is true that after she has had a child, a girl feels herself, more and more, a part of her husband's home and bongas. 'Married women with two or more children do not change their partners,' Sibu once told me. 'But when they are older, they sometimes do it as a joke.' Married men, on the other hand, range somewhat more widely and Lokhon Hansdak' said, 'At Sohrae even the old men are boys. Half the village men will take their fun if they can get it.' Sohrae, in fact, adds excitement to the marital state. It injects variety into the conjugal routine and by doing so buttresses everyday fidelity.

Yet if the older men and women enjoy the festival, it is even more important for the newly wedded. During the early years of marriage, it is the loss of her village boy which most upsets a young wife. At Sohrae she is free to meet him again. Even if her husband is present, a girl is not deterred from seeking out her friend.

262

There is moisture on your hands
Sweat on your eyes
O my love, who are you?
Feel with your hands
Touch me with your thighs
I am your former lover.

263

We are going on the road
There are limes in the way
One I have eaten
Two I have tucked away
O take them for yourself
For once you were my lover.

Sohrae, in fact, is a way of easing the shock of parting, of weaning a girl from her village lover, of reconciling the young of both sexes to the disciplines of marriage. Without this outlet, many marriages might break. With it, most Santal marriages succeed.

The festival which plays this vital role occurs in December or January after the paddy has been reaped and work is at a standstill. If a birth or death pollutes the village, the dates are changed and in order to prolong the feasting, the headmen of neighbouring villages sometimes consult each other and arrange to start on different days. Each festival continues for a week and the last should be over by the full-moon night of pus (January). It is a kind of 'harvest home' and since the rice crop depends on ploughing, it is chiefly a celebration of the cattle and of fertility.

According to an ancestral story, Sohrae was the eldest daughter of the first Santal couple, Pilcu Haram and Pilcu Budhi. They had eight daughters and seven sons in all. One day Pilcu Haram took the sons out hunting while Pilcu Budhi took the daughters for collecting potherbs. As they gathered them, they came to a banyan tree and began to eat its fruits. The daughters climbed the tree – the eldest climbing first and the others after her. When they had all climbed, the eldest was at the top and the youngest nearest the ground. Then the seven brothers came. They saw the girls eating the fruits and as they looked, Maran Buru in the guise of Lita filled the brothers with desire. So they sent the youngest brother to fetch some fruits for them. He went to the tree and since the youngest was nearest to the ground he asked her to give a fruit to him. The girl said "I will throw it

198

down" but the boy said "Give it to me with your hand". Then the girl came lower down and as she gave the fruit to the boy, he caught her hand and pulled her from the tree. When he had caught her he made the girl his wife. Then the next youngest brother asked for fruit. The next youngest sister was nearest to the ground and he made her his wife. In this way the seven brothers took seven of the sisters as their wives. When they had finished, the eldest sister was still in the tree and as there was no husband for her, she began to weep bitterly. When the brothers and sisters saw her crying, they said they would never forget her and once a year would offer her a virgin thing. From that time on an egg has been offered in a paddy field and Sohrae has been called the elder sister in memory of her.'

The festival begins with the priest and the kudam naeke or 'field' priest going to a rice field beyond the village houses. They bathe in a tank and smooth a strip of ground by washing it with cow-dung. Then they squat down facing east and trace a series of small circles. Into these circles they pour some rice, turmeric and milk and in the first circle the priest stands an egg on end. He then addresses the major bongas, asking them to bless the festival and keep it free from ill and offering to each in turn a chick or fowl. As he whispers, he takes a tiny chick from a basket, feeds it on some of the rice, touches it with turmeric and then saws its head off on the blade of a battle-axe. He lets the blood drip on the egg and the white circles, tosses the little struggling trunk onto the ground before him and lays the tiny head on one of the circles. At Sibtala where I saw the ceremony in 1943, the priest offered four chicks in this way and then sacrificed three pullets. After he had finished the kudam naeke offered two fowls to 'the bongas of the outskirts' from a separate strip a few yards to the north.

When the sacrifice is over, the kudam naeke kindles a small fire in the lee of a ridge, singes the fowls for plucking and after he has taken all the feathers out, tears the carcases to pieces. He then rolls them up into a flour pudding and bakes them on the fire in a skin of leaves. When the pudding is ready, he peals the charred leaves off and shares it with the villagers.

The priest now makes a separate fire, prepares his own pudding and after baking it eats it all except a single piece. This piece is put on the fire as an offering to wild animals so that if a leopard or hyena carries off a goat, it will only take a portion and the villagers will retrieve the rest. All the main bongas have now been propitiated but lest a bonga is omitted, the kudam naeke goes over to a field slightly apart from the rest. He searches for a thorn, squeezes his left thigh into a little ridge, pricks it three times, rubs some sun-dried rice on it, puts the blood-stained rice on a leaf and taking up a handful lets it trickle through his fingers. As it streams through he beseeches all the bongas who may by chance have been left out to accept the offering and cause no harm.

The priest then washes his feet, squats down by the circles and rinses out some leaf-cups. He takes a leaf-cup in his right hand, poises it for a moment and the kudam naeke then pours some rice-beer into it. As he holds it the priest whispers a prayer letting the rice-beer gently swill over and souse the circles. When the prayers are over, the rice-beer in the cups is drunk by the priest and the rest is swilled down by the villagers. As the beer is being drunk, the headman addresses the company. He reminds them that 'the elder sister' has come and that they are about to embark on a week of enjoyment. He tells them that boys must observe their clans and sub-clans and may not go to 'sisters'. They must not 'dirty their blood' or pollute the bongas. But apart from this they are now free to do as they like. 'Take the ripe', he says 'but do not take the unripe and if you see anything, say nothing.' Similar injunctions are given to girls. The village people reply that they are putting twelve wads of cotton in their ears and will see and hear nothing.

The stage is now set for the most dramatic part of the ritual – the driving of the village cattle over the egg. At Sibtala in 1943 the shadows were lengthening as the cattle slowly sauntered in. When they neared the field the priest went and oiled the horns of two cows directly descended from the cows of his ancestors. The herd wheeled round and came up into line before the field. Two drums began to beat. The leading cows sprang up into the field, smelt the circles, nosed the leaf-cups and went slowly on. More came up and passed through. And then more and still more until the last cow had gone and the egg remained standing, lonely and erect. The herd was then brought back and sent through one more. Again the cows went slowly up, sniffed the circles and passed on. More and more went through and still the egg stood safe. At last when only ten remained, a brown cow took fright, and in a lumbering gallop, struck the egg a glancing blow. The cow rushed on towards the herd and its owner clasped it with a cry of joy.

The egg was then fried and eaten by the kudam naeke. The remaining carcases of fowls were cooked with rice and in the chilly sunset, the cow-herds and villagers squatted round and shared the feast.

The next stage occurs much later in the evening. A little band of three drummers with one or two singers goes briskly round the village. At each house they go to the cow-shed and in the light of tapers address songs to the cows.

264

Who has made the earth?
O who has made the cows?
Thakur made the earth
Thakur made the cows.

As a song ends, they raise a trilling shout, and when the singing is over, they sweep on to the next house with a clamour of drums. At this visit it is only the cows and not the bullocks or the buffaloes that are addressed and nothing is done beyond this salutation. As I watched it in 1943, I was irresistibly reminded of waits. The long white tapers made from jute sticks, the flickering red of the tips, the cold night air, the sharp stars, the staring cows, the exaltation of the drummers – all combined to recall the simple mysteries of Christmas.

When this public celebration of the cows is over, each family comes and stands before its cowshed, rubs the horns of the cattle with oil and throws rice over them. A little later all the girls and women assemble in the street and songs are sung to welcome in Sohrae.

265

Elder sister, elder sister
Go out, O elder sister
The festival like an elephant
Is coming near
You with a lota of water
I with a cup of water
Let us go and bring it in
The festival like an elephant
You with a plate and water
I with a long-tailed cow
With the tail of that cow
We will fan and bring it in.

266

Elder sister, elder sister
Go out, O eldest sister
The festival like an elephant has come
How shall we welcome it
How shall we receive it
Sister, O elder sister

How shall we bring it in?
With a glad heart
And a sound of joy
We shall open our hearts' door
And take it to our hearts.

267

With a lota, with a vessel
Elder sister
We will bring water
To sprinkle on Sohrae
We will take the buffalo cart from the headman
And like an elephant
We will usher Sohrae in.

As they sing the women dance slowly in a curving line, keeping up a gentle oscillation of their bodies, bending their knees and jerking their haunches with passive composure.

The second day begins with a male dance before the headman's house. The dancers commence with a form known as danta, move on to a gunjar, thence to a matwar mucet' kher and wind up with a series of women's dances danced by men – two don, two lagre, two dhurumjak', then one don, and finally a kulhi enec', drifting down the village road.

For these dances, the men form a loosely strung out line on the arc of a circle and go slowly round and round while the three drummers parade and posture inside the ring. In the danta the line goes in a series of three forward steps with a slight recoil at every fourth step. Every now and then it turns briskly round, each dancer wheeling about and clapping his hands while occasionally the line goes jerking back in a series of stiff little jumps. As the line revolves, the men sing danta songs, bringing each song to a wild conclusion with a shrill O-ho-ho-ho-ho.

268

Beat the sticks
Crash the sticks
Knock the sticks
Together
All of us know
We are the sons
of Pilcu Haram.

269

Beat the sticks
Knock the sticks
Knock the sticks
Together
The old man
Squats by the fence
He has a coloured stick
He mumbles in his jaws.

270

The black hen has many chicks
'Yo baba he he he'
And many are the sons
Of Pilcu Haram, Pilcu Budhi.

271

Mother, the headman's serving girl
Is husking the paddy
She has put it out to dry
She is sitting down
And the husks
Are going up her.

272

One went to the tank
One to the river
Lovely were the ornaments
Lovely were the clothes
Brother, call them back
O call them back.

273

In the field of sugar cane
The jackal went
No it is not a jackal
But boys who saw some girls.

From the danta the men move to gunjar. This change is made through a tahareta or transition song which announces that a new stage is about to start. When it is over the dance-form changes and instead of shifting round a circle the line strides outwards in a long mannered walk, turns round and then moves back.

When the gunjar has been fully danced a matwar mucet' kher is taken up. The men walk slowly round the circle with their left arms stretching out like wands, until one of them calls out, 'And now, boys, take your sticks and go to the cows'. This concludes all the male dances and female dances are then gone through by the men – each pair of dancers denoting a husband and wife and the dancing aiming at bringing long life to every married couple in the village.

When these are over the men drift down the village road and the women break in and take their places. This dance by the women is not a celebration at the headman's house but a solemn ambulation of the entire road. The women form a line across the street. They start at the headman's house and then slowly dance their way along the road up to the village limits.

Here they execute a turning figure which is known as dhurumjak'. This dance has its own set of songs and as the line slowly pivots round, the women sing:

274

The cows have risen up
And my lover lurks in the pipal
By the banyan stands my husband
And the cows have risen to their feet.

275

Mother-in-law
In the stony river
The fishes glint
Take a hook, brother-in-law
And let us go and fish.

276

Boy, the bush is burnt
Under the banyan
The grove of banyans
Is burnt and clear
Boy, do not ask
What is my clan
Take me to the raja's darbar.

277

On the headman's smooth verandah
I was grinding kode, boy

But when I saw and heard you
How my body trembled.

When the turning is complete the line works slowly back along the road until it reaches the other end. Here the dhurumjak' is again performed and the line again returns. When some of the women tire, others take their place, and for the rest of the day and night, the line is moving on the road. As it goes up and down, the women dance the Sohrae with a gentle bobbing sway and sing a round of Sohrae songs. These deal mainly with the ways of lovers and provide, as it were, a running commentary on what is happening behind the scenes – girls encouraging the boys, boys running after girls, clandestine engagements occurring, husbands and wives keeping out of each other's way. Marriage itself is mocked, brides are jokingly consoled and over everything there is an air of laughing relaxation, modest fun and sportive daring.

278

Sit down, stand up
O friends, we have no food or drink
But in the eyes' meeting there is pleasure.

279

In the thick forest, father
A dove has been decoyed
In the middle of the village
The headman was enticed.

280

In the upper village
O you two girls
A green boy
Is playing on a drum
Girl, we will dance
Out of the house
Swinging our legs
Holding our cloth.

281

Aunt, the jamun buds are scarlet
The tip of the plantain sways
So long as I have no husband
I shall nod and sway my body.

282

Boy, beat the drum
And like a plantain
Sway your body
Play the flute
Make it sound
Like the calling of a quail.

283

There is a gander
That wanders in the streets
The gander has a necklace
What will you do with it, girl?
For like a tall bamboo
Your husband comes.

284

Brother, brother, elder brother
Give me a turban
And I will go
And tease the girls.

285

Sister-in-law
From the tree
The parrot cried
In the locked house
The fiddle sounded.

286

Because of our love
You keep a comb in your hand
You get up
In the morning
You comb your hair
O my love
Wait this year
Wait next year
The year after
I will make you mine.

287

Spider, spider
Spin me a thread

Tie the heart of my parents, spider
And I will put a silver bangle
On both your wrists.

288

Father, the parrot
Bleeds and bleeds
O milk-tree
You have murdered me.

289

Mother, father
The drums sound in the village
And like a lotus leaf in water
My body trembles as I hear them.

290

Father, from the east
And the west
A bridegroom comes
With ornaments of gold.

291

Elder brother
The litter sways
The tasselled hat falls down
O little girl
Do not let the tears fall.

292

Out in the street, the headmen
Have tied two litters
And the wind is sweeping down
O east wind, western wind
Do not blow on them.

293

With poles of silver
The golden litter shakes
Hold it gently, brother
With your two hands take it
I am one sister
They are seven brothers
Hold it gently
Take it in your hands.

294

Under the flowering tree
My lover wanted
Twelve rupees
I wept five nights and days
My lover wanted
Twelve rupees of me.

295

O my love, come and talk in our village
If you want milk, I will give you milk
If you want curds, I will give you curds
But only with a pigeon's soup will you be happy.

While the women are dancing down the road, the men take the yokes of carts and ploughs to a tank. They bathe and wash the yokes and then bring them back and stand them at the entrance to the cow shed. Then at midday each family worships the shed. The head of the house first cleans a patch of ground with cow dung, puts some rice on a leaf and mixes some rice-beer with it. He then brings a pig and a few fowls and sprinkles water on them. He grasps the pig, sprinkles vermilion or flour on its head and presses its snout on the rice. As soon as the pig has gobbled up some rice, he lifts it up, and lays it on its side. A member of the family presses its body down and the head of the house gives it three heavy hammer blows on the head with the butt of an axe-head. The blood is made to drip on the rice and after that the limp body is put aside. Three fowls are now sacrificed by clubbing their heads with the axe-head and the blood is added to the rice. The family head now offers rice-beer to his ancestors, purifies the rice with water and the ceremony ends with all present bowing to their dead. After this the pig is cut up and its heart is cooked with rice.

Towards the end of the afternoon, the cowshed is made ready for blessing the cattle. One of the women cleans a patch of ground about two yards square with cowdung and when the surface is dry, the mistress of the house traces on it some diagrams of the shed, the cowherd and the cattle's hooves. She uses a gluey white liquid made from rice pounded up with atnak' leaves and soaked in water. When the floor is done she also puts a few white patterns on the yokes.

A little later her husband goes into the private room, takes out the boiled heart and rice and sets it out on leaf plates. He squats before the plates, takes pinches of the food and offers them in turn to the family dead. Between each offering, he rinses his fingers. Some of the portions are then

antal bridegroom and
est man
antal women setting out
or 'the water marriage'
antal 'maids-of-all-
ork'

38 Planting the wedding
   pillar
39 Santal wedding: the
   mock battle
40 Sohrae festival: the
   priest propitiating the
   'outskirt' bongas

Sohrae festival: cattle approaching the egg
Sohrae festival: the senior priest installing the flag
Sohrae festival: Santal boys shooting at the plantain post

44 Sohrae festival: bait
   a buffalo
45 Baha festival: the th
   mediums are posses
   by Maran Buru (lef
   Five-Six (centre) ar
   Jaher Era (right)
46 Baha festival: sacrif
   a chick in the sacre
   grove

put aside for the male members of the family and two are eaten by himself.

The blessing or kissing of the cows takes place a little later in the evening. The women stand on the white diagrams holding lighted tapers and facing the cattle. The eldest holds a winnowing fan with dub grass, rice and a small light in it. As they stand they chant to the cows. When the incantation is over, they throw the grass and rice over the cows, and sing a round of blessing songs. For the rest of the night the girls dance up and down the village street or steal away with the boys.

Early the next morning, a conference is held at the headman's house to decide whether the important rite of khuntau or baiting is to be performed. Baiting of the cattle can be done only if there is no trouble in the village, all the cattle are healthy and no death has occurred in the preceding year. Five boys go round setting up a thick and strong pole in the village road opposite each house. A strong rope is brought and a sanctuary or 'circle of privilege' is marked out on the ground around the pole. Inside this circle, the bullock or the buffalo may kill its assailant and no one will blame it. The radius of this circle is roughly the length of the animal.

The circle is then plastered with cowdung and white diagrams are traced on it with liquid flour. These diagrams have a bewildering variety. Each sub-clan has its own pattern and each area has different forms. A formal approach to the animals now takes place and while the little band of drummers is shouting out the songs, a libation of rice-beer is made at the manjhithan. Rice-beer is then offered before the central pole of the cowshed, and flour and vermilion are rubbed on the horns and foreheads of the chosen animals. Garlands of paddy sheaves are put on their horns and necks and a fillet with three cakes is hung on their brows. Women of the house then bless them by circling a winnowing fan, rice, dub grass, three balls of flour and three of cowdung over their heads.

The chosen animals now come out and are tied securely to their stands. At Candarpura in 1942, the poles were twelve feet high and bunches of orange flowers dangled from their tops. The headman chose two bullocks for the fight – Saura (Tawny) and Pond (White) – and a brief ritual of salutation was gone through. The headman and three elder women came in turn, faced east, touched the fringes of the circles and saluted the bullocks, and then the jogmanjhi, facing west, touched and saluted. The stage was now set and out onto the road came a boy leaping and springing. Round and round the bullocks he went darting in among their horns, twirling a jute stick and smiting the heavy brows with a winnowing fan. Three men followed him – one with a shield, one with a basket and the third with a fan. They circled round the animals, uttering savage cries, stirring them to fury and crashing the shield on their horns. The white bullock got wilder and wilder. It sprang and lunged, butted and pawed but every time it charged the halter checked it and it went racing round the pole. After the sport had lasted twenty minutes the matadors left it and went on up the road to the next animal. In this way the road was covered three times and not until twilight were the tired excited beasts returned to their stalls.

296

Elder brother
You went out
As the cock crowed
You went away
As the peacock called
And did not tell me any secret.
Whether to bait the buffaloes
Or bait the bullocks
You said nothing
And you went away.

297

Dhani, Dhani, Dhani
What sort of man are you?
The bullock kicked my fan
Elder brother, elder brother
What sort of man are you?
The buffalo kicked my shield
Elder brother, we shall bait
A buffalo or a bullock
The friends are coming
Take them to their seats.

When the ceremony is over and night falls, three boys and three girls are chosen by the jogmanjhi to guard the poles. They go dancing up and down the village road keeping watch over them and from time to time other boys and girls come and dance as well. At the same time, more trysts are being kept, girls are quietly meeting their village lovers and young and old have fun.

The next morning the five boys who put the poles up take them down and each house gives them half a seer of rice, some lentils and any vegetables they can scrounge from the garden. The booty is taken to the house of the jogmanjhi and all the boys and girls gather for a feast.

In 1942 at Sibtala, there was no baiting as the conference decided against it, so the third day passed instead in a public blessing of all the cattle. The village formed the men and women into two bands. One group of women went dancing round from house to house, carrying a winnowing fan with a little light. At each house, the mistress put some dub grass and rice in the fan and the whole band stood before the cattle, chanting the names of the bullocks. When each animal's name had been proclaimed, they sang some blessing songs, sprinkled the grass and rice and then went off in a solemn bobbing dance to the next house, and so on round the village. While the women moved slowly on, a band of male drummers went briskly round the village, visiting each house with a great thunder of drums, singing songs and then moving on. The rest of the day went in dancing, drinking, and flirtation while through the night a changing line of girls danced slowly up and down the road.

The fourth day ends the ritual with a burst of merry-making. The village divides itself into its various age-groups, paddy is tied to their arms and each goes round levying a toll at every house. They dance into each courtyard, dance round it and then go dancing out. They carry a basket in which the tolls are put and as each house pays its share they dance in triumph round it.

The tour ends in hysterical excitement. Everyone is wearing mock finery. A bamboo fillet masquerades as a silver necklace. A torn sack is hailed as a silken sari. Old women pretend to quarrel and battles of hips go fiercely on. There are mock fainting fits and mock medicines.

At the end of the village, the women form a ring and shift round with their arms drooping forward, gently clapping their hands. After moving up the circle, they turn and face outwards; and then move down, bending forwards and clapping their hands in time with the steps.

The fun goes on late into the night and only as the stars pale do the groups crawl limply home.

The next day the village goes out to fish. The object of this expedition is to get some fish and crabs for the feast on the following day but it is also a part of the general jollity. The boys and girls go in separate groups and sing love songs and joke together. If they get a lot of fish and crabs, they cook a few when they get back. Otherwise they are put by for the next morning.

The following day a very early meal is cooked. Each family makes as many different kinds of curry as it can and the fish and crabs of the previous day are cooked and eaten. After that the men and boys set out for a hunt. This hunt lasts most of the morning and ranges over any neighbouring jungle. The booty usually consists of a hare or two, a squirrel, a fox or a jackal, and some jungle fowl. The men bring some sal leaves back from the jungle and when they get home each house offers some rice-beer to its ancestors, while the headman gives rice-beer at the manjhithan. A boy then takes a drum and goes to the jogmanjhi. The jogmanjhi cuts down a plaintain tree and takes it to the end of the village. The plantain is then set up and all the village youth troop down. On the way to the plantain the tails of any animal or birds killed in the hunt are tied to the centre pole in the manjhithan. At the top of the plantain a flour cake is put and the village boys shoot showers of arrows at it. As soon as the cake is hit the boys rush and scramble for it. During the shooting one or more jokers appear each carrying an enormous bow which towers against the sky. At Gidni in 1944 they used white jute sticks as arrows and roused roars of laughter at their wavering wiggly flight. The jogmanjhi then cuts the plantain into three and bends each section double by giving it a nick in the middle. He then takes the boy who shot the cake on to his shoulder, carries him to the place from where he shot it and there the boy does johar to the village. After that the boys go to the jogmanjhi's courtyard, dance the paik dance and take some rice-beer and puffed rice. They go on to the headman's house and after that to the priest's. At the priest's and jogmanjhi's houses they throw a piece of the plantain on to the roofs and at the headman's they put it on the manjhithan.

At Gidni in 1944, the headman shot an arrow into the air and all the boys aimed arrows at it as it fell. If a boy hits the arrow five years running, the headman presents him with a dhoti. After this there was round after round of gymnastic feats, frog-hopping, contests in pulling, lifting by fingers, double somersaulting and walking on the hands. When all was over, the boys danced the paik and went back to the village.

When the boy's sports are finished the girls gather at the jogmanjhi's house, dance three times up and down the village and sing goodbye to Sohrae.

298

Elder sister
I will catch it by the hand
I will pull it by the leg
The festival like an elephant
Is going away.

Sohrae, Sohrae
It was good while you were here
It was different while you stayed
Come again in time
Joy, do not cry
Joy, do not mourn
On the due day come back.

The jogmanjhi then tells them that the festival is over and they must sing the Sohrae songs and dance the Sohrae dance no more.

A little later when the festival is over, a supplementary rite occurs on the first day of the new year. Each family takes a pair of bullocks and a plough to its best rice field and ploughs one or two furrows. They then go on to their manure ditch, and turn the manure over with a mattock. With this act, the celebration ends and all is set for the coming year.

CHAPTER XII

Breakdown and Divorce

If, for many couples, the Sohrae festival tempers the shock of parting and makes easier the loss of early freedom, there remains a small minority who even after marriage are still unreconciled to their parents' choice. It is true that, outside Sohrae, the girl is supposed to see her village boy no more.

300

Friend, we have left going
To the rice field in the jungle
They have given you a wife
They have found for me a husband
O my friend, when we meet now
We must never flutter our eyebrows
Or show the teeth in our mouths.

But mutual affection may prove to be too strong. If a girl has a boy in her village, she sometimes leaves her husband's house and goes rushing home. 'If,' said Dhunu, 'the boy says "Even though you are married, I will never leave you," the girl cannot stay. She has to leave her husband.'

301

O my love, do not weep
Do not mourn
I will come and go
And share your love.

The boy, for his part, may find it equally impossible to get his former girl out of his mind.

302

Sister, that young boy
He did not leave me
Even in his wedding litter
He was making eyes at me.

303

In a litter, in a palki, father
You brought me a wife
But though you brought her
I will not leave
My village girl.
O daughter-in-law
You whom we have brought
Why are you weeping?
Your son goes still
To his village love.

304

For sex and love
Let my house go
For sex and love
Let my door go down
But I will never leave
The rapture of my village love.

In these circumstances, one of two things may happen. Slowly and reluctantly the husband and wife may begin cohabitation and even if their thoughts are still on their former friends, they may gradually come to accept each other as permanent partners. This may not happen quickly – it may even take from two to three years – but if the former friend has not precipitated a crisis, the difficulties and dangers of a long post-marital intrigue will in the end begin to tell. If in the meantime a child is born the girl's resolve may weaken. 'It is when she gets a child,' Dhunu said, 'that the link tightens. It is then that they settle.'

The other alternative is the break-up of the marriage. If the boy and girl are quite determined, nothing that the parents or the other partner can do can prevent a final breach. Dasma Tudu of Haruadangal was in love with a village girl but his parents married him to a girl of Beda Chapar. They brought the girl but he refused to sleep with her. He continued going with his village girl and would not leave her. In a year the village girl was pregnant. The parents of his wife came and took her away and after that Dasma brought the village girl to his house and made her his wife. In Jilwa a boy was married to Sukhi Soren of Kalhajor. But he also declined to keep her and kept returning her to her home. Here also a village girl was the cause of the trouble and in the end Sukhi's parents agreed to a divorce and the marriage was dissolved. In Jitpur a girl was married to a boy in Tilabad but she also had her own boy in her village and kept returning. She stayed a month with her parents and then 'intruded' on her lover. Similarly in Elajpahari, Kebol Soren was only a small boy when his parents married him. His wife kept staying in her own village as a boy there was her lover. From time to time Kebol fetched her but she invariably went back. When Kebol saw that she did not want him, he decided to take another wife.

When this happens, the boy and girl finally have their way. Once it is clear that either partner to a marriage is quite unwilling to live with the other, divorce is the accepted tribal remedy. A village meeting is called, claims are adjusted and the marriage is dissolved.

With the passing of this first disruptive period, the risks of failure grow perceptibly less. Provided that the partners can 'break the tie of their friend's love' their earlier experiences often act as a brake on later ones. Young Santal wives do not generally let 'their eyes wander'. Similarly married men, once they have settled down, prefer to maintain the married tie rather than indulge in new experiments. Adultery is very rare and although it is sometimes hinted at in songs, infidelity is not a frequent cause of broken marriages.

305

I am a married girl
And you have still no wife
Like an owl
You look at me
With your great eyes.

306

My husband is sleeping
And my lover
Fidgets and calls
In my heart I say
I must go and meet him
But my husband is lying
Stretched upon my clothes.

More important is the illness of a husband or wife. In Bandubera a boy divorced his wife. 'She was never coming to me,' he said. 'When she came, she always got ill.' In Kendpahari, Make Hembrom was divorced because all her children died. In Bankati, Rasika Marandi had married a girl of Ranidinda. She lived with him for three years but as there were many deaths in his house, she at last went home. She refused to go back saying 'If I return, I shall die.' In this case, there were also other factors. One night when her father-in-law was drunk and was taking her home from Ranidinda, he caught hold of her and spoke to her by name. This breach of taboo greatly offended the girl but it was ultimately the fear that she would die which made her abandon the marriage.

While I was camping at Ranga in 1944, a case which was clearly psychological came before me. In Ghatiari, Chambra Soren had married Sona Hembrom. Sona used to dream and three times during her dreams she bed-wetted. Chambra then took her to her mother and married a girl from Katara. Sona who was a fair good-looking girl asked for a divorce and this was granted while I was still there. A day later there was a wedding in the village and Sona was dancing with the other women with complete nonchalance as if nothing had ever happened.

In another case, Demda Murmu met Saura Hembrom at a hook-swinging at Ghager. They at once fell in love, went to the boy's house and were very happy. A little later, the girl became pregnant, was ill and could not work. Then her mother-in-law began to grumble at her. A boy was born but her parents-in-law did not pay for the birth ceremony. When the girl regained her strength they took her back. A little later she once again fell ill. Owing to fever, her milk stopped and she returned to her home. Her parents-in-law did not let her take the child. She got well but all the time that she was ill no one came to see her. Her brother then sent the jogmanjhi to find out whether her husband was taking her or leaving her. The parents-in-law replied, 'We are neither having her nor bringing her. Let her stay as she is.' When it was clear that her illness had destroyed the marriage, the matter was taken to a meeting and the girl was given a divorce.

If it is wrong to fall ill, it is even more serious to be extravagant or to waste the family resources and if a wife is convicted of either of these charges, her husband can divorce her. The breach of an important taboo has similar consequences. In Surjudih, Lubia Soren's wife kept her menstruation rags in the grain bin. Lubia, to his great horror, found them there one day and at once moved the village to sanction a divorce. If he had not done so, he believed that all his wealth would have been lost. Finally, witchcraft is so serious that if the woman is a widow even her sons can 'divorce' her and expel her from the home.

When a marriage has broken down, the husband and wife with their relatives attend a village meeting and if divorce is approved, one of two procedures is followed. If the woman has received vermilion on her forehead and is not a witch, a ceremony known as 'the tearing of the leaves' is done. This simple rite is almost everywhere the same and it will illustrate the practice if I describe the divorce of Sumi Hansdak' of Mahagama from Surai Murmu of Chota Ranga. In this case there was little difficulty in reaching an agreement and after the girl had been awarded seven rupees as chadaodi or divorce money and her father five rupees as wedding arrears, the partners stood before the villagers. Each took a single mango leaf and when everyone was ready, they tore it down the mid-rib. The headman then said 'Before the villagers, you have torn the leaves. From today you are apart. If you meet at a chata or a pata and are caught together, you will have to pay another bride-price.' After this, the two saluted the assembly and went away. If vermilion has not been put on the girl's head or the woman is adjudged to be a witch, no leaves are torn and the parties merely meet the villagers, pronounce the divorce and go away.

Simple though this ceremony is and calm and self-possessed though the partners may appear, the breach is far from being a trivial matter and indeed it is often the prelude to months of uneasy disquiet. The man may have ceased to like his wife but while she was in the home someone at least was there to be his housekeeper. When she has gone he must either live with his father or brothers or do the housework himself. Moreover being of an age when marriage is normal, not to have a wife gives him the awkward feeling that he is now to some extent 'different'. Divorce ends one marriage only to make a second even more necessary.

For women there is still greater dislocation. With divorce a girl loses her status as a wife and all the respect which accrued to her as the manager of a separate household. She returns to her village and joins her father's family. Here she is known as a chadui or divorced girl. She shares in the housework but always with the sense that her proper place is in a home of her own. It is not surprising that within a few months, she also has only one obsession – to find another partner. This obsession is so marked that a number of songs and proverbs describe a chadui's arts. 'A chadui and a green bulbul – they sing in a thousand ways.' 'A chadui decks herself out like a banded flute.' 'A chadui has the head of a maina. It is always neat and preened.' 'A partridge decoys and a chadui deceives.'

307
In the upper village
They were dancing lagre
I went and danced
But my luck was out
I met a chadui.

308
Thinking it was fresh
I took a cooked bel fruit
Thinking she was not yet married
I rubbed vermilion on a chadui.

309
Large is the village
And with three parts
And the two girls are chaduis
Do not call out as you dance
For the two girls are chaduis.

310
Little boy
Do not go down
To the lower fields
A chadui girl
Is in the upper village
Suddenly
She may say to you
'Keep me.'

For the woman, in fact, divorce involves an agony of frustration that can end only with another marriage.

Yet although marriage is the goal, chaduis are far worse placed for securing it than their former spouses. It is true that a divorced man is considerably less eligible as a husband than a bachelor but sooner or later he succeeds in getting a bride. A chadui on the other hand has often to overcome considerable difficulties. If she has received vermilion from her former partner, she remains his wife in the after-world and can therefore offer only very limited rights to her second husband. She is actually in a far better position if her first marriage was less respectable. In that case 'her base will be cracked' but 'her head will be intact' and as a consequence her second husband can enjoy her 'for ever'. For this reason, chaduis usually stand the best chances with widowers or with men who have themselves been divorced.

Yet in certain circumstances a divorced girl can none the less do well for herself. If she is beautiful and a boy falls in love with her the fact of the previous divorce does not prevent his marrying her. Choto Soren was a servant in the house of Ramdas Hembrom of Saraipani. The daughter of Ramdas had been divorced. Choto fell in love with her and after commencing their union by 'meeting at bedtime' they were duly married. Kailu Marandi of Katikbhita was still unmarried. He met a divorced girl of Hijri and because she was very beautiful he fell in love with her. He induced his parents to accept the marriage and the two were married.

If a boy is poor, he sometimes marries a divorced girl in order to save the expenses of a wedding or to marry in a rich family. Mangat Hembrom of Bokoa was very poor and still unmarried. He could not afford the ordinary wedding expenses so he married a divorced girl of his village.

It is when her first husband is a ghar jawae or her father agrees to bring one for her that a divorced girl stands the greatest chance of securing a husband who has never been previously married. Here the prospect of a comfortable living with adequate lands outweighs the disadvantages of possessing another man's previous wife.

311

Unmarried boy
If you will keep me
Although I am a chadui
I will give you
Twelve bighas of land
Unmarried boy
If you will take me
Although I am a chadui
I will keep you
Like a Babu of Jamtara.

When at last a marriage is arranged, its exact form depends on several circumstances. A divorced husband, wedding a previously unmarried girl, can do so by the standard ritual. Similarly if the bride is divorced but has escaped a bonga relationship with her first husband, her second wedding can be as gay and public as a first. If, however, 'both base and head are cracked', she can no longer enjoy the brief glory in the lifted basket and must submit to the following less honoured ceremony.

On the wedding day the bridegroom stays at home and a small party from his family or village goes to the woman's house with the bride price. After eating a meal, paying the money and giving the woman a cloth they return bringing her with them. The bride and bridegroom are then taken into a room and in the presence of the two headmen and jogmanjhis and a few villagers, the central rite is performed. This consists of the bridegroom smearing vermilion on a flower and inserting it in the woman's hair. When Khade Kisku took a divorced girl as his second wife he put vermilion on a dimbu flower with his left hand. Then, again using his left hand, he took the flower and put it in the girl's hair above the left ear. This use of the left or unclean hand was quite deliberate for it symbolised the soiled nature of the newly taken wife. On the other hand, when Lokhon Hansdak' married a divorced girl, he put vermilion on a flower but used his right hand in putting it in her left ear. He avoided the left hand since he himself belonged to the special sub-clan of Cilbinda and his second wife had therefore the privileges of a first wife and was not 'soiled' by her former connection. At the time the flower is given, the witnesses shout 'Haribol' as in a standard wedding.

When vermilion has been thus applied, it affects the girl in the following ways. In the case of certain sub-clans – Cilbindha Hansdak', Rokbutur Marandi, Goda Marandi, Manjhikil Marandi, Kuari Hembrom, Khanda Soren – it extinguishes the bonga relationship with the woman's previous husband and once she has had a male child by her second husband, she is fully qualified to assist him in his worship. In the case of all other sub-clans, however, the vermilion has only very limited implications. It enables the woman's daughters to be lifted in a basket and to be given vermilion at their weddings. It does not, however, qualify the woman herself to assist her husband in serving his bongas. It is at most a hollow substitute, a means of conferring a superficial dignity; and it is public recognition rather than the vermilion which now makes her a valid wife.

CHAPTER XIII
Santals and Sex

I THE PRIMARY CHARACTERS

From early youth until the onset of old age, sexual intercourse is one of the chief ingredients in Santal happiness. In the years preceding marriage, it is the natural end of romantic love. When he thinks of his girl, a boy 'burns with heat', the two 'ache for water' and they seek together a passionate release. Their attitudes are expressed in a host of love songs, sung either privately in the forest or openly in the village – at weddings, at the Sohrae festival and at social dances. In the case of forest songs, the references to sex are frank and unabashed. In the case of other songs, the implications are similar but the treatment is more symbolic.

312

The hot earth
Scorches the feet
The hot sky
Is burning the body
O my love
Give me a gold umbrella
To cool my mango body.

313

Girl, in this great heat
Where have you been?
You have seen my lover
I was in his arms.

314

A mango and a tamarind
How I long for them, O friend
In the plantain, the honey
Is dripping, dripping down.

315

You took me from my home
You snatched me from my friends
To a stony lonely field you took me
And you made me ache for water.

316

Fumble at the door
Then for the legs of the cot
O my love
Grope your way in
To the legs of the inner door.

317

At the big river
The stony river
How I thirst for water
I am a grown girl
I am not a youngster
O my love
Do not shake my body.

318

O my love
Have me, have me quickly
If you do not want it
Put back my clothes.

319

I am lying between two stones
And the babblers are calling
O eat my body
Eat and eat my vulva.

320

Pull down the sal sapling
And hang your quail upon it
O my love
Take me to you now.

321

On the mountain a crab
Rustles in the leaves

On the hill a crab
Slowly drags along
If I had seen my friend
I would have killed myself with running
I would have died from striking my brow
If I had seen my girl
How the lily would have burst into bud.

322
As we climbed the hill
The rice that had no husk was flowering
Girl, the elder brother
Calls like a dove or a pigeon.

323
As I could see this fruit, the mango
How I want you, my love
The juice drips from the tip of a bunch of plantains
And I am filled with it, my love.

In the years that follow marriage, intercourse becomes more and more a nightly conjugal routine. 'When they are young,' said Dhunu referring to couples that are happily married, 'they come together five or six times a night. They are on the same cot. They have delight. When there is a child, they take each other two, three or four times. Up to forty a man must have it twice or thrice a night and after forty never less than once.' 'Not everyone has the same power,' said Sibu. 'A weak man goes to his wife every night at bed-time and again just before he gets up. A man who is hungry, who has gone without it for days, will come ten times in a night. When a boy and girl are first married, they have each other five times a night and twice in the day. After that, they go four times in the night and a fifth time when they have drunk rice-beer.'

324
Why are the boys and girls
So happy in this village?
When you pick a vegetable
It shoots again and again.

This frequency of intercourse seems due to various factors. There is no doubt that Santals enjoy it. They regard it, in fact, as one of the best things in life. It does not seem to produce premature exhaustion but rather to have a tonic effect. To move through Santal villages is to feel immediately that here is a people who are truly well. At the same time there is nothing coarse or gross in this nightly copulation and their general sense of refinement is not at all affected. More than many people, in fact, Santals seem able to make the most of sex without destroying its finer aspects.

A feeling that the primary characters are to some extent responsible is reflected in various myths. In a story which explains the origin of the clitoris, both penis and vagina are shown as detachable. 'In olden days, when boys went down to bathe, they would take out their moustaches, beards, hair and penises and lay them on the ground. Girls also took out their vaginas. One day three girls were washing when a jackal came. He made off with their organs and ate them up. The girls came out and found their vulvas gone. They chased the jackal and came on Maran Buru. Maran Buru went after the jackal and killed it. He cut it open and inside he found not three but four vaginas. Maran Buru told each girl to take her organ. The girls took them. Then Maran Buru said "What shall I do with the fourth? If I give it to one girl, she will have two and all her daughters will be like her." So he cut it into three and put a third in each vagina. The piece became the clitoris and since then the vagina has this organ.'

Another myth relates how the vagina was formerly in the armpit and the penis was as long as a rope. 'In olden times, the penises of boys were twelve cubits long and were kept coiled about the waist. The vaginas of girls were in their armpits. One day a girl was in her courtyard frying mahua flowers when a boy passed the fence. As she fried the flowers she lifted her arm and he caught a glimpse of her organ. The boy stood there gazing with desire, his penis tingled and he passed it through the fence and put it in her. When the penis touched her, the girl started. She seized a ladle and dealt the thing a blow. The boy winced and holding his penis like a rope he drew it back and rushed away. In his pain he ran about, not caring where he went. If a mouse crossed his track he trod on it and in this way he accounted for twelve basketfuls of mice. The mice were mad with fear and ran to Cando. When Cando heard their story, he was greatly grieved. "If men do this," he said, "they will never be good." So he called the animals, birds and insects. They resolved that while the penis of the man must be made short it must stay as long as twelve cubits but by the measuring standards of a mouse. So a mouse began to measure. When it had measured twelve lengths with its foreleg, it began to gnaw the penis. As it finished gnawing, a lizard nodded and said, "Do not bite more. Let it stay like my head." So they left it. Since then whenever a man's penis stands up, it nods like the head of a lizard. As they did this, Cando also shifted the woman's organ from the armpit and put it in the fork of her thighs.'

In another story, the sexual organs are credited with separate characters. 'When Maran Buru made man and woman, he gave them names for their toes, feet, legs, thighs and bottoms but no names for the penis or vagina. So the two organs ran away. They went to the forest and climbed a tree. Maran Buru followed them. He said, "Why have you run away?" They said, "You have named the others but us you have not named." Maran Buru said, "I will give you names so that at every moment men and women will call upon you." So he named the penis "Babu" or "Young gentleman" and the vagina "Mai" or "Daughter". Since then their names are heard at every moment of the day.'

This conversational intimacy is carried even further in a story of the clitoris. 'If the vagina is small and there is difficulty in child-birth, the anus says to the vagina "Do not tear me. You drip water on me when you clean the pot of curds. Spare me now." So the clitoris is torn instead.'

If the organs themselves seem in part to determine the amount and frequency of copulation, enjoyment on the other hand is proportionate to the sizes of the different parts. These are all appraised from different angles and the mons veneris, the pubic hair and the clitoris are regarded as playing roles almost as important as those of the penis and vagina. The mons veneris for example should surmount the vagina 'like a small honeycomb.'

325
My love
Like a ripe mango is your body
And like bel fruits are your breasts
O my love
Like a bees' comb is your hill.
Whose joint cracks on it?

326
In the burnt forest
The wasps have made new nests
Your small vagina
Swells and swells.

327
The comb of the bees is soft
O my love you may take me

As a still unmarried girl
For I have a juri
Lovely as a bud.

328
In the rice field was her clitoris
And her mound was the breast of a dove
Like the horns of a young buffalo
She spread her thighs out to him.

Pubic hair should be a small protecting fringe.

329
To left, to right the bushy hair
And in the midst the little hole.

330
The pubic hair flutters
And the cock flaps his comb
When my sister's husband took me
I rode away and away.

In a similar manner, the clitoris should fulfill the function of a regulator. 'If the penis is small, the clitoris presses on it. It stops it from going out. If the penis is large, it is the clitoris which widens the vagina.'

Yet while these organs have each their separate roles, it is the penis and vagina which must fit. The girl's organ, in particular, must be neither over-large nor over-small. If it is jalak', 'the lips stick together and the hole is too narrow'. In big girls, a nawa pandhi is large but not unsuitable. 'It is a new shoe. The lips are large but the channel is neat. It bites the penis.' A short plump girl has a cucruc' mai 'with lips as small as a leaf-cup'. The vagina of a thin girl is birju, 'weak and powerless, without a trace of sweetness'. A rongo organ has no pubic hair – 'only a dark mark'. But these deficiencies are minor besides a vulva that is khalak' – 'big and loose as a large leaf-cup, so empty that it never bites'. To give satisfaction, in fact, the vulva must be firm and narrow so that it 'sucks the penis as a calf sucks the udder'. When such an organ is found, Santals are quick to voice their approval.

331
It hurts her
When you have it

It aches
When she is not had
How lovely is her small vagina.

332
Seeing my clumsy walk
They do not have me
But in my narrows
What sweetness have I.

Against a girl's neatness, a boy should offer size. A penis that is kutis tonka leka, 'like the beak of a little bird', cannot reach 'the place where desire dwells'. Yet even here a certain moderation is advisable. 'To give pleasure the penis should be as long as eight fingers are broad. A horse's penis, that is the best.' If it is larger, it verges on the absurd. It is when penis and vagina fit – when the strength of the one matches the trimness of the other – that copulation yields its greatest joy.

2 THE RIGHT TRUE END

In the light of these erotic standards, how then do Santals envisage 'the supreme embrace'?

The first act of sex is often distressing. 'When a girl has a boy for the first time, the tears come. The way has to be made. It is then it hurts. After that, she is happy.'

333
From who knows when, Rajaram
Have you been longing for me?
You are splitting me down
Like the new shoot of a kend
O Rajaram, you are fully grown
And I am still untried
Work your waist gently.

In many cases the girl's hymen is still intact and its rupture causes her to bleed.

334
In the morning you are drawing water, sister
But what is that blood upon your skirt?
Brother, you know the way a girl is born
A green kingfisher I caught up in my lime.

335
If you would eat fish
Go to the pool among the rocks
For a young unmarried girl
Has drugged the water with her blood.

In yet another song an encounter with a virgin is described as a fight
between a cow and a buffalo with the girl pretending that the blood on her
cloth is the sap from a tree.

336
Girl, on the cloth for your breasts
What blood is this?
Mother, it was you who told me
To take the buffaloes with the cows
There was a fight
Between a cow and buffalo
I lent against a munga
It is the blood of the munga, mother.

Yet once the first distress is over, the girl herself is ready for her boy.

337
Dug with a stick
Cut with an axe
My vagina
Strained to and fro.

338
The first time
And she sobbed and sobbed
But in three days
She smiled and smiled.

Once defloration is accomplished, Santal boys and girls spend longer
on their first approaches and intercourse is often preceded by a variety of
caresses. Kissing is frequently indulged in though not as fully as in ancient
India or in the modern West. Fellatio and cunnilingus, I was told, were
never practised; the thighs, buttocks and private parts are never kissed
and in fact it is a form of derisive taunting to suggest to a boy that he
should kiss a girl's sex. If a boy is shy, a girl sometimes says, 'Be ready or

I'll make you kiss my vulva', while if a boy is making unwanted advances, the girl says, 'Be off or I'll rub my privates in your face.' But the rest of the body – above the waist – is considered the lips' property. 'The boy takes the girl. He holds her in his arms. He kisses her lips, her cheeks, her breasts. Their tongues meet. He devours her with kisses. When the boy stops, the girl begins.' Equally important are the hands. 'As they lie together, the boy catches her haunches. He holds her breasts. His hands fondle her buttocks. He strokes her breasts. He caresses her sex. He touches her clitoris. Then the girl fondles his body. They lie and their hands go everywhere.'

When, at last, they are ready, there is a fairly wide choice of posture though the technique known as gitic' durup' – lying and sitting – is by far the most favoured. 'The girl lies on the ground. The boy squats before her. He lifts her thighs.'

339

Sister, the boys
All know too much
When they lift the thighs
It opens like a horn
And the fruit of the kend
Nods to and fro.

'If the girl is on a cot, the boy sits at the end. One leg is on the ground, the other on the bed. He draws her to him. He holds her shoulders. If the cot is strong, he straddles it and lifts her thighs.'

340

Broken are the strings of the cot
And it sags in the middle
O come to me if you are a man
If you are a bonga go away
I am opening my thighs
And closing them
About your waist.

While this posture is believed to be the best, it is not however the only method which is tried and when a boy and girl are wildly in love or are in the early years of marriage, they explore a variety of positions.

Jambro deper, for example, is 'loving like pythons'. 'They lie on their sides, locked in each other's arms. Then the boy enters.'

230

In taber deper, the usual Western method is employed. 'The girl lies on her back. The boy lies over her. He goes between her thighs. But there is little joy.'

341

On the ground
I lie above her
And it creaks and creaks.
Like the palm of my brother's hand
It pierces and goes in.

Sometimes 'the boy sits and the girl squats on his lap. Her legs clasp his waist. Their faces meet.'

342

From the east are labourers
Who are working on a road
O brother-in-law
Make a path through me
On the ground is the dust
And the boulders are rough
Take me on your knees
And make your road.

343

Since there was no room on the floor
You had me on a rice bale
It was so cold you sat me on your knees
And from your lap you glued me to you.

Another form is 'standing' or thad deper. 'If it is muddy and they cannot sit, they stand together. The boy puts a leg between her thighs. Then he enters.'

344

Girls, for eating kend and tarop
Come to the field with the hesel
The kend we will eat
Tarop we will eat
And standing we will take each other.

231

345

Girls, let us go to the rivers
And catch some fish together
When the fish are killed
We will stand and have each other.

In yet another form, 'the girl lies on her chest with her buttocks pro-truding upwards. The boy takes her legs. They clasp his waist. He goes between them.'

Sometimes 'they lie together with his penis locked in her thighs.'

In bituc' deper, 'the girl kneels down. She bows her head on her hands. Her haunches are round and lovely. The boy kneels erect and goes to her.'

346

O you blind one
O you slow one
Come to our house
And I will show you my bottom
Through a hole in the wall.

A variation of this is engot' deper. 'The girl stands and touches her toes. Her buttocks are large and the boy goes to her from behind.'

When at last the organs meet, the best lover is one who can prolong his action without too much violence.

347

Boy, put your hands on my chest
And your legs in my thighs
And like a quail that flicks its tail
Slowly and gently sway your waist.

3 THE POETRY OF SEX

In *A Dream in the Luxembourg*, Richard Aldington writes:

'I shall say no more,
Nothing of how we were lovers
How I was her lover and she my woman
Though once I meant to tell her – the real her
How in the dream she was so beautiful

And so ardent a woman lover,
And all we did and all we said.
But I cannot tell it even to her,
For the mysteries that are spoken by two bodies
The bodies of two lovers, so ardent, so beautiful,
Cannot be said in words, even a lover's words,
Even when the lover is a sort of poet.'

With sex so large a feature of Santal life, it is not surprising that Santal poetry should deal so often with the union of lovers. As we shall see, there is one occasion – the annual hunt – when a positive premium is placed on grossness, vulgarity and crudeness. At other times, the emphasis is all the other way – on refinement, delicacy and beauty. Symbolism, which is second nature to Santals, comes into its own and the 'right true end of love' is described in terms of natural phenomena – birds, animals, trees, flowers, fruit, rivers, clouds, storm and rain. There can be little doubt that by this instinctive recourse to parallels drawn from nature and to symbolic imagery of this kind, Santals are able to communicate intimacies of feeling that might otherwise defy sensitive expression.

348
On the mountain the kend
Has fruits both large and small
Slip on the ground, girl
Wait a little for me
And I will pick them for you.

349
To eat figs
You took me to a strange forest
We have eaten figs
We have come back
I could not think
You would not keep me.

350
As soon as you come, you say
Give me, little girl, a vessel of water
O middle brother, if I fly away
Who will give you water?

351

By the mountain stream
A spring is by the plum tree
And you are fetching water
Give me some cold water, girl
To cool my burning body.

352

As I climbed the hill
My turban fell
O my love
Search for my turban
Had we been lovers still
I would have looked for it, O friend.

353

On the bank of the river
The bushes are in fruit
The horned owl
And the bearded kingfisher
Have finished their eating.

354

The owl calls 'kor kor'
The kingfisher 'kir kir'
Where did you catch them with your lime?
In the field I caught them
Where once we had our love.

355

I went by paths
I met her in the way
She said
Give me a red flower

356

Seeing the milk flower, mother
I picked and put it in my hair
I broke the stem
The tree withered
That boy
Has taken away my heart.

357

Over the hill
The wind goes
And the rain drifts down
O my love
The thatch of the big house
Was carried far away
And the rain
Is dripping down.

358

To the east and west were clouds
In the north and south
Was lightning
The wind and rain came down
But do not cry, my love.

359

In the upper lands the clouds have gathered
And the storm is coming up
O dark girl, we will take the leaf of a palm tree
And stop the wind and rain.

360

O my love
Let me come
From the house to the street
I will make your water flow
To the depth of a hand.

361

O my love you are taking me
Over the two rivers
If one day you do not keep me
I will go
To my father's house.

362

From the spring
In the mountain
The clear water flows
I put my pot on my head
I took a pot at my waist

And the water
Splashes on my body.

363

You are on that side
I am on this side
Wait till I cross the river
I have caught my foot in the weed
I have broken my sweet pot.

364

Take the buffaloes to the forest
And pick and pick the flowers
At the spring with the plum tree
I will thread the blossom
And, Durga, you can thread me.

365

On the higher land were cows
By the river there were buffaloes
We were threading green flowers
We did not notice it was midnight.

366

Below the garden by the stony spring
We sat together
Uncle, I shall call you uncle
But do not call me daughter
The waters of two rivers
Are flowing into one.

CHAPTER XIV

Marriage and Fertility
the Baha Festival

Although the act of marriage means ultimately a fuller sexual life, sex is very far from exhausting the aims and objects of the institution. Once a Santal pair have settled down, their ambition is to have a child. A young wife feels incomplete without a baby. She must become a mother to secure adult respect. Moreover when the couple start a separate home, the house will need a child – 'to give it life'. 'For love and joy we want sons' said Salkhu Soren. But even more important is the economic urge. A wife will be handicapped in running the household if there is no daughter to assist her. A husband will find it difficult to cultivate his fields if there is no one to graze the cattle or assist with the ploughing, while in old age a son is his principal if not his only support. To have a child before marriage, not to have a child after it – these are among a Santal's greatest dreads.

367

When the sal trees are in leaf
On the mountain
How lovely they look
Wealth in the house
A door in the doorway
But without a child
There is no beauty.

368

The mother set me up with money
The father gave me a tank
But I have no children
To whom shall I give
A share in the tank
Cando, if you will give me children
Give me a child of gold.

For ensuring this family objective, Santals turn primarily to their bongas. We have already seen that in terms of strict theology the gift of a child depends on certain aspects of Thakur Jiu, the Bidhi Bidhanta. 'Unless these will it, no child can come.' It is natural however that Santals should view the situation in the light of their dual world. They are aware of bongas at every step and even if the Bidhan Bidhanta are the fundamental operative units, it is necessary that nothing should occur to blight their wise intentions. To ensure children as well as to promote prosperity, the major bongas must therefore be honoured and the first means is the Baha festival or feast of flowers, held in March.

This festival, with its long ancestral usage, is believed to have started in the following manner. 'In olden times, when all the forests were thick and dense, the great trees were the abode of bongas. The Tudus were iron-workers and every day went to the forest for charcoal. One day two Tudu boys were making charcoal when they saw some bongas approaching. They were struck with fright and ran away. At a short distance they found an atnak' tree. The trunk was hollow and in their fear they went inside. Since their home was near the tree, the bongas gathered by it and began to dance together. The Tudu boys stayed trembling in their hole. Then they resolved, 'This is the haunt of bongas and whatever we do we are bound to die. But before we die let us dance with them.' Thinking this, they came out of the hole and, since all the bongas were naked, they began to call out. As they called, they ran among the bonga boys and girls holding out a flower for them to sniff. As a bonga girl smelt the flower, the Tudu boy fondled her breasts. The girls were filled with confusion and began to dance bending low. As the hands of the Tudu boys were smutty with charcoal, the breasts of the bonga girls became black. From that time on the nipples of women have been black like the ends of a drum.

'The bongas were delighted with the two Tudu boys and taught them everything about dancing and bonga service. They also taught them their names – Jaher Era, Maran Buru, the Five-Six, Gosae Era, Pargana bonga, Manjhi Haram, and the bonga girls, Hisi, Dumni, Chita and Kapra. By the grace of the bongas, the two boys learnt all the ways of singing and of bonga service and became the gurus or teachers of the twelve clans. They went round the twelve countries and made disciples from all the people. When people heard their skill in singing and saw their knowledge they were amazed and even today their prowess is celebrated.'

369

O you two drummers

Playing the drum
You do not know
The beat of the songs
Give your drums to the two Tudus
And they will beat the tunes.

'From the day they got this knowledge of the bongas, Santals are observing Baha as their first festival.'

This account is supplemented in another version. 'When there were only Santals, the clan of Tudus did the work of blacksmiths. Two brothers went to the Urmi forest to make charcoal. It became night. They started to go back. In the way they saw three bonga girls dancing. Behind them, the Five-Six were dancing sogoe fashion, with their clothes rustling. The bonga girls had sal flowers in their hair. Their cloths were tied. There were no buffalo horns or drums. The two brothers were afraid and hid in a hole in a fig tree. The bonga girls with the Five-Six came near them. They danced round the tree. The younger of the brothers said "Our lives are gone. There is no chance of saving them. Let us go and dance with them." So the two brothers came out. The younger went dancing, sogoe fashion, with them round the tree. He went round three or four times. His hands were black with charcoal. He caught a breast of one of the bonga girls and his touch made it black. The girl saw the black on her breast and bowed low. The other two bowed down with her. They danced until cock-crow, bending their bodies and swaying their arms. The Five-Six danced with them. When it was dawn the bonga girls told the Tudu boys to start a festival because they had danced with them. The Tudu boys said, "What shall we call it?" The bonga girls said, "Call it the Baha festival because we danced with flowers in our hair." Then the Tudu boys left them and went to their village. In the village they called the villagers and asked them to start the festival. They told them about the bonga girls but the villagers did not believe them. That evening a buffalo horn sounded in the priest's house and a drum began to beat. No one was playing the horn and the drum was beating of itself. As they sounded, a man was possessed with the Baha bonga and rushed to the forest. At that time, there were no jahers or sacred groves. He swept a patch of trees and went round and round it. The priest followed him with a vessel of water. They made the first grove. The next day they put stones by the trees in the name of the Five-Six and all the village girls came and danced round them, bending down their bodies. They did this once a year for five years. After five years the Baha bonga came on a man and said that they must sacrifice a black calf to the Five-Six every five years and take a new dhoti, a new broom, a new basket, bonga bells, a new earthen pot and a bow and arrow, an axe and an iron chain when they went to the grove. Since then they are doing this.'

Finally, a third account throws light on Gosae Era, the lonely figure who is a member of the company but is kept slightly apart.

'At the time of the first ancestors,' Sangram Hembrom told me, 'there were five brothers who lived in the forest. Their mother was with them. They used to hunt the whole day and bring back peacocks and any game they killed. Their mother stayed at home and cooked for them.

'One day they were hunting and came on a Hindu girl of the Kamar caste. She was lovely as a flame. The youngest of the five brothers set his heart on her and said he would take her with him. He asked his brothers and took the Kamar girl away. It was then the practice that on returning from a hunt the eldest brother would give their mother the same number of arrows as there were hunters and the mother would give out rice as many times as there were arrows. That day, instead of five they gave her six arrows. Their mother said, "For whom have you given me an extra one?" They said, "We have brought another with us. We have brought a Kamar girl back as a wife." Their mother said, "Do not bring her here. She is not of our caste." That night they gave her rice and kept her. The next day they put up a separate shed a little apart and she lived with them there. As they had brought her they did not send her away. The mother of the boys is Jaher Era. The Kamar girl is Gosae Era. The five brothers are Moreko Turuiko (the Five-Six). Because of this, Gosae Era is always kept apart.'

But although the festival is a massive propitiation of the major bongas, its ritual is also a miming of fertility. On the first day, sheds are erected, the Baha hunt takes place and the grove is swept. On the second, trees are shot at, the flowering forest is celebrated, flowers are thrown into the aprons of the women and a water-battle is waged in the village streets. Children are not expressly demanded but everything is done – by symbol, poetry and action – to simulate their gift.

The festival commences with the villagers washing and the priest, the godet or messenger and a few others going down to the grove in the morning to get it ready for the rites. They put up two sheds of sal branches and thatching grass – one at the three trees for Maran Buru, Jaher Era and the Five-Six and the other at the mahua tree for Gosae Era. The sheds sometimes have great straw tassels and at Dhamna a straw monkey dangled from a branch. The priest then bathes and goes round cow-dunging a little patch at the tree of every bonga. The party then returns to the village; and either puts some thatching grass on the manjhithan or gives it a new roof. The priest now breaks his fast and presents those who have made the sheds with food and rice-beer.

In the afternoon, he gets together all his gear – a mat, a small open bowl of water, a new broom, three new winnowing fans, bangles, necklaces, a bow wrapped in cloth, an arrow, a new basket, a battle axe, two buffalo horns, a new earthen pot and a skein of thread. He purifies them with water and places them in the courtyard.

The village meanwhile goes out on the Baha hunt. All the men and boys take bows, arrows and axes and the crowd makes a long round of the fields. The hunt ends at evening and the men then assemble at the priest's house.

When I saw the festival in Karhabel in March 1943, the priest put out the gear in the courtyard and squatted down beside it. The godet faced him. Some girls went dancing out of the house and after a few circles in the village street began to break away. A faltering gasping blare was sounded on a buffalo horn. The priest's wife handed him the three new winnowing fans and in the gathering darkness a chorus of a dozen men started up the Baha songs.

370

Under the rafters
Who is sitting
Who has taken his seat?
The priest is sitting
Under the rafters.

371

Who will cut
The wood for Maran Buru?
Who will thatch
The shed for Jaher?
The priest will cut
The wood for Maran Buru
The priest will thatch
The shed for Jaher.

372

What has the priest brought?
What things has he set down?

He has brought
A bowl of oil
He has put down
A box of scarlet powder
He has brought
A winnowing fan of bamboo
He has set down
A basket of bamboo.

373

Ja Gosae
We have washed
And cleaned our heads
In whose courtyard do you sit today?
In whose courtyard do you sit erect?
In the priest's courtyard I am sitting
By the small path I sit erect
In the priest's courtyard
Is liquor made from flowers.

374

Chita, why are you late?
For whom do you delay?
Ja Gosae
For whom do you delay?
My father's kinsmen are away hunting
My brothers beat the jungle
Chita, because of this you dallied
For this you made delay.

As the songs went on the priest sat gravely holding the fans while from time to time a drum-beat sounded.

After an hour's singing, three mediums – the men who were to be seized with Maran Buru, the Five-Six and the Lady of the Grove – went out and washed. Again the drum-beat sounded and they came back and sat before the basket. Again the horn blared and the priest brought out some sun-dried rice and placed it on the fan. Then with slow and solemn fervour, the songs began again.

375

On the top of a pipal
The barbet calls

On the branch of a banyan
The woodpecker sings
The year has turned
The year has come again
The woodpecker calls
Turning it has turned
The barbet sings
Coming it has come
The woodpecker calls
The weevils have gone
Away with the river
The insects have gone
Into the sea.

376

In the shade of a pipal
At the foot of a banyan
A barbet sings
The land is aflame
The land is burning
The woodpecker calls
The year is new
The year has come again
The barbet sings
Who chose the spot for dancing?
Who made the dance start?
The woodpecker is singing
The Five chose
The spot for dancing
The Six have made the dance start
The barbet sings
The place for dancing
Is chosen, chosen
The dance is starting
The woodpecker sings
The dancers are starting.

Suddenly the three began to shake their heads in a wild frenzy. First
one and then another gave a piercing howl, their arms shaking and jerking.
The priest said, 'Who are you?' and the men answered, 'Maran Buru',
'The Five-Six', 'Jaher Era'. A moment later, 'Jaher Era' had seized the

basket and with trembling hands had put on the necklace and bangles and snatched the broom. 'The Five-Six' seized the bow and arrow. 'Maran Buru' took the axe and the three men in all the frenzy of possession went stumbling out of the house and over the fields to the grove. As they hurried through the gloom under the starlight, 'The Five-Six' leading and 'Jaher Era' twirling the broom, they let out grisly shrieks. When they reached the grove, they went from tree to tree, shrieking and sweeping every shed and patch. When all the stones were swept and visited, they hastened back to the village.

When the party returns, the priest washes the feet of 'Jaher Era' and 'The Five-Six 'and puts the broom back in the basket. Then each of the mediums washes the priest, pouring water first on the priest's head and then on his own. Finally the bow and arrow are put in the basket and the three mediums squat in a row. The priest now issues them with fans and rice. The three jerk their heads and the rice trickles through their hands. They toss it six times over their hands and the priest says 'Gosae, today the places in the grove are newly cleaned. The priest has bathed. Tomorrow we shall worship in the Flower's name. Bring no ill meanwhile. Give no hurt. Make everything go well. If in the cleaning anything is amiss, con-done it.' The mediums reply, 'No ill will come.' Then the priest says, 'Go back to the forest. The horse and the umbrella are weary. Seek for your pipal and your dimbu leaves.'

When the bongas have 'left', rice-beer is drunk, dancing starts and songs are sung throughout the night. These songs have a variety of themes. Some are celebrations of the hot season and the flowering forest.

377

On the rol mountain
The rol tree is in flower
And the flowers hang.
On the rol mountain
The rol tree is in fruit
And the fruit swings.
On the meral mountain
The meral tree has flowered
And the flowers sway.
On the meral mountain
The meral tree has fruited
And the fruit hangs.
The blooms, the blooms are white

And the fruit hangs
The fruit has filled the branches
And the fruit hangs.

378

The pipal leaves sway 'hipar hipar'
The banyan leaves go 'nohar nohar'
The pipal tree, the banyan
The pipal leaves
Are a red sari
The banyan leaves
Are a silk cloth
The pipal and the banyan
I went below the pipal
And its sap dripped on me
I went below the banyan
And its sap fell on me
The pipal tree, the banyan.

379

In the pipal tree the barbet sings
On the branch of the banyan
The woodpecker calls
The year is turning
The barbet sings
The year has turned
The woodpecker calls.

380

Ja Gosae
The Five, the Five brothers
The woodpecker calls
The Six, the Six sisters
The woodpecker sings
The Five have chosen
The place for dancing
The barbet is singing
The Six have said
The dancing must start
The woodpecker sings
The place is chosen
The barbet sings

The dance is starting
The woodpecker sings.

A few refer to the earlier ablutions and dwell on washing and fishing.

381
Gosae, O elder sister
The river is full
The river is in flood
'Seke seke' sounds the water
'Rule rule' goes the stream
The fish has risen
The fish has come
Let us make a net
And pull it to the shore.

382
The river has filled
The river is in flood
Parrot, go back
My heart is in my lover
My husband's brother has my life.

383
'Titriti rankilo'
A ring was on the finger
'Ritriti rankilo'
A ring was on my toe
Where, elder sister
Is the ring on the finger?
Where, elder sister
Is the ring on your toe?
Golden sister
The ring on the finger
Golden sister
The ring on the toe
I was washing my body
At a pool in the sand
The ring was on the finger
I was drawing
Water at the spring

246

The ring was on my toe
In the pool in the sand
The ring fell from my finger
In the spring water
The ring slipped from my toe
My lover has found
The ring of my finger
My husband's brother
Kept the ring of my toe
Tell him to return
The ring of my finger
Tell him to give me
The ring of my toe
The ring of my finger
Is not with my lover
The ring of my toe
Is not with my brother-in-law.

Yet other songs describe the Baha hunt.

384

The two hunters on Logo Buru
The two beaters of Ghanta bari
Come to the hunting
Go to the chase.

385

The hunters have hunted
The beaters have beaten
In what forests did they hunt
Where was it that they beat?
They have hunted the Sin forest
They have beaten the Man forest
They have caught a new-born tiger
Ja Gosae.

386

The young dog loiters in the forest
The curled hawk rests on the hand
Let us go to the hunt
Go to the chase
The young dog noses in the forest

The curled hawk rests on the hand
Let us go to the hunt
Go to the chase
Let us lead the young dog
Let us carry the curled hawk
Let us go to the hunt
Go to the chase.
Throw the ringed stick
Leave the milk, the parched rice
Let us go to the hunt
Go to the chase
The young dog returns from the trail
The hawk has soared out of the hand
Come and return.

Later the same night, the priest and his wife lie down on mats in the courtyard and a line of girls dances round them through the gloom. The dancing goes on until morning and at day break they sing as follows:

387

The dust rises
The sky is hot and red
Who is it that has risen?
The land is dusty
The sky is hot and red
The dust gathers on the land
The sky is hot and red
A sun of brass comes up
The land is dusty
The sky is hot and red
A golden star
Comes out
The dust rises
The sky is hot and red
The sun has risen in the sky
The dust flows on the land
The sky is hot and red
The star has shone
The land is dusty
The sky is hot and red

The dust flows
The sky is hot and red
The morning star has climbed
The dust rises
The sky is hot and red
It has risen and risen.
The dust rises on the land
The sky is hot and red
The grass shrivels in the heat
The dust rises
The sky is hot and red
The grass is burnt and withered
The dust rises
The sky is hot and red
The grass has grown green
The dust gathers
The sky is hot and red
The grass is green
The land is dusty
The sky is hot and red.

The second day sees the climax of the festival. The godet is sent to collect the bonga fowls. The priest's wife prepares some wet flour. The priest himself chooses a new fan and puts in it some oil, flour, rice, vermilion and a wedge of wet cowdung. All the time, a line of girls goes slowly round the courtyard, their bodies bending and their arms swinging slowly in the baha dance.

The stage is then set and about the middle of the morning, the priest goes to the grove and boys and girls dance behind him. When the priest reaches the grove, he places the winnowing fan, the battle-axe, the bow and arrow and the broom in front of the three major trees and then very slowly and with great care links the three trees with a girdle. He takes a strand of cotton and moving widdershins, goes round the trees three times. A little later girls and women come dancing to the grove. They form a number of rows and with hands tightly clasped, come skipping and tossing over the fields. As they advance, drummers move before them. At the grove they form a single line and then dance slowly by the trees, rounding their haunches, bending their bodies and swinging their arms so that they almost touch the ground.

As they dance the women sing:

388

Chita, beneath a pipal give me oil
Kapra, below a banyan bring out oil
Chita, under a pipal
Bring water for my feet
Kapra, under a banyan bring me oil
Yesterday I brought rain
But the well is dry
I gave you rain two days ago
But the spring is dry
Where the girls wash their hair
Whose share of water
Has dried in the well
Where the girls wash their hair?
Whose water
Dried in the spring
Where the girls wash their hands?

389

Kapra, do not wash
In the water of my well
Do not clean your hair
In the water of my spring
Go to the river
Stand in the middle
Wash your body
Clean and rinse your hair.

390

The trees
The forest
Has decked itself in beauty
I will go for leaf-cups
And make my body
Beautiful with flowers.

391

Gosae, Gosae
Who will wear the flowers?
Gosae
Who will put them in a basket?
Jaher Era

Will wear the flowers
Gosae Era
Will put them in a basket.

392
'Tiriri rankure'
A ring on the finger
'Tiriri rankure'
A ring on my toe
'Tiriri rankure'
Rings on all the fingers
'Tiriri rankure'
Rings on all my toes.

393
In the forest the horns are sounding
Who are playing
The horns in the forest?
Who are singing?
In the forests the horns sound.
The Five are playing
The horns in the forest
Jaher Era is singing
Where the horns sound.

About noon the priest begins his rites. Jaher Era, the Five-Six and Maran Buru again possess three men and they squat in a room jerking their heads. The gear is set before them. Then suddenly with a howl, 'The Five-Six' seizes the bow and arrow, 'Maran Buru' grips the axe and the broom is taken by 'Jaher Era'. The three leave the room and once again set out in a hurrying dash across the fields. When I saw them go at Dhamna in 1945, 'Jaher Era' was leading – stumbling over the ridges and jerking the broom. The party reached a mahua tree and circled round it. 'The Five-Six' stood by the trunk, shot an arrow into it and all three gathered the fallen flowers. After that they again dashed on, a crowd of men and boys rushing behind them. At a sal tree, 'Jaher Era' suddenly stopped and 'The Five-Six' took another arrow and shot it into the tree. A bachelor boy then took the axe from 'Maran Buru', climbed the tree and cut some sprigs of blossom. After that, laden with flowers, the three went hurrying to the grove.

While the party is rushing through the fields, the women at the grove continue their swinging dance and celebrate the expedition as if it were a hunt.

394
The tiger cub roars hudure hudure
The leopard cub snarls nuhure nuhure
Go and see the young tiger
Go and bring the young leopard.

395
Ja Gosae
He is an only son
And we are only two
Do not send him to the hunt
There is thirst for water
There is a young tiger.

396
Let us get a young dog
Let us keep a brown hawk
And go to the hunt
Go to the chase
I have found a young dog
I have kept a brown hawk
Let us go to the hunt
Let us go to the chase
Let us lead the young dog
Let us hold the brown hawk
And go to the hunt
I will bring
The breast of a partridge
I will bring
The leg of a hare
Let us go to the hunt
Go to the chase
I have brought
The breast of a partridge
I have found
The leg of a hare
Pierce the lungs of the partridge

Cut the lungs out
Let us go to the hunt
Go to the chase
The young dog lingers in the forest
The brown hawk rests on the hand
Let us go to the hunt
Go to the chase
I have put in the pot
The breast of the partridge
I have set apart
The legs of the hare
Let us go to the hunt
Go to the chase
The breast of the partridge
Has been burnt black
The legs of the hare
Have turned to cinders
Let us go to the hunt
Go to the chase
Wife, wife
O you green pigeon
Where will you rest and stay?

As the mediums return the sacrifice begins. The priest makes a circle on the ground with flour. Sal and mahua blossoms are put in it and the dancing stops. The priest now offers a fowl to Jaher Era, sawing its neck on the upturned axe. As he offers it, he says, 'Jaher Era, in the name of Baha, I make this offering to you. Let nothing bad or sick invade the village. If the cows and goats wander and stray, bring them safely home'. As the blood drips on the mark for Jaher Era, the medium plunges forward, sucks the hot blood and the women sing songs in her honour. The same is done for the Five-Six but the songs change to songs in its honour. Finally Maran Buru is reached, a third white fowl is offered and the songs change once more. Water is then poured on the three mediums, the priest and the godet', and the bongas are 'released'.

A bachelor boy now climbs a sal tree in the grove and throws down blossom. More mahua flowers are brought and the line of women again goes dancing round the inmost trees. A little later rice-beer is offered at the stones. The priest now takes his stance, the ground before him is swept and the women sing:

397
The Five, the Five brothers
Clean their house with milk
The Six, the Six brothers
Clean their house with curds
Whose is the cock?
Whose is the pea-hen?
The cock is the Five's
The pea-hen is Jaher Era's
From the east the rain sweeps
In the Sita Nala the water streams
Elder sister, let us beg
A sal flower from the Five
If they withhold it
There is blossom with the Six.

Each girl or woman now comes up in turn holding out her skirt like an apron. As she stands before him, the priest tosses a sprig of blossom into it, and the girl then tucks it into her waist, makes a low johar and returns to the line. There she puts the blossom in her hair or ears. When all the women have received flowers, the line reforms but instead of going round and round the three inner trees, it goes out onto the edge and starts a dancing progress round the whole grove.

The villagers now drift back to their houses to sacrifice fowls and pigs, while the priest stays alone in the grove to consume the brown fowl. Later, the villagers return and in a great dancing procession escort him to the village. A boy bears a basket of flowers, another carries the new pot while the priest bears a winnowing fan, a vessel of water and some further flowers. As he enters the village the priest goes from house to house. At every door, a girl washes his feet and he gives her a flower and sprinkles her with water. If the women regard him as a brother-in-law, they souse him with water and give him rice-beer to 'dry his clothes'. A great dance then takes place before his house. The girls swing round and round. The drummers leap in a frenzy of excitement and a general water-festival ensues. Bowls of water are brought out. The women dash the water at each other. Boys bring out bamboo guns and shoot water at the shrieking girls. The girls rush round throwing water at the boys. As they do so they taunt them saying, 'You have brought a Kamar girl!' This goes on until the first fury is over. Then when the sun has set, lagre dances start up again, and the village goes dancing into the night.

398

At the end of the fence
They are singing loud
Beyond the gate
There are singers
How shall I go out
How shall I win my way?
Inside is the father-in-law
At the gate is the mother-in-law
How shall I creep out?
How shall I break through?
Within the house is a lighted lamp
It is burning like a torch
How shall I creep out
And go to them outside?
The bangles clatter
The toe rings clink
How shall I go out?
How shall I steal my way?
O elder sister
We are two sisters
We are wives
Of two brothers
How shall I go out
And win my way?

CHAPTER XV

Marriage and Fertility
the Jiwet' Karam

I THE INSTALLATION OF THE KARAM TREE

If the Baha festival is a collective effort to woo the bongas and ensure that marriages are fertile – the Jiwet' Karam ('a Karam for the living') is a private ceremony that supplements this worship and avails of yet another source of help. Unlike the Karam festival of the Uraons, it is not an annual ceremony nor one that the village itself must regularly perform. It is rather an optional act sponsored by individuals in which the villagers assist. The standard ceremony, with slight modifications, is also performed on five further occasions. Manjhi Karam is done when a new headman first assumes office and seeks to associate his term of service with fertility and welfare. Dangua Karam is done, once in five years, when village boys and girls are ripe for marriage and their early wedding, with many children, is desired. Guru Karam celebrates the starting of an ohja's practice while Cela Karam marks the end of the pupils' class and celebrates their initiation. Mak' More Karam is done in continuation of a Mak' More festival as a thanksgiving for ending sickness. Finally Upas or Janam Karam celebrates the chance appearance of a Karam seedling on a man's private plot. Each ceremony focuses on the magical properties believed to be inherent in the Karam tree and by honouring the Karam seeks to obtain an increase in wealth and progeny.

The standard ceremony which is often held in September begins after dark when the villagers go to the man at whose instance the Karam will be done. When all have assembled, they begin to sing

399
Jogmanjhi
Jogmanjhi
O jogmanjhi
Get the light ready

256

Prepare prepare
I will touch the wick with flame
Make the lamp ready.

The women then set out the various gear – a new winnowing fan, a battle-axe, vermilion, oil, dub grass, cotton, gur, milk, paddy and rice-beer.

The jogmanjhi then gathers everything up and as he sallies out into the darkness, the crowd goes singing with him.

400

Arise, headman
Come, O village five
Let us find and bring the Karam
Come with us, O five
And we will bring the Karam
Come with us
Ram, Lokhon
And we will cut
A Karam in the forest
Come with us
Bhorot, Catur
And we will cut
A Karam in the thick, thick forest.

When they reach a karam tree, the crowd surrounds it while the jogmanjhi washes his feet and sprinkles the tree with water. He now lights a lamp and sets it by the trunk and choosing a fork with two small branches, he winds the cotton round the two stems. He then dabs oil on the fork and makes three vermilion marks on each of the branches. As he does this, with grave methodical slowness, the band of villagers address the tree:

401

O Karam
Why have you come?
Why have you arrived?
O Karam
I have come for you
For you I have arrived.
Jogmanjhi
Do not touch it

Leave it alone
First wash your feet
And sprinkle it with water
Jogmanjhi
Bring a skein of thread
And tie the Karam branch.

402

Karmu
I shall not go
O Karmu, return
Go back
Karmu, for your love
I fasted
Ten years
For the sake of Karmu
I have eaten nothing
Twenty years
Do not weep, Karmu
Do not mourn
I will take you
I will bring you
O Karmu
I will set you in my lap
I will put you on my hip
Karmu, Karmu
I will lift you in my arms
O Karmu
I will wash you in milk
I will wash your hair in curds
O Karmu
I will keep you ever at my waist.

The jogmanjhi then offers rice-beer and either water or milk to Maran Buru and prays 'O Maran Buru, we are making you this offering. We are doing the Karam ceremony. Till today this tree was in the forest. Tonight we shall take it to the village. Let it stay green. Let everyone dance and sing. May there be no ache of belly or head. Give us your blessing.' Two young unmarried boys are now produced and made to clasp each fork. The jogmanjhi unwinds the cotton and with two quick strokes of the axe he severs the two stems.

403

Karam, Karam
The Karam has been cut
Karam is not cut
The ashes all are cut.

The whole band of villagers now dance around the tree. Dhurumjak' songs are sung and with the two boys going ahead, the villagers return in a long straggling procession. As they reach the house of the host, they halt and a girl welcomes the boys, the jogmanjhi and the guru by washing their feet. As she does so, the villagers sing:

404

O Amki Devi
Bring a plate of brass
A pot of water
I have brought a tree
From Brindaban
O mother wash my feet.

The jogmanjhi now takes a digging stick and makes a small mound of earth.

405

Jogmanjhi, bring
A digging stick of gold
A digging stick of silver
Dig deep a hole
And plant the Karam branches.

The two boys bend down together and at the same moment plant the branches side by side. The jogmanjhi again winds the cotton round them and two girls from the host's family plaster the mound with water and cowdung.

406

Jogmanjhi
Bring a skein of thread
Jogmanjhi
I have planted
Two Karam branches

259

Jogmanjhi
Tie the twin strands of branches
With your thin thread
Bring water of the sea
Amki Devi
And clean the dancing ground.
Jogmanjhi, I have brought
Sea water
I have brought
Cowdung
I have cleaned
The four corners.

After this, women from the host's family come out and circle winnowing fans above the branches. A lamp is lit and a cloth stained with turmeric, is draped around the stems.

407

Mother, do the circling
Of the two Karam branches
The circling
Of the twin branches
Mother bring a length of cloth
And swathe the Karam branches.

The villagers squat in a great circle round the tree. The guru faces east and a long recital of the Karam sermon then follows.

2 HOW THE WORLD BEGAN

'In the beginning,' the guru says, 'there was only water and below the water earth. Thakur Jiu made the water creatures – crabs, alligators, crocodiles, raghop' boar fishes, prawns, worms and turtles. Then Thakur said, "What shall I make? I will make man." He made two people of mud. As he gave life to them, the sun horse came from above, trampled on them and broke them to pieces and Thakur was grieved. Then Thakur said, "I shall not make men of mud. I shall make birds." He made a goose and gander by rubbing dirt from his chest. He held the two in his hands and they were good. Then he breathed on them, life came and they flew in the air. They could not find a resting place so they perched on Thakur's hands. Then the sun horse came on a thread of gossamer to quench its thirst. As it drank, foam dripped from its mouth and floated on the water. Then Thakur said to the birds, "Go and settle on the foam." When they sat on it, they floated on the face of the water and the foam bore them like a boat. Then they said to Thakur, "We can move now but have no food."

'Thakur called the crocodile. It came and said to him, "Thakur, why have you called me?" Thakur said, "Can you bring earth?" The crocodile said, "If you ask me, I will try." It dived in the water and began to bring up earth but all of it dissolved. Then Thakur called the prawn. It came and said, "Thakur, why have you called me?" Thakur said to it, "Can you bring me earth?" The prawn replied, "If you ask me, I will." Then it swam in the water and brought up earth but all the earth dissolved. Then Thakur called the crab. It came and said, "Thakur, why have you called me?" Thakur said, "Can you bring up earth?" The crab said, "If you tell me, I will." Then it went into the water and brought earth in its pincers but all the earth dissolved. Then Thakur called the worm. It came and said, "Thakur, why have you called me?" Thakur said, "Can you bring up earth?" The worm said, "If you tell me, I will. But the turtle must stand on the top of the water." Then Thakur called the turtle. It came and said, "Thakur, why have you called me?" Thakur said, "No one has brought earth from the water. The worm will bring it if you stand on the surface." The turtle stood firmly on the water and as it stood, Thakur tied its four legs at the four corners. Then the worm went into the water. It sucked the earth in with its mouth and excreted through its tail on to the back of the turtle and the earth settled on it like a skin. The worm went on bringing up the earth until it finished the whole world. Then it stopped.

'After that, Thakur had the earth levelled with a clod-crusher. Some clods stuck to the crusher and became mountains. The foam on the water settled on the raised and levelled earth. In the foam Thakur sowed some sirom seed and the first grass grew. Then he sowed the karam tree, and then sal and mahua and after that all the plants and trees of the world. The earth was hard and firm. On the clumps of sirom grass the birds made their nest and laid two eggs. The female sat on them and the male brought food. They hatched their eggs and two human beings were born – a boy and a girl. Then the two birds said, "Thakur, how shall we feed these human beings?" Thakur gave them cotton wool and said, "Squeeze the juice from what you eat, soak the cotton in it and let the children suck." And in this way they grew. Then the birds wondered where they should keep them. They asked Thakur. He said, "Fly and find a place for them." They flew to the west. They searched and found a place, Hihiri Pipiri. They came and told Thakur. He said, "Take them to it." They took them on their backs and brought them there. The names of the two human beings were Pilcu Haram and Pilcu Budhi. Neither had clothes and they lived, happy and unashamed.'

3   SEX AND INCEST

'One day, Maran Buru in the guise of Lita came to them and said, "Where are you, children? How are you? I am your grandfather. I have come to visit you. I see that you are happy, but there is one delight in life which you have not yet known. Brew some rice-beer; it is very good." He showed them how to make the ferment. The three went to the forest. Lita showed them the root and they dug it up. When they had brought it, Lita said to Pilcu Budhi, "Wet the rice for us." She wetted it. Then she powdered it to flour, they crushed the root, mixed it with water and from the water and the flour they made a pellet. They kept the ball shut up in a basket with straw. At dawn next day, at the same time that they had made the ball, they opened the basket, threw the straw away and having dried the ball on a sieve, they kept it ready. Then they collected panic and millet grass, husked it, cooked the rice, cooled it, added the ferment and made a bundle of it in leaves. After five days it fermented. In the evening they poured water over it. Then Lita said, "First pour a little for Maran Buru. I shall come and see you again tomorrow." So the two made three leaf-cups and filled them. One they offered to Maran Buru and after that they drank. As they drank they began to make love and making love, they drank and drank the rice-beer until both were drunk. Night came and they slept together. At dawn Lita came. He called to them, "Grandchildren, have you got up yet or not? Come out." When they came to their senses and saw that they were naked, they were ashamed and said, "Grandfather, how can we come out? We are feeling very bashful. We are naked. Last night we got drunk on rice-beer and what a bad thing we did."

'Then Lita said "No harm is done." He laughed and went away. Then Pilcu Haram and Pilcu Budhi covered their bodies with banyan leaves and hid their shame. They had children, seven boys and seven girls. The eldest boy they named Sandra, the next Sandhom, the next Care, the next Mane and the youngest Acaredelhu. The eldest girl they named Chita, the next Kapu, the next Hisi, and another Damni. They lived and grew up there. The father with his sons would go off one way to hunt. The mother with the daughters would go off another way for vegetables and leaves. In the evening, they met together at their home. One day the boys went to one forest and the girls to another. When they were tired of gathering vegetables, the girls went to a banyan tree and began to play by swinging on the roots. Then they began to dance the dahar dance and to sing:

408

Mother, the ants
The ants are swarming
Under the branches
Of the banyan.

'The boys who were tired of hunting brought a deer. Hearing the girls singing, they said, "Listen". They left the deer and went to the girls and began to dance with them. With the dancing, they all felt happy. The eldest boy chose the eldest girl, the youngest boy, the youngest girl and in this way each obtained a partner. The eldest boy and the eldest girl went to look at the deer. The rest sang:

409

Under, under the banyan is a young deer
Mother, look at the young deer, the young deer.

They paired off. When the father and mother found that they had paired they said "Let us marry them". They built a house and divided it into seven rooms and brewed rice-beer. They all drank and the father and mother put a couple in each room; the eldest boy with the eldest girl, the youngest boy with the youngest girl till each of them were married.

'After they were married, children were born. Then the father and mother said, "When there was no one else, we two met and had seven sons and seven daughters. We have married these brothers and sisters. Now we shall divide them into clans, so that a brother may not marry a sister." So they made seven clans – Hansdak', Murmu, Kisku, Hembrom, Marandi, Soren and Tudu. They lived there and many days went by. They became more and more.

'Then they went to a place called Khoj Kaman. While they were there, men grew wicked and became like buffaloes. When he saw this, Thakur became very angry and decided to destroy mankind if they did not return to him. He searched for them and said, "Return to my ways." But they did not heed him. Then Thakur called Pilcu Haram and Pilcu Budhi and said, "Your children are not heeding my words so I shall kill them. Go into a cave on the mountain and you will be saved."

'The pair heard Thakur's words and went to the mountain cave. As soon as they had entered, Thakur rained down fire for seven days and seven nights without stopping. He killed every human being and animal; and only the two in the cave at Harata were saved.

410

Seven days
And seven nights
It rained with fire
Seven days
And seven nights
It did not stop
O two, where were you?
Where was your shelter?
On Harata
Within the mountain cave
We stayed and had our shelter.

Then the rain stopped and the pair came out. They built a house, had children and became more and more. From Harata they moved to Sasanbeda and there once more made clans. They formed the first seven and added five more.'

4 THE ORIGIN OF KARAM

The guru now comes to the origin of Karam. 'One day in Sasanbeda,' he says, 'the Marandi clan were making merry. They took a Karam branch and set it up. They brewed rice-beer and throughout the night they danced around it. Two goatherds saw the dancing and could not put it from their minds. As they grazed the goats, they would plant a Karam in the sand and dance before it. The goats strayed and ate the crops. People were angry and two of them, Karmu and Dharmu, seized the branches and threw them in the river. A branch fell in the Somae Sokra stream and drifted down. The other stuck on a bank. From that day on, the luck of Karmu and Dharmu ended. Their food shrank before they could eat it. Their wages vanished. They decided to destroy all that they had made. They took their sisters, Noso and Baso, and began to break the ridges in their rice land. As they hacked at the clods, Thakur came. He said, "Why are you breaking your fields?" "Because our food vanishes." "I gave you the Karam," Thakur said, "but you did not use it. You pulled it up. You threw it away. Now you must find it."

Then the two brothers and sisters gave up damaging the field and Karmu left to find the Karam. As he went, he saw a bair tree but the plums were full of maggots. "I have lost my luck," said the bair tree. "No one eats my plums." A little further on he saw a fig tree but the figs were full of insects. "Bring me back my luck," said the fig tree. Then he found a Gwala or milkman. When the calf stayed, it pulled at its mother. When the calf went, the cow followed it. "My luck is out," said the Gwala. "Get it back for me." Then he saw a woman. As she washed her clothes, they stuck to the rock. "Find me my luck," she said. Then he saw a woman with a bundle of thatching grass upon her head. "I cannot take it down," she cried. Then he saw a man on horseback. "Whenever I want to go forwards," said the man, "the horse gallops backwards; and when I want to go backwards, it rushes forwards." "I will help you if I can," said Karmu. Then he saw a man glued to a stool. "I cannot free my bottom," he said. "If I get the Karam," said Karmu, "I will help you."

'So he went and went till at last he reached the river. The Karam branch was floating in the water. "Why have you come?" said the branch. "It is for you that I have come, for you, Karam." But the branch sang:

411

I shall not return, Karmu
I shall not go back
In your anger, Karmu
You cast me away
In the pool of the Somae river
I have floated in the water
I have drifted to the sea
I have floated
I have come
To the sea.

Then Karmu said, "Come with me, Karam. Come with me. Take pity. For ten years I have fasted." But Karam sang:

412

Karmu, do not weep
Do not wail
I shall not go, Karmu
I shall not return
In your anger, Karmu
You cast me away
And I drifted to the sea.

Then Karmu said, "Come with me, Karam. I will wrap you in my cloth. I will clasp you to my breast. I will wash you in milk."

'The branch was still drifting. It was going down with the stream. Karmu entered the water. He stood on a fish. He caught the branch. He drew it to him. He wrapped it in his cloth. He clasped it in his arms. He set off for his home.

'As he went, he met the man with a stool on his bottom. "You cannot free yourself," said Karmu, "because you never welcomed strangers. You never gave them seats." "I will never do so again," said the man, and the stool left him. Then Karmu saw the man on horseback. "You never lent your horse to others," Karmu said. "Take my horse," said the man, "and ride it as you will." And he gave the horse to Karmu and went on. Then he met the woman with the bundle of thatching grass stuck to her head. "When others had straw in their hair," he said, "you never took it out." "If I see any," she said, "I will tell them." "Then throw your bundle down," said Karmu and she did so. Then he met the woman who was washing clothes. "You stopped others from washing," he said. "You dirtied their clothes." "I will never do it again," said the woman. "Then pull your cloth from the rock," said Karmu. Then he met the Gwala or milkman. "You have many cows," he said, "yet you never give their milk to others. You must give away some cows." "Take whichever cows you will," said the Gwala, and some cows went on with Karmu. Then he saw the fig tree. "You will have no more insects," he said. Then he saw the bair tree. "You prick anyone who picks your plums," Karmu said. "Take what plums you will," said the bair tree. Karmu took them. The tree did not prick him and the plums were free of maggots.

'Then Karmu reached his home. Cows, goats and sheep were with him. The wife of Dharmu heard him coming. "Karmu is coming," she cried. "He is dead," said Dharmu. "He is coming," said his wife. Then they went outside and saw him. The street was full of animals. He opened the cowshed. Those that went in were cows, goats and sheep. Those that went on were deer and nilgai. Then they feasted him and danced. They planted the Karam in the village street. They bowed before it. They circled it with paddy, dub grass and bhelaonja fruit. They sang and danced and the Karam bestowed on them its luck.'

5 THE KARAM DANCES

As the sermon draws to its close, tension relaxes, men and boys straighten up and soon there are separate groups dancing the rinja in the village street. A few go off to drum for the girls while others form a loosely strung out circle. The girls go edging round clapping their hands, while the men and boys perform some agile figures. They start by strutting round the circle, each dancer moving his arms with bold truculent jerks. Then the line faces inwards, they hold hands and the circle goes swinging round in a fast careering rush. When they have danced this through, they stand behind each other in a tightly fitting line. They grip each other's shoulders, lock the left foot in the calf of the man behind and the whole line goes stiffly hopping round. A little later, the spirit of joking daring quickens, they divide themselves in two, one line standing on the shoulders of the other and the line which is now two lines goes slowly marching round. When they have covered the circle several times, they face inwards and the top-most line of dancers changes position. Each man now stands with his legs spread-eagled on the shoulders of the men below him. He holds the arms of his companions and a circle of inter-gripping limbs is thus imposed upon the lower ranks. When all is ready, the band starts to move and the towering edifice of forms goes tottering round the street. As the line revolves, the drummers, each on separate mounts, go quickly past it.

Throughout the night, dances of this type go on. Rice-beer is drunk and an air of riotous gaiety infects the village. As the dawn comes up, however, the dances gradually slacken and with the singing of bhinsar or dawn songs the dancers go to their homes.

413
Rise, sun and moon
Rise on the Karam
In your light, O friend
I will do the bhinsar dance.

414
When the dogs bark
The day breaks
When the peacock calls
The dawn comes.

415
Rise, drunk brother
The horse is starting
The dogs bark
The night has turned to dawn.

416

Get up, big bullock
And go and graze the grass
Above you, the golden vulture
Hovers in the sky.

417

O vulture, eat the flesh
But leave the bones
The bones will go
To the deep deep sea.

When these dawn songs are over, the girls and women fade away. The men dancers change their mode, running slowly out and back, whirling their hands aloft and swinging round. Then suddenly the drums stop and the dancing is over.

6 THE CONSIGNMENT TO WATER

While the dancers are back at their houses, there is a slight pause, but before the sun gets high, the last rites begin. The village again gathers at the branches and a circling ceremony is done once more.

418

O mother, father
Give me a brass plate
And fine fine paddy
Prepare the green grass
And I will do the circling
And bid goodbye to Karam.

The jogmanjhi takes the two boys who assisted at the cutting and in one act they pull the branches up. The guru then presents some Karam leaves to the two girls who plastered the mound and they either exchange the leaves or put them in each other's hair. Other pairs then ask the guru for leaves and if he gives the leaves to them, the bestowal and subsequent exchange give to each friendship the status of a 'Karam twig'. While this is going on, a number of songs evoke the final scene. They depict the stream or pond. They refer to bathing and washing and the cleaning of the hair. They describe the happy scenes of flirtation which streams witness. Finally they summon the Karam branches for their last immersion.

419

Whose is the pond, the pond
Whose is the tank
The tank with flowers?
The pond, the pond
It is the mother's pond
The tank, the tank
It is the father's tank with flowers.

420

In the pond of mustard, mother
What is creeping?
In the flowering tank, father
What things are growing?
In the pond of mustard
The betel nut has crept
In the tank of flowers
The champa bloom has come.

421

Who are those two girls bathing?
I have smelt the oil of their hair
Who are those two girls cleaning their tresses?
I have smelt their scented oil.

422

The two girl friends were washing
And I smelt the oil of their hair
The two girl friends
Were cleaning their tresses
And I smelt their scented oil.

423

My love plays his flute
By the river or the stream
My friend plays his flute
By the shore of the sea.

424

Rise, O Karam
Rise to your feet
Let us go, Karam
To wash and clean our hair.

425

Where, O Karam
Will you wash your body?
Where, O Karam
Will you wash your hair?
At the last ghat, my Karmu
I will wash my body
At the meral ghat, my Karmu
I will clean my hair
At the last ghat, Karam
The water is like milk
At the meral ghat
The clay is soft as curds
At the last ghat, Karmu
You will wash in milk
At the meral ghat, Karmu
You will clean your hair in curds.

When the bestowal of the leaves is over, the two boys dash wildly to
the water and cast the branches in. As they float away, other boy dancers
crowd in and some last songs are sung:

426

O Karam you are going
To the banks of the Ganges
O Karam
You are leaving me
On the dancing-floor
Stay, O Karam
Stay and come back
O Karam
Catch the reeds
In the river
Catch the bushes.
Dancer, do not weep
Do not mourn
In a year's time
I will return.

427

The water of the well is dry
The water of the pot remains

In the hand is the gold umbrella
On the head is the silken cloth
They are going from the dance-floor
The water of the well is dry
The water of the pot remains
In the hand is the gold umbrella
On the head is the silken cloth
The Karam branch
Is drifting to the sea
O brother with your goats
I saw the Karam
On the way
O brother, tending sheep
I saw the Karam
Going down
The dance, the dance is ending.

When the immersion is over, the boys troop back, the girls and women gather in the street and the festival ends with the dancing of lagre.

This standard ritual is slightly altered on three occasions. If the ceremony is a Mak' More Karam, the animals and birds which were vowed are first sacrificed in the sacred grove and the village boys and girls dance round and round the trees. As the sun goes down, they return to the village and after night fall, the men and boys go to the forest to bring the Karam in. If the ceremony is Upas or Janam Karam, the villagers first go to the new Karam seedling, the twigs are wound with cotton and the ordinary ritual is then performed. The plant is not however harmed. Instead the jogmanjhi digs the earth all round it and the Karam host then gently pulls it up and puts it in a pot. The plant is then carried back in the lap of the host or his wife and is set down in their private shrine. After that the sermon is recited and dances go on through the night. Finally in the case of Dangua Karam, the ritual is virtually the same except that after the circling ceremony, the women bring out some cucumbers. These are tucked in a winnowing fan and covered with paddy leaves. As they show them to the people, they say 'Here are the babies.' After that the women cut up the cucumbers and the company consumes them.

CHAPTER XVI

The Wanted Child

I IMPOTENCE AND STERILITY

These two ceremonies – the Baha and the Karam – at once bring into
motion various powerful forces. They ensure the continuing good wishes
of the major bongas and tap the luck associated with the Karam tree. They
provide, in fact, a fertilising background in terms of which each husband
and wife must make their efforts. If, in spite of this, no child results, there
are several explanations to account for their failure.

Before marriage, impotence is sometimes encountered.

428

Across the mountain we wandered
On the whole mountain we went
And everything we would we did
But your penis did not fill me.

429

Sister-in-law,
You are gathering cowdung
And I am with the buffaloes
O boy with cut hair
Strike quickly and firmly
O you elder brother,
You are only babbling and fumbling
Take your worm from my belly.

After marriage, it can also occur but is generally believed to be rare. At
Chirapathar a girl complained of her husband. 'He sleeps with me only
like a brother or sister. He is lazy. He has no penis. What use is he?' In
Dhawa, Nunulal Baske was taken to Nawadih as a ghar jawae or permanently inducted son-in-law. He remained for two years in the house but
never went to his wife. At last the girl lost patience and demanded a

Baha festival: Santal
women dancing round
the sacred grove
Baha festival: Santal man
climbing a sal tree to
gather flowers
Baha festival: Santal
women revering the
priest

50 Baha festival: the wa
   battle
51 Jiwet' Karam cerem
   the rinja dance
52 Karam dancers in a r

itlaha : the drummers
itlaha : the crowd
advancing
hotu Ramu Murmu of
mtala

56 Santal girl with mirror
57 Santal girl
58 Santal mother and daughter
59 Santal girls

divorce. 'He never talks to me day or night,' she said. 'He never fills my mind. He has not got any penis. He is not a boy.'

If a boy is pressing unwanted attentions on a girl, temporary impotence can sometimes be secured by magic. 'The girl must hold her breath and then either tie her hair in a bun, take a ring off one finger and put it on another or untie her cloth and retie it all in one breath. If she does this, his penis will not stand.' If, however, the boy knows that she has done it, he can untie the hair or the cloth, take the ring away and his virility will return.

Another method is to root up a little catom arak' plant with the toes and put it in the hair, all in one breath. This also is believed to make a lover impotent.

If a boy is permanently incapable, there are various prescriptions for effecting a cure. One is to mix the white of an egg with a bidi bhelom root and to take it three times at cock-crow and sunset for three days. Another is an obvious example of sympathetic magic. 'Kill a wagtail on a Saturday. Powder its feathers. Drink them with mahua liquor and the penis will wag once more like the bird.' A third is based on the view that impotence is partly psychological. 'Kill a male sparrow on a Sunday. Roast and eat the flesh. Then if you believe that all is well, your penis will stand.' A fourth involves propitiation of the Rongo Ruji bonga. 'Take urine and a big cock. Say "Rongo Ruji bonga, my penis is not standing. I offer this to you. Make it stand." Take out the cock's testes. Then take and crush the bark of a merso loa tree. Mix with one of the testes. Fry the other and eat it. Take a living codgoc' fish and insert the mixture in its mouth. Fry the fish alive. Take out the mixture and eat it. In two days potency will return.'

In certain extremely rare cases, frigidity in the woman is thought to be responsible. Sibu knew of two sisters in Sadhudih. 'They never let any boy go to them,' he said. 'Some boys even left their girls and tried to have them. Their brother tried hard to cure them. He offered first a fowl, then a pig, then a goat but it was all to no avail. They had no interest.' On the other hand, Duli Murmu declared, 'I have seen the sons and daughters of my grandson married but never a girl who did not want a boy.'

If impotence is clearly not to blame, physical defects are sometimes believed to play a minor part. 'A girl does not get a child if her root is wrong.' 'If her child's house is dirty, the flower withers.' 'If her menstrual blood comes black or white or if the womb gets out of place and leans one way, no child can come.' Similarly, if the man's urine is red or his semen 'weak and thin', nothing can be hoped for. The size of the sexual organs, on the other hand, is irrelevant. 'A large or small vagina,' said Dhunu, 'a big or little penis – a child comes all the same.' More usually, however, it is witches or bongas who are blamed for childlessness. 'A witch,' said Sibu, 'can blast a girl. She inverts her womb and blackens the flower. Sometimes the witch induces her own bonga husband to intervene. The bonga seduces the girl. He enjoys her body. His semen spoils her flower. After that no child is possible. If a girl takes a bonga lover of her own accord, no children by her human husband can survive.'

If sterility persists, a guru is consulted and various medicines are tried. These are often efficacious if taken in the prescribed manner. The following recipe was tried with complete success by the father of Sibu Tudu of Tetaria. 'Steal secretly a gulanj flower from the head or ear of an unmarried girl. Mix with a mandargom flower. Grind and make two pills. Bathe on a full moon night. Offer a little to Jaher Era and vow a goat. Take one pill yourself and give the other to your wife.'

Another prescription is 'Take the umbilical cord of a ram. Powder it with the root of a chat pat creeper. Mix with three pinches of black pepper. Take at dawn on the day the period ends. This will give a boy. If a girl is wanted, substitute the cord of a ewe.'

Duli Murmu who told me this prescription keeps several cords in stock at a time. When she treated the wife of Fogla Hansdak' of Sahajuri, 'the medicine at once shot up like the seed of a plant' and the woman conceived the same month. Unfortunately, Duli had muddled her cords and gave a sheep's cord in mistake for a ram's. As a consequence, Fogla got a daughter instead of the son which he had wanted. If the cord of a woman's first child can be procured, the same mixture is made and taken. If the first child was a girl, the woman will then get a girl and if it was a boy, she will get a boy. When a woman has taken this medicine she can drink rice-beer but must on no account touch mahua liquor until the child is born. A Santal woman of Balidih who did this at once miscarried.

If medicines are tried but to no effect, the woman goes to an ojha who divines whether bongas are 'blocking the way'. If a bonga is diagnosed, the ojha transfers it to a fowl and the medicine is tried once more. The wife of Matla Hansdak' of Sahajuri consulted Duli and took her medicines. Nothing happened so they then consulted an ojha who detected a bonga and 'dispersed' it. This time Duli made no mistake and the same month that she gave medicines a boy was conceived. This expedient however has one serious disadvantage. If a child is conceived, the parents are required to name the child after the ojha or his wife and can only avoid this rather distasteful consequence if the ojha agrees to waive the condition and they pay him five rupees.

If, as a last resort, the couple have approached the bonga that is latent in a Hindu shrine, a similar condition affects the naming. Gulu Murmu of Baghmara had no children so with his wife he went to the jaithan or Hindu shrine in Jiakara. He promised the godling a goat if he got a child and when, within a year a son was born, he gave the goat and named the boy Jiaram. Kesar Baske of Rakh had no children so he took his wife to the local dibithan or shrine to Devi and made a sacrifice to the godling, Kalyaneswari. He also honoured his pledge and when a son was born he named it Kalyan Baske.

2 ADOPTION

If in spite of medicines and offerings, a child still fails to come, the couple conclude that the Bidhi Bidhanta have willed it otherwise. They are not however entirely devoid of other remedies and in certain circumstances the husband tests his fertility by taking a co-wife. A Santal of Sarauni failed to get children, so, at his wife's suggestion, he married her sister. Jagan Tudu of Bhalke had no children so, with his wife's consent, he took a second girl, had children by her and both wives lived happily with him. Dhapra of Taldangal also had no children. He took a second wife, got children and all were happy.

Not every Santal however cares to risk a co-wife and a much more common remedy is adoption. When this is resorted to, the first and most usual course is to adopt a youth from among the husband's relatives. These afford him a range of choice though it is not as wide as one might at first expect. He cannot, for example, adopt a brother, the son of a paternal or maternal uncle, a grand-uncle, a paternal or maternal uncle, or the son or grandson of a grand-uncle. He is debarred in fact from adopting anyone on the tribal level of a brother, father or uncle. But there is no objection to taking, among others, the son or grandson of a brother, the grandson or great-grandson of a paternal uncle or the great-grandsons of paternal grand-uncles. Similarly although it is rare to adopt a man whose age is more than thirty, adoption at any age from birth to early manhood is often done.

In such cases, the boy is of the same sub-clan as his adopting father. He already has full access to his bongas. All that is necessary is village approval and even if certain relatives object, the decision of the villagers is final. When the village has approved, the adopted son changes his residence, and unless anything is specifically reserved for him at the time of his adoption, he loses all rights in his own father's household. He can no longer demand partition on marriage or claim a son's share on his father's death. He becomes, in fact, the son of his adopting father – with almost all the privileges of a natural son. He cannot claim partition after marriage but in all other ways it is as if he had been born in his new family. If he is unmarried, his adopting father will arrange and pay for his marriage and the first grandson will be named after him. If the adopted son is married and has children, the next son will take the adopting father's name.

A second course is to choose a youth not from the relatives but from an outside family. This may occur when the brothers are on bad terms or when the adopting father has married a widow with children and adopts a stepson. Here also village opinion is decisive but the process itself is considerably more complicated. Since the boy is necessarily of a different clan or sub-clan, it follows that his bongas will be different from those of his adopting father. To become a son therefore he must change his bongas and to do this he must submit to a replica of the naming ceremony and undergo the rite of bonga tala. For this, the adoptive son and the village males are shaved and go to a tank for bathing. Flour is put on the chests of men and women. A midwife announces the clan of the adopting father and the new name which the adopted son will bear. Finally rice gruel with nim leaves is drunk. When the ceremony is over, the youth is deemed to have shed his former bongas. He can now share in the family's sacrificial meat and can even, if necessary, be married in his former clan. The change of bongas, in fact, makes him the man's own son.

Yet a third type of adoption is when the adopted youth is either the son of a sister, the son of a daughter of a paternal or maternal aunt or uncle, the son of a stepchild, the son of a wife's elder sister or indeed of anyone with whom sexual relations by the adopting father are forbidden. In such cases not only the bongas but the clan of the boy will be different and in that respect he will be in the same situation as a stepson or outsider. He will not however be 'brought into the bongas'. The reason for this is that bonga tala would give his adopting father an incestuous relationship with the boy's mother. When, therefore, the boy's mother is such that intercourse with her by the man would lead to outcasting the boy is adopted by a simple declaration in the village.

Anpa Murmu of Banspahari had no sons so he adopted a son of his sister. The boy's name was Munshi Marandi but since his mother was Anpa's sister, no change of bongas was possible and Munshi retained his own name and clan. Similarly when Bando Murmu of Ero adopted Kanhu Hembrom, the boy was the son of Bando's grandfather's sister's son and Kanhu's own father was younger than Bando. The latter accordingly stood in a forbidden relationship to Kanhu's mother. Bonga alteration was impossible and Kanhu was therefore adopted by a simple declaration. If Kanhu's father had been older than Bando, the incestuous relationship would of course no longer have existed and the acquisition of new bongas would then have been essentially necessary.

There remains a fourth type of adoption – that of a girl. When this occurs, a brother's daughter or brother's granddaughter is usually selected but an outsider, a stepdaughter, the daughter of a sister, the daughter of a stepchild or a girl from the family of the adopting mother is sometimes taken. If such a girl is already married, her husband may be made into a ghar jawae by 'being brought in' while if she is still unmarried her wedding may be done in ghar jawae form with village approval. When the girl is drawn from a brother's family, her name and clan continue as before but if she is a stepdaughter or outside the father's family, the adoption is done by change of bongas. If, however, she is the daughter of her adopting father's sister or the daughter of a stepchild or if sexual relations by the new father with her mother would amount to incest, change of bongas is dispensed with and she acquires the status of adopted daughter by a simple declaration.

Ram Murmu of Bandorkonda was married to Solma. They had no children and later Solma left him and lived with Pandu Hansdak'. A daughter, Khandi Hansdak', was born to them but after Pandu's death, Solma came back to Ram Murmu and brought Khandi with her. Ram then adopted his stepdaughter, brought her into his bongas and named her Raimat Murmu. Raimat was the name of his mother and Murmu was his clan. When Raimat grew up Ram married her to a ghar jawae and she later inherited all his lands.

In a case from Bandarjuri, Thakura Hembrom had a single daughter and a son. The girl had a love affair with a Dom and but for the fact that she left Bandarjuri and 'became dead' the village would have done bitlaha. Thakura then married a widow with two daughters. He arranged husbands for the two girls and sometime later a stepgranddaughter was born. The child's father died and her mother remarried in another village. Thakura then adopted his stepgranddaughter, but since relations with her mother (Thakura's stepdaughter) would have amounted to incest, change of bongas was impossible and the adoption was completed by a village declaration. After that Thakura took village approval and married the girl to a ghar jawae. The ghar jawae died and in 1942 Thakura brought a second ghar jawae. When at last Thakura himself died his own daughter tried to get her father's land but a little later not only the village but a meeting of five headmen all awarded the lands to the adopted girl.

In all these cases, adoption is for 'the mutual help, the one of the other', and for this reason it is always a permanent relationship which is intended to end only with death. If, however, friction develops, adjustments are sometimes necessary. If an adopted son is already related on his father's side, the adoption can be cancelled. If, however, his bongas have been changed, the adoption cannot be cancelled and the only remedies are partition and separation or the adoption of further children to off-set the recalcitrant one.

CHAPTER XVII
The Bonga Lover

During the years preceding marriage and, in fact, throughout a Santal's lifetime, the bongas continually impinge on Santal affairs. We have seen how the putting of vermilion on a girl involves a change in her bongas, how sexual relations with certain persons pollute the bongas and how at weddings the village bongas are closely associated with some of the ritual. It is not surprising, therefore, that before and after marriage an even more intimate relationship is sometimes believed to develop. The bongas, it is thought, are not invariably strange invisible forces obsessed with Santal life but are sometimes met with in the guise of boys and girls.

430
At noon I went for water
I met a bonga or a boy
If you are bonga, drag yourself away
If you are lover, stay with me and come.

431
Two bonga girls
From the tall hill
Have come below to bathe
They have washed their skin
They have cleaned their hair
Their sex is shining white.

432
From the pool, the pool
Two bonga girls came up
And we have learnt from them
The ways of magic.

These reports of romantic encounters are rare in Santal life but a number of folk tales describe in vivid detail the core of the experience. None of them need to be taken too literally yet they should not be too lightly dismissed. They reveal how deep is the Santal involvement with bongas and how aware most Santals are of the dangers and mysteries – as well as of the delights – of sex. The desire of bongas to intrude on Santal life, their fascination with mortals, their willingness to exchange their own kind of life for that of Santals, their need to fraternise – these project a kind of alter-Santal which over the centuries the tribe has felt it necessary to invent. During my years among the Santals, I never met anyone who actually claimed to have had a bonga lover. At the same time, I never met a Santal, apart from Christians, who denied that bonga lovers existed. Bonga lovers were in many ways what Santals hoped for and expected – a boy or girl who by their enterprising adventures fused the normal with the supernormal, the natural with the supernatural. They demonstrated what all Santals believed – that despite sickness, catastrophe and death, life at its most mysterious was on their side. The bonga lover was, in last analysis, a loving bonga and through these accounts of supposed experiences Santals revealed their ultimate confidence in life itself.

Dukhu and his bonga wife
A boy named Dukhu met a girl by a pool in a dry river. The girl was a bonga and the two fell in love. The girl brought him rice out of the bushes. Dukhu ate it and to test her love gave her his leavings. The girl ate them and they decided to get married. Dukhu asked her to take him to her parents so one day she led him into the pool and as he went in, the water never came above his ankles; and somehow they passed along a broad road until they came to the bonga girl's house and this was full of tigers and leopards and snakes. After they had had their dinner, she took him back and he knew that she was a bonga but still he could not give her up. After that they met each day at noon. Dukhu's brother's wife came to spy on him but though she went and watched every day she only saw him sitting alone and the bonga girl was invisible to her. But one day she saw him disappear into the pool and come out again. Dukhu's father decided to find out who had made his son disappear and so he baled the water out. At the bottom lay a great fish, for the bonga girl had turned into it. Dukhu's father killed the fish and cut it up but when the pieces were put in a pot to boil, out of the pot jumped the bonga girl. The boy and girl were then married but the bonga girl warned her husband never to strike her on the head. One day the boy did so and the bonga girl taking her child with her left the house and was seen no more.

The bonga girl
In a spring by a mango tree there lived a bonga girl. She fell in love with a
boy and took the guise of his elder brother's wife. The boy asked her why
she was alone in the jungle. She replied that she had words to say to him.
'What is it,' said the boy, 'that you could not say it in our house?' 'Little
one,' she said, 'today my mind has gone out to you, to talk and laugh.'
'But if my brother finds us, he will be angry.' 'Your brother need not
know.' So the boy said, 'Let us do it quickly' and they made the matter
round. After that, they spent the whole day flirting and dallying and at
night the boy drove in the buffaloes. The girl went ahead and the boy did
not know she was a bonga. In this way they met for a year. One night the
girl woke him and took him to the rock by the mango and a little later he
was back in his house. In the morning he said to his sister-in-law, 'Where
did you take me last night?' The girl said, 'Nowhere'. Then the boy said,
'A girl like my sister-in-law took me to the rock'. That night the girl and
her husband lay awake and when the bonga girl came, the boy called.
They lit a lamp but the girl was gone. Then the bonga girl came again and
said, 'Today you must have told them.' The boy said, 'You have never told
me who you are.' The noise of their talking roused his father but when he
lit a lamp the girl was gone. Then they left the lamp burning and the girl
came no more. Next day the girl changed to another girl and lured the
boy with her singing. They began to talk and flirt. Then the girl said, 'You
do not know me, friend? It was I who came to you in the night.' The boy
said, 'Why have you deceived me? Why have you gone about as my
sister-in-law? Who are you?' Then they stayed together and though the
night came up, they still stayed on. The girl took him to her bonga house
and the buffaloes went home alone. In the morning the boy returned, told
no one and left the country.

The young man and the bonga girl
One night a young man was driving home his buffaloes. He saw a girl
standing by a pipal tree. The girl was a bonga girl who had been expelled
from a man and fastened by thorns to the tree. The young man did not like
to leave her so he told her to go with him to his house. He freed her from
the thorns and they went to his house. That night his parents gave her a
mat and the girl slept apart. The next morning, she rose early, collected
the dung from the cowshed, swept the courtyard and went and fetched the
water. The boy's mother was delighted and they decided to keep her as
the boy's wife. That night the two slept on the same cot and made their
minds one.

THE HILL OF FLUTES

Sometime later the girl said to the boy, 'We are now husband and wife. We are here not for a day but forever. If we ever quarrel, you may beat me with a stick and strike me with your fists but there is one thing you must never do. You must never trample on me or kick me either with your toes or with the sole of your foot. If you kick me, I shall leave you.' When the month of November came, the boy put some vermilion on a flower and put it in her hair and in a year they had a child. The girl settled down and the family grew rich. They had another child. One day the boy drank rice-beer and then in fun began to quarrel with her and gave her a kick. The girl wept bitterly and upbraided him, 'I told you you must never touch me with your foot. I am taking the two children. I am leaving you.' Then she left the house. The boy's father pleaded with her but she said, 'Your son did not listen. He has sent me away.' When she reached the middle of the field, she and the two children burst into flames and vanished in a flash. When the others saw it they were full of fear for they thought she might have eaten them but the young man was overwhelmed with grief. A little later the family grew poor and were never rich again.

The music master
In a certain village lived a Banam Raja or music master. He had a fiddle shaped from a coconut and every evening he played upon it. There was no one in the whole countryside who could play the fiddle or sing like him and he would go on playing long into the night. A bonga girl was fascinated with his singing and every day when he played she came dancing to listen. As she came each day the two talked together and gradually became friends. The bonga girl sang songs of the bonga land and taught the music master all her music. One day when the music master had lost his fear of bongas, the girl suggested she should marry him, but the music master did not agree as he already had a wife. But the bonga girl made love to him and said, 'It does not matter. You may keep me also. I will behave well with my co-wife. The people of my house have agreed to my marriage with you. Come with me today and see our house'. One day when the music master had agreed he went to the bonga land with the girl. The girl's father and mother knew of their coming and were waiting for them. They welcomed them fitly and washed their legs with water. After staying there a few days the music master took leave from his bonga wife and went back to the land of men. When he got back his wife asked him where he had been. At first he did not tell her but she pressed him and then he told her. When his wife heard she was very angry and one day in a fit of anger she threw his fiddle in the manure pit. That evening the notes of

282

the fiddle came up from the pit as if a man was singing and playing. When the music master's wife heard it she was filled with amazement and knew that her husband was in fact a friend of the bongas. Then the woman began to ask him, 'What is the bonga land like? Is my co-wife ill-disposed towards me?' He replied, 'Why should she be cross with you? She married me knowing you were there. If there is any ill-feeling, it is on your side'. When he gave her this reply his wife wanted to know more of the bonga land and the two talked together. 'What is the bonga land like?' 'The same as this.' 'What do they eat and drink?' 'As we do.' 'Do they have dal and rice?' 'They take it from ours.' 'How do they differ from us?' 'Hardly at all. The two lands are the same. There is no difference in fields. The men are short and both men and women have long hair. Most of the men have top-knots. They wear their clothes like us. They sleep on the floor. Snakes are their stools but the snakes do nothing to them. The feet of bonga boys and girls face backwards. When you go into their land for the first time it is like going through a cave or a crack. When you go through the hole or crack it feels like the land of men. Bonga girls come and bathe in the tanks and pools in the land of men.'

The wife of the music master had a great wish to see the bonga country. So one day he took her there and the bongas showed her every kindness.

A bad woman

In a certain place there lived a man and his wife. The husband was always doing good and wished well of everyone. But his wife was always behaving badly. Since the husband was good, everyone liked him. If strangers came to the house he showed them every courtesy but when the woman saw his conduct she was always annoyed. The man and woman had a daughter. When the girl came of age they could not get a husband for her since no one cared to be the woman's son-in-law. One day, the girl's father tied up some food and set out in search of a husband. He had not gone far when he met a jugi. The old man told the jugi he had come in search of a son-in-law. The jugi looked at his book and said, 'Today the omens are not good. Go back home and start tomorrow at cock crow. The man you meet first will be your son-in-law.' The old man did as the jugi said and returned to his home. The next day he again went out at cock crow and after going a little distance met a youth covered with itches. The old man called him son-in-law and brought him home. When his wife saw the son-in-law, she was angry and welcomed him rudely. A few days later, the old man and his wife died and from that day the boy's appearance changed and his full beauty came.

Now the husband was a bonga boy who had taken another shape for blinding men but neither the girl nor anyone knew he was a bonga. The girl had a younger brother and her husband said to her, 'As your parents are now no more we are like orphans. Let your brother go anywhere he likes but never to the place where your parents are buried'. One day the boy chanced to visit their place of burial. Close to the spot was a pool and the boy saw some bongas bring an old man on a litter and after washing him carefully put him back on it and return. A little later, he saw the bongas bringing a bound woman and beating her. They set her down in the water and still beating her they took her away. When the young boy returned home he told his elder sister all that he had seen and his sister told her husband. Then her husband said, 'The old man and woman he has seen are not others but your mother and father. That is why I told you not to let him go where your parents are buried. Since your father was a good man he is now in happiness and since your mother behaved ill on earth she is now in trouble. Your father brought me in but your mother did not like me.' When the girl heard his words she was sad at heart and asked him how he knew that the two were her parents. Then her husband replied, 'I am the master of all the ants, flies and animals. So why should I not know? That was why I told you not to let him go there.' Then the girl knew that her husband was not a man but a bonga. And when he saw she knew, the bonga vanished and went to the bonga land.

The husband of the bonga girl

There was a river and in the river was a bonga pool. Bonga girls used to go and bathe in it and once when a boy was grazing his buffaloes, they took him away. Near the pool was a village and one day a village boy saw the bonga girls bathing. The boy was dazzled with their beauty and made up his mind to drag one to his house. So day after day he went and watched them. One day the girls had taken off their clothes and in a carefree way were bathing naked in the pool. The boy seized the clothes of a girl and when their bathing was finished all save one dressed and went away. As the girl had lost her clothes she could not return to the bonga country and for days she wandered in the land of men. She borrowed clothes from a Santal girl and went about like a Santal. She made friends with Santal girls as they went for leaves and from going with them she at last discovered which boy it was who had stolen her clothes. When the bonga girl had traced her clothes she went day and night to the boy to ask him for them. From talking together the two became flower friends and fell in love but the boy refused to give the clothes to her. One day he said to the girl, 'If you will marry me I will give you the clothes, but otherwise I will not give them to you.' Without her bonga clothes the girl could do nothing for all her power was in them. As the girl was helpless she replied, 'I am willing to marry you but you must never make me clean the cow-shed and when we quarrel do not kick me.' The boy said, 'Let it be as you wish.' The two were married and after living as man and wife they had a child. One evening in the cold weather all the women were warming themselves at a fire when the bonga girl burnt her child. The child's father kicked her and in a trice, the bonga girl began to glow with light and vanished in a flame.

The girl with the long arm

There was a Raja with a son. When the boy grew up the Raja arranged his marriage and on the wedding day the bridegroom's party set out with the noise of bands and drums. At the bride's house there was great joy and when the feast was over the bride and bridegroom mounted the same litter and set out on the journey home. As they went along, the litter bearers grew tired, and after a while they put the litter down by a spring in which a bonga girl was living and they themselves went off. When the litter bearers had gone, the bonga girl came out of the spring, pulled the bride from the litter and put on all her things. Then she entered the litter and seated herself by the boy. An hour later the bearers returned and lifting up the litter they again started for home. When they reached the house they took the bride out with great joy and after feasting, each went away. No one knew who the bride was as all of them thought she was the Raja's new daughter-in-law. The bridegroom also did not know and the two lived together and presently had a child.

One day when everyone was out at work, only the girl was at home and a young boy came to the house to borrow some tobacco. The girl was sitting in the courtyard feeding her baby and from where she was, she stretched a hand to a shelf inside the house and gave the boy tobacco. The boy saw her do it and when he returned he said, 'What can she be? From right inside in the courtyard, she put a hand inside the house and reached a shelf. How long her arm is!' When the villagers heard this they began to wonder. Another day the girl was treading the pounder and her baby was asleep in the courtyard. That day all the people of the house had taken the cows to rest at midday and a cow came towards the child. The girl put out her hand from where she was standing. Her hand went out into the courtyard and she said, 'Hey cow, mind you don't trample on my baby.' At this, everyone was frightened and said, 'She is not a human being.' So they dug a well and pushed her down it hurriedly and heaped the earth above her.

The boy and the bonga girl

In a village there lived a young married boy. His father had buffaloes and every day the boy took them to graze by the river and scrubbed them in a pool. Sometimes he also grazed them at night. By the pool was a small patch of forest and on its edge was a great mahua tree with spreading branches.

One day at noon he took the buffaloes to the pool for washing. As he came to it he saw eight or nine naked girls. They had put their clothes on the bank and were bathing in the water. When they saw the boy they scrambled out and rushed to get their clothes, looking glasses, combs and hair pins and vanished in a flash.

Now the boy had set his mind on meeting the girls and wanted to take one of them. One day he left the buffaloes on the high land by the river and going to the pool before noon he hid in the bushes. He hid so well that from outside no one could see him. At noon, the bonga girls again came down to bathe. They took off all their clothes and put with them their combs and looking glasses. Then they went into the water to bathe. In the water they played and disported themselves and none of them knew the boy was hiding. When the boy saw they were busy bathing he dashed out of the bushes and collected up the clothes, looking glass, comb and bun of false hair of one of the bonga girls. As he did so, the bonga girls saw him, scrambled out of the water, gathered up their clothes and were gone in a flash. But the girl whose clothes the boy had taken stayed as she was. The girl asked him for her clothes but the boy did not give them to her for he knew that the bonga power lay in her mirror. Presently he gave her the clothes and made her wear them but the looking-glass he kept back and did not give her. The bonga girl besought him and besought him but he did not give her the looking-glass. Then the boy said to her, 'I am going to keep you.' And he took her to his house. The bonga girl was very lovely but the boy told no one that she was a bonga. After that they lived together as man and wife. The boy put the mirror in a little box, nailed it down and put it in a chest.

As they lived together they had two sons. But the husband still did not tell anyone that the girl was a bonga. The bonga girl entreated him continually for her looking-glass but the boy never gave it. Many years went by but whenever the two were alone the bonga girl kept asking. The boy grew tired of being pestered and thought, 'Many days have passed. She is the mother of two children. Perhaps she will not go back now.' But still he had some doubt. At last when he was tired of all her asking he said to her one day, 'Very well, I will give it back to you.' He opened the box and gave the looking-glass to her. No sooner had the bonga girl received it than she vanished in a flash and was never seen again. The boy was full of grief but though their two sons stayed with him he never met her again.

Bonga dancing

There was a cowherd boy who used to graze his buffaloes all alone. He had a flute and from time to time played sweetly on it. There were two bonga girls and when they heard the flute they lost their hearts. One day they went to him in human form and the three of them laughed and joked together. The next day the two girls went again and said to him, 'You have seduced us with your flute. We have come to make you our bridegroom.'

The boy saw that the girls were not human girls but bongas. So when he said he would not keep them, they spirited him away. They took him to their country and made him sit on a stool of snakes. Before he sat down he was full of fear but nothing happened and gradually he became accustomed to it and minded it no more.

One day the two girls took the boy to a lagre dance. Only bonga boys and girls were dancing and at the dancing ground he found Pargana bonga. Pargana bonga was taller than the others and as the dance went on he sat on a large coiled-up snake. When the two girls and the boy arrived Pargana bonga said, 'Who is this?' and the two girls replied, 'He is our husband.' Then the bonga boys took him as a friend. They danced with fine and lovely skill and the girls sang against the boys. Through staying with them the boy learnt all the ways of bonga singing and drumming.

One day the boy had a longing for his old land. The two girls made him ready and knotted in his waist some flat rice, sugar and cakes. But when he reached home and undid them, he found only leaves, river scum and cow-dung. After that the boy was never spirited away but whenever he took the drum, he made the dance go as it had never gone before.

The cowherd and the bonga girl

There were seven brothers and the youngest was a cowherd. He grew friendly with a bonga girl and one day she said to him, 'I will not let you go. We will stay together.' The boy said, 'I will stay but if I do not take the cows and buffaloes back who will do it?' Then the bonga girl said, 'Take them but return at once or I will turn into a snake and kill you. And leave your flute and fiddle with me as a pledge.' The boy reached home and said, 'A bonga girl has kept my flute and fiddle.' 'Where?' 'In that stone cave.' Then his father went to the cave and sang:

433
Shall I call you daughter-in-law?
What shall I call you?
Give me the boy's flute
Give me back his fiddle.

But the bonga girl said, 'Father, send your son himself.' The father went home and told his wife. Then his wife came and sang:

434
Shall I call you daughter-in-law?
Or what shall I call you?
Give me the boy's flute
Give me back his fiddle.

But the bonga girl said, 'Send your son.' After that the elder brother went and after him the six brothers and all sang to her. Then the youngest said to them, 'None of you have brought the flute and fiddle. Now she will come as a snake and bite me.'

One night when all the brothers were asleep, the bonga girl came rustling like a snake. The boy remembered and began to sing:

435
Get up, father, get up
The cobra is approaching.

But his father lay still. Then he called to his mother:

436
Get up, mother, get up
The cobra is approaching.

But she also did not stir. Then he spoke to the eldest brother but he did not hear. Then he called to all the six brothers but none of them moved. When all hope was gone, the boy seized a knife. The snake came straight into the house and caught him in its folds. But still no one heard and the snake began to swallow him. As it swallowed the boy cut its belly with the knife and when he had cut all of it the snake died. In the morning, the brothers woke and the boy showed the dead snake to them. He said, 'Father, it was the bonga girl. She came like a snake. I called and called you but none of you heard me and none of you came.'

CHAPTER XVIII

Woman as Witch

I THE CAUSES OF DISEASE

Once a Santal has a wife and children, his main ambition is to be happy in his family. Such a state depends on numerous factors – on mutual consideration by husband and wife, on willing co-operation in the day's work, on filial affection and respect, on non-intervention by bongas, on kindliness within the tribe. But even more important than any of these things is physical well-being. Free from sickness, Santals have poise, buoyancy, and a quite extraordinary zest for life. An air of exhilaration surrounds all that they do. They live because they want to live. Sap their health and the zest for living weakens. There is something abnormal, against life, in being ill. A fraction of disease, they feel, may just conceivably be 'natural' but the greater part involves hostility – a malevolent intrusion by harmful bongas, a callous neutrality by their bonga guardians, a will to harm them by other Santals. To enjoy happiness it is necessary to be well; to be well it is even more necessary to be happy.

When a person falls ill, conceptions such as these determine his treatment. The first step is to summon a guru or physician in the hope that the illness is only physical. The guru takes the patient's pulse, identifies the disease and describes the herbs to be gathered and applied. These are often quite successful and if within a week the patient is well, the bongas are absolved and only the body is blamed. If the illness persists and the herbs achieve little, the suspicion grows that other forces are at work and the guru makes way for the ojha or medicine-man.

This healer differs from a guru in that besides knowing medicines, he is also on special terms with bongas. He possesses a saket or tutelary spirit of his own through whose offices he can sometimes remove the cause of illness. When he meets the patient, he begins by taking his pulse. From this he infers which bonga is at fault and at once applies a mantra or charm. If this is successful, the sick person rallies and gets well. If it fails, the ojha resorts to a second expedient and proceeds to divine the cause of sickness by a method called sunum bonga. This process of divination is one of the most expert tasks in Santal life. The ojha gets ready some mustard oil and water and begins by taking two sal leaves. He creases the leaves and intensifies their markings. After that he dips a finger and marks each section with a drop of oil, declaring as he does so, which mark will stand for natural causes, which for bongas, and which for ancestors and allotting yet another mark for witches. When all the marks have been put, the ojha touches them with his finger and conjures the oil to declare the cause of illness. He then puts the other leaf on top and presses and rubs the two together, conjuring the leaves also to divine the cause. Finally, he removes the covering leaf and examines the disposition of the oil. According as the oil has run, the ojha announces the cause.

If the illness is due to natural causes, medicines are once again tried while if an ancestor is responsible, a sacrifice is performed. In Kusma, the mother of Ranjit Hembrom began to have fits. Sunum bonga was done and it then transpired that for three years Ranjit had omitted to make the usual offerings at Sohrae. Ranjit delayed no longer, the sacrifice was done and his mother recovered.

If a bonga is at fault, the ojha takes a little rice, sets it on the leaf, touches it with the patient's left hand and then runs it through his fingers. He then goes out to a field behind the house, scratches his thigh and mingles the blood with the rice. He then locates the bonga and scatters the rice round him, saying, 'Bonga, you have attached yourself to this Santal. Today I have caught you like a fish or a crab. Leave him from now on. May all disease and sickness go. Ease his pain and may he recover like spring water. You are my Thakur and father.' After that he scatters rice for the bongas of the village boundaries saying, 'Gosae, now you are here, you are in the stumps and roots, you are in the water, among the creepers, those who can walk come here, those who cannot, favour us from afar.' After invoking these bongas, he prescribes a medicine and gives it to the patient.

If the conjuration of a bonga and the taking of medicine still have no effect, the ojha is asked to vow an animal to his saket or tutelary bonga and beseech him to cure the patient. If the patient recovers, the sacrifice is performed. The wife of Bijai Hembrom was collecting mahua flowers in Dhamna when a splinter from a snake's bone ran into her finger. The place festered, blood poisoning set in and for five days she lay unconscious. When an ojha was called, Bijai at once promised to provide the ojha's saket bonga with a goat if his wife recovered. The ojha thereupon recited some charms, gave the woman medicine and conjured his bonga to dispel the sickness. A little later the poison dispersed and the woman recovered.

When she was fully well, Bijai sent the ojha a goat and two pigeons for offering to the bonga and also paid him the sum of five rupees for his services.

If the disease is an epidemic or disom duk, the headman must intervene and promise the Five-Six a Mak' More festival. If none of these agencies is diagnosed, there remains a sinister possibility – that witchcraft is at fault, that the disease is due to a conflict with a female member of the family or of the village and that the whole relationship between the sexes is somehow out of gear.

2 WITCHES AND THEIR POWERS

We have seen how in spite of romantic relations before marriage and later tenderness in the home, woman is from time to time regarded as imbued with strange mysterious powers. She cannot for example climb a roof because the nearness of her sex may pollute the bongas. For the same reason, she must keep herself away from the trunks of trees in the sacred grove. In copulation the vagina is sometimes described as 'like a bonga'. The whole process of attraction – the power of girls to inflame passion, to subdue boys to their will – makes them seem from time to time a source of danger. Even in the happiest of households a woman's will may sometimes conflict with a man's and on account of her feminine character she may appear intractable to masculine treatment. When, therefore, the basis of ordinary life is threatened by illness, a woman's pique is at times held to be the cause and it is perhaps significant that in the following myth, the origin of witchcraft is ascribed to tensions in the family.

'One day the village men assembled. "We are men," they said. "Why are we disobeyed? If we say a word or two to women, they reply with twenty words of anger. We can bear this state no longer." Then they said, "Let us go to Maran Buru and learn an art so that these women will respect us more." At midnight they met in the forest and called to Maran Buru. "Grandfather," they said, "many men are so harassed that they have come to see you." Maran Buru came to them. "What is troubling you, grandchildren?" he said. Then they told him their trouble and implored him to teach them how to keep their womenfolk in order. "What can I teach you?" asked Maran Buru. "Mark these leaves with your blood." Hearing this they were frightened and said, "We will come tomorrow to give you our blood and learn the art." Then they went away. But the women were hidden and had heard everything. Then the women said, "Look at these men. From before they pestered us and were always after us like dogs.

Now we are old they think us good for nothing. They have decided to kill us. Let us see who kills whom." When the men reached home, their women welcomed them so lovingly that they thought, "When they are good to us like this, what need is there of controlling them any further?" Next day the women gave the men their rice and in the evening plied them with rice-beer. When the men were drunk, the women put on dhotis and turbans and sticking some goat's hair on their upper lips, they went to Maran Buru. "Grandfather, come quickly," they said, "Our women are troubling us day and night." Maran Buru came and the women said, "Give us the leaves. We will mark them with our blood and rid ourselves for ever from this pest." Maran Buru brought out the sal leaves. Then the women sat on mats and marked their husbands' signs with their blood. Maran Buru then taught them the incantations and gave them the power of eating men. Next day the men woke up and found that the women were still far from mild. "Let us go," they said. "Whatever Maran Buru says, we will learn the art." At night they went to the forest and called on Maran Buru. "Grandfather, the women are too much for us. Teach us," they said. When Maran Buru heard them, he said, "But I have given you the art once. Do you want to learn it again?" Then the men said, "When did you teach us? Since we came that day, we have not been to see you." Then Maran Buru replied, "But I have certainly instructed you. Look at your blood marks." The men saw the leaves and said, "The marks are ours but we did not give them. Who gave them we do not know." Then Maran Buru put his hands to his cheeks and divined what had happened. "The women have treated me like a child," he said. Then in anger he said to the men, "Give me your marks and we will see how these women have tricked us." The men marked the leaves and Maran Buru made them expert in the art of witchfinding. But despite this skill, women always get the better of men.'

This view of sickness as in some way connected both with conflicts in the family and with the mysteries of sex is illustrated in the various customs which surround a witch's training. Her power to be a witch begins at puberty and in many cases a girl is seduced into learning the art as soon as she starts to menstruate. An old woman dilates to her on the powers that witchcraft will confer. She tempts the girl to hear the witches' songs. She tells her not to be afraid. She mesmerises her with tales of other witches. The girl listens with fascinated horror and presently, she yields. When she has consented to listen, the witch starts to sing the songs. These are very difficult to obtain but I was able to secure two examples from Santal men who had gone with witches in their youth.

437

I have cut the plaintain grove
I have taken off my clothes
I have learnt from my mother-in-law
How to eat my husband
On the hills the wind blows
I have cut the thatching grass
I have grown weary
Weary of eating rice.

438

The weapons are ready
The axe glitters
Over the smooth verandah
The wasps are swarming
O Bagru, leave us
Kill the young servants
Kill the girls, the boys.

Once a girl has heard such songs, she must either become a witch or die.

After the songs have been heard, the next stage is the introduction to the bongas themselves, for a witch must not only be married to a bonga but must learn from him the art of killing. This is sometimes a dangerous interlude since if the bonga husband does not like his bride he may sometimes kill her instead.

In Jhimoli Ragda Hansdak' was grazing his buffaloes at night when he heard a child crying. He hid himself and from where he crouched he saw a woman with a little girl beneath a cotton tree. The woman was calling out to a bonga to come down and marry the child. The bonga was unwilling but at last he came, paid twenty five rupees as bride-price and took the child. When Ragda heard the witch's voice he recognised her as his own wife and the child as his niece. A few days later, Ragda's niece fell ill and since the bonga had never wanted to marry her, there was little hope and very soon she died.

Finally a young witch must qualify for full membership by 'eating' one of her own family. For this purpose she herself either assists in the 'killing' or shares in the flesh after the 'killing' has been done.

Rengta Kisku of Dumdumi was attacked and mauled by two bears. A jan guru or witch-doctor was consulted and declared that Rengta's sister was under training as a witch with her husband's elder sister. To complete her course, they had marked down Rengta for killing and his sister had attacked him as a bear in order to eat his flesh. The two girls were severely beaten and Rengta's sister then admitted that she had tried to 'eat' her brother and had become a bear for doing so.

In Rajpora, the little daughter of Juna Hembrom was selected by her two aunts for training as a witch. They decided that the girl must 'eat' her own father and one day as Juna was going out to plough, the two women took the girl with them and felled him with the blunt end of an axe. The women then took out his liver and cooked and ate it behind a house. The little girl did not take her share but hid it under a stone. A little later her father fell ill and in remorse the girl told her grandmother all that they had done. A jan guru who was consulted confirmed what the girl had said and by applying special medicine Juna was saved.

Once a girl has been initiated, she must observe the discipline of witches and her first duty is to assist at the ritual and attend the witches' gatherings. These assemblies sometimes take place every night but more usually on Saturdays or Sundays or at even longer intervals. A godet bonga is deputed to summon the members. He goes through the village carrying a black hen and as soon as the witches hear it they rise and hurry to their posts. Sometimes another bonga is sent to lull the village into a trance so that no one may detect the women at their revels. The place for meeting is either the manjhithan, the sacred grove, a lonely dale, a great tree, the end of the village or a cross road. As the witches leave their houses, they strip themselves naked and put on girdles of brooms. Each leaves a broom on her bed and her bonga familiar transforms it into a temporary image of herself.

When the company has assembled, they honour Pargana bonga and then proceed to business. Sometimes they mount a tree and are then transported to a place where seeds of sickness can be found. Sometimes they copulate with their bonga husbands or dance in the sacred grove, the brooms jerking and swinging on their buttocks. Two village boys are made to act as drummers and a folk-tale records how two boys grew fond of the witches' company and every night performed this service for them – the witches dancing the Sohrae and lagre dances from the manjhithan down to the grove and the boys drumming and dancing naked before them. But their most important task is to select persons for 'eating' and decide how best to kill them.

When a person has been chosen, there are five ways of killing him. The first and most immediately lethal is to 'extract' the lungs, liver or heart and then to 'cook' and 'eat' them. This method is generally favoured but is fringed with certain conditions. Only certain persons can be ended in this manner and then only by the most strict observance of certain rites.

The first assumption is that although the witch herself may do the killing and herself 'eat' the victim, she can only do so by means of powers given to her by the bongas. She must therefore first take a bonga's permission before she starts her murderous work and while the bonga in question need not be Manjhi Haram or Pargana bonga, at least one bonga approved by Pargana bonga must consent to the act. If Pargana bonga demurs, the witches sometimes abuse him and make him kiss their privates.

In Rajdah Doman Marandi chanced to offend the wife of his eldest son. The woman was a witch and in consultation with two others, she decided to kill and 'eat' him. But they had first to secure the bongas' approval. One night therefore they entered Doman's house, lifted him on his cot and carried him to the manjhithan. There they asked Manjhi Haram to approve the 'eating'. Manjhi Haram declined so they carried him to the sacred grove. There also Pargana bonga refused but advised them to consult the ato or village bonga in the village pool. The women again picked up the cot and with Doman still asleep carried him to the pool and there the ato bonga gave them permission. After that they took him to the end of the village and between a jack fruit and a mango they 'cut out' his heart.

A second and equally important condition is that at least one member of the victim's family must herself be a witch. In most cases the witch, already in the family, does the killing but if she does not actually strike the victim she must assist at the operation either by touching him with her hands or with a knife or by pointing him out with her fingers.

In Jordiha a band of witches took Barka Tudu to the sacred grove. There they tied a rope round his neck and marched him round the grove till he fainted. His daughter who was one of the witches then 'killed' and 'ate' him. Sometime later Barka fell ill and when the villagers accused his daughter of 'eating' him, she confessed that she had done so at the instance of her mother.

Hopa Murmu of Boha was in love with a girl who was a witch. He himself was a witches' boy and used to play the drum when the witches danced. As he was married to another girl, the witch said 'I will kill her.' With Hopa's aid the witch and a friend split open the chest of Hopa's wife and 'took out' her liver, lungs and heart. They cooked them in flour, 'ate' them and the next day the girl died.

If no member of the inner family or household is a witch, the killing is postponed until a girl in the family has been seduced and converted into one.

Mongla Soren of Mohonpur had two daughters aged ten and eight.

Two old women and two young girls of the village were witches and one day they proposed to 'eat' the younger of the two daughters. Since there was no witch in the family, they first seduced the elder daughter and having made her into a witch they induced her to touch her sister. The girl did so, the women 'extracted' her heart, cooked it in a pot and a little later the girl died. The women then demanded Mongla himself but the girl refused to touch her father and on this the witches made her ill. As she lay on her cot, she told her father everything, the pargana of Katikund was consulted and the witches were warned that they would be beaten to death unless they cured the girl. A little later the girl recovered.

In Amtala, there were two witches – the wife of Mongla Murmu's nephew and a woman of the village. They decided they must eat either Mongla or his brother, Chotu Ramu Murmu, but no one in the family was a witch. They decided therefore that Mongla's daughter must be converted and one day they took her to the jungle. At first the girl refused to help but the two women then called a tiger, mounted the girl on it, caught her by the legs and threatened to kill her if she did not surrender one of the two men. On this the girl agreed, the two women went to her house and there the girl folded her hands and pointed at her father.

When bonga approval has been gained and a witch secured in the family itself, the next stage is the 'extraction' of the vital organs. This need not necessarily be done at night but the family witch must herself be present. Sometimes the heart only is 'extracted' and at other times only the liver or lungs. When the viscera have been taken out, the wound is closed but sometimes other objects are inserted in their place.

In Kukurtopa, Keso Murmu combined the offices of headman and village priest. The Sohrae festival came round and on the night before it was due to start, Keso suddenly felt severe pains in his belly. The pains subsided and the next morning he performed the sacrifices. But a few hours later he again fell ill and everyone thought he would die. His son went to call his uncle and as he was telling him, his aunt cried out, 'Why should not Keso have a pain? He has never paid me my fee as matchmaker?' Everyone was alarmed when they heard her say this. The whole village met and the woman was told to cure Keso at once. She took some oil, massaged Keso's belly and the pains eased. A little later Keso defecated and a tuber cut flat on both its sides was found in the stool.

In Saharghati, the daughter of Mongal Soren 'opened' her father's chest and belly, took out his lungs and liver and put a pestle and datauni back in their place. When her father fell ill the girl confessed she had done this and was a witch.

When the liver, lungs or heart have been 'extracted', they are cooked with rice, a portion is offered to the bongas and the rest is then eaten by the witches. If the entire organ is completely consumed the victim's soul or jivi can never return, the man is doomed and nothing can now save him. If however only a part of the organ is extracted or if a portion of it escapes the eating, the jivi can sometimes be regrafted onto his body, and the man saved.

In the case from Amtala, which I have already described, Mongla Murmu's daughter first pointed to her father and her cousin's wife, then 'opened' the man's chest and extracted a piece of his heart. The two women took it to the forest, cooked it in a new pot with sun-dried rice and ate it. As they cooked they invoked three bongas – Ger Naran, Indi Naran and Pahar Nangin and offerings of the pudding were made to them. They gave the girl a share but she hid it under a stone. Some days later Mongla fell ill and it was only after his daughter had confessed and the three bongas had been appeased that he at last recovered. If all his heart had been 'extracted' or if all of it had been 'eaten', Mongla would have died.

In the case from Rajdah in which Doman Marandi was taken on a cot and operated on at the end of the village, the three witches 'took out' his heart, cooked it with some rice, danced round the hearth and finally ate the pudding. They did not however completely eat it and the pot with its leavings was put back in a house. After that they carried Doman home and put him in his usual place. The next morning when Doman woke up he did not notice any pain but was vaguely frightened and disturbed. He suspected that witches had been tampering with him and when the villagers went to consult a jan guru or witch-doctor about another case, he went with them and told the jan guru what had happened. The jan guru said that witches had 'eaten' his heart, and that his son's wife was responsible. In this case Doman ultimately recovered but only because a part of his heart had not been eaten.

After the victim's organs have been 'eaten', it is only a question of time before he falls ill. The witches usually select a date for his death and some days earlier the fatal sickness starts. Sometimes they kill him almost immediately while at other times they allow a month or two to elapse and then the crisis comes.

In the case from Rajdah, nothing happened for several weeks. In September, Doman's heart was 'eaten' but his death was settled for the full moon day in January. It was not until two months had gone by that he fell ill.

When the sickness starts, only the prompt discovery of the cause and the chance that a part of the organ has escaped consumption can prevent the witch from accomplishing her object.

If a witch fails to secure the approval of Manjhi Haram or Pargana bonga or if no one in the victim's family can be suborned, the method of 'eating' has necessarily to be abandoned and the woman is compelled to employ one of four other methods.

These differ from the first in that the witch herself is no longer the agent of murder and the victim does not necessarily belong to her family. She is merely its instigator and the work of destruction is done by a bonga instead.

The first method is when a bonga is himself the death-dealing agent and afflicts the victim with disease. In an account by Bompas, a witch summons a bonga and says, 'Brother-in-law Ramjit, there is something that you must do for me; my nephew is ill; he must die on such and such a day; that day I must see the smoke of his funeral pyre; but you must save me from the witch-finder'. On the day before that fixed by the witch, the invalid became unconscious and was at the point of death.

The second method is for the bonga not to do the killing himself but to provide a death-dealing agent in his place. Bompas, for example, has described how a witch was incensed by her brother-in-law and summoned a bonga from a pool. 'When the woman saw him her tongue flickered in and out like a snake's and she made a hissing noise, such as a crab makes. Then the woman began, "Dharmal Chandi, I have a request which you must promise to grant". And when the bonga had promised she proceeded, "You must have my brother-in-law killed by a tiger the day after to-morrow" ... and the bonga promised to do what she asked and disappeared.'

In Bewa the son of Jagan Tudu was bitten by a dog. Next night while he was making water he felt his grandmother touch his chest. The following day he died saying she was a witch who had killed him through the dog.

Yet a third method is to localise a bonga in a stone and then to bury it in the house or cowshed of the victim. 'Such bongas,' says Kolean Haram, 'are called thapna bongas. They are of two kinds, one is a white stone, on which vermilion has been put and hair wound round; another is a silk cocoon with one end cut off and inside it a little of every kind of grain and a white stone marked with vermilion.' If anyone steps on the stone he steps on the bonga and is at once struck with disease or death.

Finally the seeds of sickness can be strewn in the village, buried in its lanes, or sprinkled in wells and hollow horns. These seeds are sometimes brought from the Kundli tank near Barhait. 'All the witches of the world come to it,' a Santal told me, 'and there is a place where they assemble. In this tank the seeds of sickness are to be found and the witches go there for getting their supplies. They put the seed in little earthen vessels or in the shells of water snails. For taking the seed away, they yoke rutting buffaloes to carts. When they wish to bring sickness to any country or village, they bury some of the seed at the end of the village street and at the manjhithan. Then when the time comes, the sickness from the buried seed spreads. The people and animals of the village feel pain and die.'

Once witchcraft is suspected, the village musters its energies. The headman begins by publicly warning all witches to desist from their work. After that, a number of freshly cut sal branches are set up by a stream. Each branch is made to stand for a particular household, a particular bonga or a particular woman. Some rice is scattered and Sin Cando is asked to make the guilty 'branch' dry up. Some hours later the branches are examined and if the leaves of one have withered, while the others are still fresh, the villagers believe that they are on the track of the witch. In some cases, only a single branch is set up – each leaf serving for a female member of the victim's family – while in other cases it is only these members who are tested by being given branches. When the leaves have suggested a verdict, the villagers approach a jan guru for confirmation. They do not voice their own suspicions but wait for the jan himself to disclose the name. The jan offers some rice to a number of bongas, blows on a shell, rings a bell and then goes into a trance. While he is in it, he describes the village of the patient, names the family members and at last declares whether a bonga or a witch is responsible for the sickness. If a witch is at fault, he then pronounces the fated name.

If this coincides with the verdict of the leaves, the woman is presumed to be a witch but before action is taken against her, a second jan guru is normally consulted. If a second, third or fourth jan guru differs, the matter remains inconclusive. The woman will still deny the charge and even if her relations accept the diagnosis, they are debarred from acting on it without a second guru's agreement. Moreover the woman herself may go to the jan guru, interrogate him and if necessary discredit his opinion. In Bordoha, the son of Dibia Hembrom fell ill. Witchcraft was diagnosed and the jan guru declared that the child's own mother had 'killed' and 'eaten' him. The woman indignantly denied the charge, took all the villagers back with her and demanded to know how the jan guru had reached his decision. The jan guru was unnerved by the woman's protests and, very unwisely for himself, changed his ground. He said that the child had not been 'eaten' but that the woman had induced a bonga to harm him.

The villagers were greatly enraged at this change of attitude, acquitted the woman and abused the jan guru so freely that he had to shift his practice to another part of the country.

Similarly the woman herself may have other jan gurus consulted and if these reject the first guru's reading, she is virtually absolved.

If, however, the second jan guru confirms the decision of the first, the diagnosis is usually regarded as conclusive and no matter how the woman protests, she is now treated as a proved witch. In Siankhuri, the wife of Chaitu Baske was diagnosed as a witch. She appealed to five jan gurus but all of them confirmed the diagnosis and after that there was no help.

Once a witch has been identified, the action taken depends on whether the victim is still alive or is already dead. If the victim is alive and quickly recovers, nothing more is done. The taint of witchcraft may remain but it is thought that either other witches have distorted the jan guru's diagnosis or the witch herself has thought better of it and of her own accord has cured the victim.

If the sickness continues, the victim's plight gives an intense urgency to the situation and the witch herself is made to intervene, confess her crime and take the necessary measures. These vary according as to whether the witch has 'eaten' her victim or has merely stricken him through a bonga.

In the case from Rajdah where Doman Marandi was 'eaten' the leading witch was the wife of his eldest son. When Doman's condition grew critical, he told his children that there was no more time to be lost. They therefore seized the woman, kicked her, beat her, threw her on the ground and jabbed her with a stick. The woman then confessed everything, named her co-witches and said that if some fowls, a pig, a pigeon, a sheep and a goat were sacrificed to certain bongas whom she named, Doman might still be saved. These sacrifices were done the same night but it grew to morning before Doman's jivi had been brought back. The witch said that they must wait till evening and that one of her co-witches must be made to help her. One of the two was then forced out of her house, given a thrashing and compelled to assist. That night the two witches took the villagers to the spot where the heart had been 'extracted'. When it was dark and they could scarcely be seen, one of them took off her clothes and climbed a tree. While she was in its branches a bird flew out. A great while later she came down, put on her clothes and the two went straight to Doman's house. There they went to the sick man and put on his chest a piece of fresh heart. They then asked an ojha to complete the cure. The ojha added some spices, put the piece of heart in Doman's mouth and told him to swallow it. He did so, went off to sleep, at midnight felt better and by the next day was cured.

In Rajpara, Juna Hembrom was 'eaten' by his two sisters and little daughter. The child told her grandmother that she had kept her own share under a stone and had not eaten it. A jan guru was consulted and on his advice a pigeon and frog were sacrificed, their hearts were mixed with spice and Juna ate them. Shortly afterwards he completely recovered.

If the sickness is due to a witch's action but she has not 'eaten' the victim similar steps are taken to appease the bongas.

In Siankhuri, a jan guru diagnosed that the wife of Chaitu Baske was a witch and that Chaitu's younger brother was ill because she had set up a bonga. When the villagers heard this, they beat the woman and Chaitu was made to pay five rupees and give a pig, a pigeon and a white fowl for sacrifice. When he did this, his brother recovered.

If a bonga has been buried by a witch, the first task is to locate its stone.

In Haripur, Geda Hembrom and his family were ill. Two jan gurus divined that some bongas had been buried in their house and by means of a divining rod they located the two stones. When the stones were dug up they were found to have been marked with vermilion and tied in human hair. Geda then took them to a field, sacrificed a sheep, a pig and three fowls and burnt the stones and hair. After that all his family got well.

If seeds of sickness have been planted, these also must be located and the usual methods are either to divine their presence by means of little rods or to beat the witch until she confesses.

In Gorkond, Hambro Hembrom caught smallpox and when his family consulted the jan guru, the latter named five women of the village as the witches responsible. The witches admitted that they had planted seeds of sickness and after they had pointed out the places, the villagers dug up some little earthen pots. The pots with the seeds were then burnt and the witches were made to sacrifice a pig, a goat, a sheep, a pigeon and a fowl outside the village.

In Jasaidih, an epidemic broke out among men and cattle. A jan guru diagnosed that 'poison' had been buried at the two ends of the village. The villagers dug the earth and discovered some snail shells. They took them out and threw them away and after that the attacks subsided. The jan guru also identified the witches and each of them was fined twenty five rupees and made to give a fowl, a pig and a goat.

If the victim dies, shortly after the diagnosis or is already dead when the witch is named, preventive action is obviously out of the question and all that can be done is to prevent a recurrence of the evil.

In many areas the family first vent their grief by giving the witch a beating and after that a village meeting is called and the woman is punished with a fine.

Suphal Murmu of Kalipathar accused his father's elder brother's wife of killing him by beating him on the chest. A jan guru confirmed that the woman was a witch but before anything could be done Suphal had died. His father wanted to kill the witch outright but the others advised him to be guided by the village. In the end the woman was fined thirty rupees and the money was paid by her brothers.

If the witch has been suspected for some time or the village doubts if of her own will she can now abandon the art, they proceed to disqualify her from further intercourse with bongas by causing her to drink a mixture of human excrement and urine. No bonga will ever go near excrement and accordingly a witch who has once been so polluted is deprived of all her maleficent powers.

In Sapdiha, the wife of Burhan Hembrom was neutralised by being forced to drink some human excrement and urine.

In Mahagama, cholera broke out and for some time four or five persons died each day. All the villagers became desperate and seeing no other remedy, they beat all the women in the village and made them drink human excreta. A little later the cholera stopped and since then there has never been an epidemic in the village.

If the villagers are disinclined to force the woman to take the mixture, they sometimes adopt more furtive methods.

In Bhuibhanga, the wife of Surai Murmu was a proved witch. Her husband consulted Chotu Ramu Murmu of Amtala who agreed to prepare a neutralising mixture. He got together specimens of excreta of as many animals as he could and also of various men and women. He then wrapped them in some sal leaves and kept them under a stone in the forest. After that he sacrificed a pig and five days later went naked to the spot. There he recovered the packet, pounded up the excreta, mixed it with a sond-hani root and gave it to Surai. Surai mixed it with his wife's food and since then all the bongas have completely boycotted her and no jan guru has ever diagnosed her as a witch.

Yet another recipe was employed when the wife of Anu Marandi in the Nonihat circle was found to be a witch. She was bluffed into giving a few drops of her own blood. A piece of hoof from a horse which had died on a Sunday was pounded up and the blood mixed with it. This was then dropped into some rice-beer and the woman drank it without knowing. This polluted her so completely that no bongas have ever helped her since.

If for any reason excrement is not administered and in spite of fining, the witch still continues her fell pursuits, the final resort is expulsion from the village. But I know of only three instances in which this happened.

CHAPTER XIX

The Annual Hunt

I PRELIMINARIES

When the hot weather arrives, Santals gather in enormous crowds for the purpose of a hunt. This hunt occurs wherever there are hills and throughout the Santal Parganas, each mountain or patch of jungle provokes a large assembly. The hunt is controlled by a dihri or hunt-master who decides the date of meeting, determines the route to be followed and presides at the evening gatherings.

When the date is announced, Santals from far and near come trooping in. They bring their night meal with them and camp beneath the trees. Since success in the chase depends on Pargana bonga, it is necessary to win the favour of his sister, the Rongo Ruji bonga. We have already seen that this bonga is obsessed with sex and accordingly a stone in the neighbourhood is treated as her 'head' and urine is passed upon it. All who attend the hunt should not have gone to any woman the day before. Similarly, no woman should have intercourse while the male members of her family are away. If a woman does so, it is thought that her husband or son will be killed by a bear or a leopard or will cut himself while hacking at a creeper.

Once the date is decided, the dihri takes careful precautions. His wife brings a brass vessel of water, puts it inside the house and twice a day examines it for signs of danger. Both she and the dihri sleep on the ground. Each remains celibate and each eats nothing except after dark. On the night previous to the hunt, the dihri brings a pair of sal twigs and puts them on the pot of water. Two lamps are placed beside them and early the next morning, he subjects the leaves to anxious examination. If they are fresh and green, the omen is good but if they are dried and shrivelled, the hunt is expected to fail. That night he and his wife again abstain from food and sleep apart.

The following morning, the dihri's wife ties her husband in some fibre bonds, passing a loose band round his arms and chest. The dihri does the same thing in return, hobbling her legs with one set and pinioning her arms with another. The woman then takes up a squatting posture near the door of the house. A pot of water is set before her and she passes the day watching the water and never stirring. If the water gets slightly dull, she knows that some small animals or birds have been killed but if some blood appears, it means that the hunt has killed a leopard, pig or bear. Once the water has clouded or turned to blood, she can end her vigil and break her fast. Until this happens, however, she must sit stolidly on for it is the strictness of her watch, the purity of her conduct, that determines success. If she rises before the water has changed, the hunt is doomed to failure. At Jhandaburu in 1943 when the hunt secured only seven hares, three peacocks and one jungle fowl, the dihri's wife saw only a slight cloudiness in the water but many Santals doubted whether she had watched the pot correctly and some of them declared that the smallness of the bag was due to her rising too early.

Once his wife is in position, the dihri goes at dawn to do the sacrifice. He reaches the customary spot and dons a cap of flabby leaves. This is assumed as a kind of protective disguise 'so that the hunters may not be seen and the animals will remain'. He then drives two arrows into the ground two feet apart, links them with cotton and makes a row of small white circles. At Jhandaburu, he sacrificed two pigeons and six chicks, gently sawing their throats on the upturned blade of a battle-axe. As he offered, he invoked the local bonga of Jhandaburu, the Rongo Ruji bonga and the various bongas of the mountain. Finally, a little hole was dug with a spear, the dihri cut the throat of a black chick, pushed its struggling trunk into the hole and rammed the earth down over it. He then fell back in a spasm like a stricken animal while four men pounced upon him and pretended to hack him with an axe. By thus mimicking the hunters' goal, he was believed to bring it appreciably nearer. After that, the dihri carefully put away his leaf cap and removed his fibre thongs. His uncle went aside, pricked his thigh and offered the tiny drops of blood to 'whatever bongas were in the other hills' and the dihri and his assistants then washed, cooked the chicks and pigeons and broke their fast.

Once the sacrifices are over, the hunt is free to start. The men who have come in from the surrounding country go off and soon a great line is moving through the hills. The line goes up with hardly any noise. There are no drums and only when an animal is sighted does the hunt break into shouts and yells. At Jhandaburu, while the hunt was moving up the slopes, there was a strange silence all the morning and it was only when the first beat was over and the men had worked down to a spring that shouting started.

While the hunt is covering certain hillsides, the dihri moves quietly over to a selected spot a few miles away. As he climbs, his progress is marked by the dull thudding of a tumdak'. This is the only drum which beats throughout the day and the hunters tell from its sound which spot the dihri has reached. When he arrives at the rendezvous, he again puts on his leaf cap and fibre pinions and neutralises a second area. The dawn ritual is once again gone through, more chicks are sacrificed and bongas of other places in the hills are appeased. The hunt then goes into the new tract and ends at evening by a stream.

As the hunters arrive, hot and jaded from their long journey through the forest, they go and wash, get together some firewood and prepare the night meal. Any birds or animals killed during the day are divided according to custom and soon there are lines of little fires glowing in the darkness. When the hunters have eaten, the night's proceedings start. The dihri collects some of the senior men, goes into session with them and commences to hear disputes and discuss the rules of sex. Others gather and soon there is a crowd squatting at his feet. At the same time, small arenas are made in other parts of the camp and a series of nude jokers commence to entertain the hunters.

2 THE HUNTING NIGHT'S ENTERTAINMENTS

For staging these performances, a special class of Santal is required. He is not, in origin, different from other tribesmen and in fact any member of any clan may assume this strange exacting role. Once however he has yielded to exhibitionism, he is dedicated to the Rongo Ruji bonga and must continue to serve her regardless of his private whims. He must not only attend the local hunt each year but must seek out other hunts at which to parade his nudity. Should he avoid a hunt, the Rongo Ruji bonga would feel herself insulted and would punish him with headaches. At the same time the part he plays is full of danger for his stark exposed sex must on no account be witnessed by a woman. If a woman chanced to view his organ and cursed it, he would become impotent for the remainder of his life. Although, therefore, the Rongo Ruji bonga approves of his role and delights in his gestures, the joker must reward her with a sacrifice every time he returns. He must make a small white circle, and touch it with his penis. After that he must dedicate a chick, have 'intercourse' with it and then cut its throat on an axe. Once in five years, an old goat is used and after the dancer has 'coupled' with it, the head is cut off and offered. Only in this way is his strange abnormal role protected and condoned.

When the arena is ready and the squatting Santals are full of quiet expectancy, the players begin their joking turns. Two men clad in flowing white skirts and playing flutes come strutting in and commence to move about the circle. A moment later comes a nude joker, moving behind them, leaping stiffly like a frog or gently skipping in their tracks. As he bounces round, he tosses his penis, jerking it sometimes at the buttocks of the leaders and sometimes in the faces of the audience.

When I saw the dance at Jhandaburu in 1943, two parties were oscillating in different portions of the camp. In one arena, the joker had smeared his body with clay and was prancing round, bouncing a hollow gourd on his buttocks. In the other, two leaders with flutes were followed by men with cymbals while a nude joker went romping round behind. As the leaders moved with light stiff jumps, they thrust their buttocks out and lunged with their penises. The clown went briskly round assaulting their haunches, pulling out his foreskin and tucking his penis in a cord. As he did so, he shouted 'Others have great big penises but mine is so little I tie it up with a string.' Once he seized a money bag like a string condom and put his penis in it. 'Others have money,' he said, 'and they keep it in a bag. I have no money so I keep my penis in it.' Presently a singer said, 'I have a lot of land but no cattle or ploughs.' 'Then use this plough,' the joker replied and 'coupled' with the ground. 'You have ploughed the land,' the singer said, 'but given me no seed.' 'I can give you twelve maunds of gram and sow it for you,' said the joker and again he showed his sex and jerked it freely. 'Look at this beautiful gram and how it has grown. No one is watching it but I am here to see it. Come and look at it, sister.' But the singer who was now a 'girl' refused and instead sent her 'husband', the other leader. 'Why are you sending your fool of a husband?', asked the joker. 'Give me the girl instead.' Then the 'girl' came and the joker made such violent lunges that the 'girl' lost her 'bun'. 'Give me back my bun,' she said, 'and you may take me for a month and a half.' 'Not unless I can have you for three months,' said the joker, 'will I give it to you back'; and in this frantic jesting manner, the skipping lumbering dance went on.

Side by side with these acts of 'music-hall' burlesque or during intervals between them, the skirted flute-players sing songs about sex, marked by bawdy humour, obscene extravagance or coarse ribaldry. They are not unlike English songs of the type of 'Eskimo Nell', 'The Good Ship Venus', 'Whizz-bang' and 'The Ball of Kirriemuir' and just as these songs have their appropriate place in the beery atmosphere of a rugger club, these forest songs cheer the hunters while they pass the night.

Certain songs are celebrations of the Rongo Ruji bonga and treat her with rough fantastic freedom.

439

In the Rongo Ruji's vulva
A porpoise is plunging
By the clitoris, the clitoris
A little shrimp is leaning
In the groove of thighs
A bearded fish goes in.

440

The vulva of a hen
With ragged hair
The vagina of a peacock
Big as an axle
Over the Rongo Ruji
The little vulva of a sow.

A few refer to bestiality and describe encounters with birds and animals.

441

With us is a blind mare
We shut her in the house by day
But at night we go to her.

442

I went for love
And sat among the fowls
A hen pecked my penis
And they chased me
With broken axes
To the back of the house.

Other songs associate the killing of animals with the sexual act itself.

443

The drums are sounding
Through the afternoon
O brother-in-law
I hear them and my cunt
Throbs and aches.

444

Boy, your elder brother
Went to the hunt
He has stabbed a rabbit
He has slain a peacock
How my vagina
Writhes and itches.

445

My friend went
To the hunt on the mountain
A tiger or a leopard
Are pouncing on him
At midnight my sex
Aches and aches.

446

Boy, your brother
Went to the Jhandaburu hunt
He killed a peacock
But they snatched the spoil
Boy, your brother
Went to the hunt
He slew a peacock
O elder brother
Come at midnight with the spoil.

Yet further songs poke fun at intercourse or celebrate the genitals, dangling them as it were before the crowd with brutal levity.

447

Like a pounder stands a cobra
The penis, girl, stands up
The vagina swells.

448

Under the tree, father
They are cooking a penis
But they never give it to me
When I tell my father
He draws his penis out
When I tell my mother
She opens wide her cunt.

449

He is wearing a straw rope
And a mat as a dhoti
O you white haired ones
Come and sit on me
Suck his cock
Suck the genitals of old women.

450

In the priest's arse
The bees have made a nest
O you two girls
Make leaf-cups for us
The priest's mallet
Is fat and big
O you two girls
Do not go near him
The priest's mallet
Is as long as a dozen arms
Do not go near him
O you two girls.

451

Girls, do not stroll
By the edge of the river
The headman's serving boy
Is like a buffalo on heat
By the spring with the tamarind
He is rolling in the mud
Tie his legs with a fly-whisk
Fix him with a hair-pin
Hammer him with a bangle.

452

Grandmother
Give me back my pubic hair
Around your flute
I will wind it like a scarf
And all the people will see it.

453

Do not speak to me, mother's brother
Do not laugh and smile

Mother's brother, that is what I am calling you
I shall tangle you in my pubic hair
I shall batter you with my breasts
And send you staggering down.

454
Below the mountain is a shrub
That is waving to and fro
Bhaero, put your penis in
The snake is going
Into the groove, the hole.

455
Slight and thin he was
But his sex was big as a pumpkin
He only touched my door
And a thrill went through my bones.

456
When my brother-in-law takes me
It feels like being loved
It feels like being lifted.
Like a mouse in a heap of cowdung
He makes me shake and quiver.

457
Girl, on a smooth bed I lay
And who can say
When it slipped in.

458
If you must have me, take me
But do not shake me so
Only because I have no parents
You are enjoying me like this.

459
Through jungle after jungle we wandered
Through a whole forest we went
But what did you ask me?
Do not speak to me so.
Do not ask me
Within two days we shall make it
Like the gaping mouth of a crow.

460

Boy, the girl you have
Is like a fire in the forest
Or a flame
Winking in a lamp
But her cunt
Is just a big big bag.

Finally, song after song exults in forbidden relationships, harping especially on aunts and nephews and uncles and nieces.

461

At the pool by the kadam tree
You are tending buffaloes
Do not smile at me, boy
You are my uncle
My mother you call sister-in-law
My father you call brother
Do not tug at my clothes
I am finished with the village
I am done with the ties of the country
The stick of the gold umbrella
Is standing up on high.

462

Cutting thatch on the big mountain
Uncle, a thorn stuck in me
Uncle, get it out
Girl, there is no needle
And no tweezers
How can I pull it out?
Uncle, uncle
Pull out the thorn from between my thighs.

463

Uncle and niece,
We had each other
And did not feel ashamed.
The morning stars came out.
Uncle, let me go now
To husk the paddy.

464

The shade of a tree shifts round
And a bundle of leaves withers
O let me go, you blind boy
Your mother I call aunt
Your father I call uncle
O let me go, you blind one.

465

Uncle, the river flows with tossing waves.
Take me across it, uncle
I will take you over
But what will you give me?
Are you a fool, uncle?
Are you an idiot?
With what I have in me
I shall reward you.

466

To pick leaves I went
O why did you follow me?
Your mother I call sister
Your father I call brother-in-law
Boy, I am your aunt.

467

On a path in the forest you met me
On a sandy road you threw me down
Your father I call elder brother
Your mother I call sister-in-law
Boy, I am your aunt.

468

By the river in the plot of maize
We met each other
O aunt, my aunt
Let us now be brisk.

469

Boy, your mother is my sister
Your father is my brother-in-law
Boy, I am your aunt.
O my aunt

Aunt or not
I must have you.

470

I came from the street
I stood at your gate
'Aunt, aunt' I called
But you gave no answer
I pushed the door open
'Aunt, aunt' I said
But you gave no answer
From the door I came inside
'Aunt, aunt' I called
But you gave no answer
I climbed on the bed,
I whispered 'Aunt, aunt'
But you gave no answer
I lifted your thighs
Still I said 'Aunt'
But you gave no answer
I raised your cloth
'Aunt, aunt' I said
But you gave no answer
I pressed my penis in
And said 'Aunt, aunt'
But you gave no answer
I held your shoulders
I called you aunt
But you did not answer
I moved my waist
I said 'Aunt' again and again
But you said nothing
I have put your legs down
I am standing up
I am about to leave
'Who's that? Who's that?'
You suddenly blurt out.

Comic and audacious though these songs are, it is forest stories, however, that bulk the largest in a night's performance. These are told with great abandon, often in the first person, by the nude jokers themselves and

315

as they posture in the circle, the crowd accompanies their gestures with bursts of roaring glee. A short selection of these droll recitals will give some idea of the commoner subjects and their customary treatment.

The widow and the fish

In a certain village lived a widow whose husband had died after she had born a single child. A little later her body was like a girl's and when the village boys saw her, their penises stood up. All of them said how much they would enjoy her if only they could have the chance. That month, the rain poured down, and my plots filled. A ridge burst and fish collected in the pool. We began to discuss whether we would bale the water out. Then the widow said, 'As I have no land to cultivate, let me catch the fish.' As she was due to start one morning, I went there in the evening. The cowherds said to me, 'That young widow is baling the water from your field and spoiling all your paddy.' Then I went and saw her. She was stirring the mud with her feet and pouncing on the fish with her hands. 'Why are you catching fish in my field?', I said, 'You have spoilt the paddy.' She replied, 'I have baled out all the water so I am taking the fish' and she went on catching them. She had tucked her clothes up high so as not to get them muddy. Seeing her tightly bending down I got excited and going into the pool I pulled her clothes up and began to take her from behind. As no one had had her for so long, she stood quite still and let me do it thoroughly. When at last I finished, she ran up from the field and began to abuse me. 'I shall tell your wife. Why have you done this to me? What am I to you that you should force me? I shall tell the headman and paranik.' Then she gathered up her basket of fish and sped across the fields. When she reached my house, she threw the fish in the courtyard and called out, 'Because of this fish, your man has been at me. Give him two helpings of it for his supper.' As I went home I guessed that they would question me and as I entered they said, 'Is it true that you have had this woman?' I answered in a heat, 'No. I have not. She was catching fish in our field and I scolded her for spoiling the paddy. All because of this she is saying that I had her.' Then they said, 'The widow brought the fishes and threw them down. I have washed half a basketful.' I asked them to cook them and when the fish was ready, they gave me two helpings. See. I had taken her. If it had been you, you would have got a scolding, 'Why have you been to another woman?' But I enjoyed her and also got two helpings.

The suspicious husband and his wife

A certain man had a daughter who was lovely as a flame and when they saw her, people stopped and stared. Because of this her husband grew suspicious and the two began to quarrel. One day the girl who had all along been faithful said to him in anger, 'You are always hurting me. I will cheat you under your very eyes.' The boy said, 'Do you think I am blind? I will beat you till your clothes drop.' The woman said, 'We will see what sort of beater you are.' So in anger the girl exchanged flowers with a boy in the village and they agreed to have each other in the cowshed at milking time. That day the boy came to the house and the girl said to her husband, 'Father of my son, you are milking the cows so well that all the milk is going in the pot.' The husband replied, 'What do you take me for?' His wife said, 'Because you are milking with your eyes open the milk is going in the pot. If you were blind-folded you could not do it.' The husband said in anger, 'Tie this wrapper round my eyes and then see how I do it.' His wife tied it tightly round and beckoned to her friend. Then on one side the husband's milking was going gab gab and on another the wife and her friend were going cakop' cakop'. And in this way the girl tricked him under his very eyes.

As time went on, the pair still bickered and the girl decided to deceive him once again. One day she arranged to have her village boy during her husband's supper. As evening fell, her husband brought the buffaloes home. The woman made the rice hot and put her baby out on the verandah. Some bells were at its waist. At supper time her village boy came in and on his waist were bells also. While the husband ate his rice inside, the two began on the verandah. As they jerked to and fro, the bells began to tinkle and the girl chanted, bah dudur, hetan dudur, tahak' tahak'. 'Do not get frightened,' she said, 'There is still some time before he finishes. Shake me very slowly and we shall both be happy.' Inside the house the husband thought that she was dandling the child. 'Do not shake him so much or it will hurt him,' he said. Then he finished his rice and the two also completed their work.

One day the girl said to herself, 'I must have my village boy under his open eyes.' A day had been fixed for a hunt so the girl said to the boy, 'You must kill a peacock and hawk it round, saying you will part with it to whichever girl will have you.' In the hunt the boy's luck was in and thanks to the Rongo Ruji bonga, he killed a large peacock. From the day before the hunt the woman was pretending to be ill. 'I am dying,' she moaned. When her village boy got back, he began to strut about. 'Who will trade this peacock with me for a girl?' When she heard him calling, the woman said to her husband, 'Father of your son, get me a little peacock and perhaps I shall feel better.' The husband said, 'You are not hearing properly. The boy is saying he will only give the peacock if a girl does it with him.' 'What does that matter?', said his wife, 'He knows that I am ill. If he has me, he will do it very slowly.' The husband did not want such a lovely wife to die so in the hope of saving her he bought the peacock. Then the boy said to the girl, 'Are you ready?' The girl replied, 'I am very ill. Do not jerk me too much or I shall ache all over.' The boy said, 'I shall thrust it very gently.' Then the woman began to moan out to her husband, 'Hold my legs for me. His peacock is very big.' So what else could he do? The husband lifted her thighs, the boy went slowly in and for a great while they did it.

The old couple
There was once an old man and his wife. One evening when they were lying down to sleep they said to each other, 'Now that we are old, where shall we get the old joy?' The old woman said, 'Old man, are you wanting girls with tight little cunts?' The man replied, 'I am old now. No girl would take me.' The old woman said, 'Do not worry. Let me try. Catch some scaly fish from the stream and bring them to me.' The old man did as she said and brought her some scaly fishes. She washed the mud off and strung them on a thread like a charm. Then she tied the threaded fishes round her waist and hid them in her cloth. A little later she called out to the village girls, 'Come and catch some fish. Your old grandfather has stirred them in the stream.' All the girls came down and they went with her to the water. The old woman had pulled her clothes above her knees and from time to time she hitched them up. Some of the girls noticed that her bottom shone and glittered so they said to her, 'Grandmother, what is flashing from your girl's part?' The old woman laughed and said, 'Your old grandfather took a fancy to it and plated me with silver.' When she heard this, a girl said, 'Grandmother, could you get me plated too?' and the others also said, 'Get me plated like that.' Then the old woman said, 'Very well. Do as I say and I will have you plated' and she told them to come to her house one at a time. That evening a girl came to the old man and said, 'Grandfather, please give me a plating like grandmother's.' The old man said, 'Girl, it has to be measured if you would like to be plated. Come after supper.' The girl ate her food and went to him. He made her lie down on a mat. Then the girl took off her clothes and with a thread he measured her place. The girl said to him, 'Grandfather, have you taken my measurements?' The old man said, 'Girl, I must measure inside also.' The girl said, 'What will you measure with?' The old man showed her a stick and said, 'With this.' The girl said, 'No, no. It will hurt me. Measure me the way you measured grandmother.' The old man said, 'Because she is mine I

have measured her with my prick. But you are not my wife. So how shall I measure you with it?'. Then the girl said, 'What does it matter? Measure me with yours.' Then the old man copulated with the girl and said, 'Now I am making you your charm.'

In this way the old man got all the young girls of the village. He was delighted at the old lady's skill in getting them for him and said to her, 'Well, old woman, you have made it seem like old times to me. I will get a strong one for you also.'

One day he said to her, 'Old woman, get out your fine new clothes and at noon today tie them up and go over to the further village. In the evening put on your new clothes and come back with the dirty ones tied in a bundle on your head. As you return and come near the cowherd boys, mince your steps a little. If the boys follow you, break into a little run but see that they do not catch you.' The old woman did as he said. When the boys saw her they began to say, 'Where does that girl come from? Let us see the house she goes to.' The boys watched her and she entered the old man's house. When they had brought the buffaloes home, they went to the back of his house and called out, 'Grandfather'. The old man came out and said, 'Yes, boys. What are you making all this noise for?' A grown-up boy said, 'Nothing, grandfather. We saw someone going into your house. We want to know who it is.' The old man laughed and said, 'I know you. You young thieves are always after that.' Then the boy said, 'Grandfather, we want to come in. Do not be cross with us.' Then he said, 'Very well, boy. Come in as you wish. The girl will sleep alone in that room.' In the night the boys came back. They went in one by one. Each fumbled in the darkness, found her and had her. When they had finished, one of them said, 'Well, chaps, whether it was because I was the last or not, I thought it very large and loose.' Another boy said, 'I also found it very loose.' Then they began to think, 'Is it possible that the old man has cheated us?' Next morning they were taking out the buffaloes when they asked him, 'Grandfather, is the girl who was there yesterday still here?' The old man said, 'What did you do to her that she ran away at cockcrow?' At the grazing ground the boys said to each other, 'Was it perhaps the old woman that we had?' So they looked at their organs and on one of them they found a white hair. Then they said, 'Yes, it was indeed the old woman that we had. The old man took us in completely.' In this way the old woman, long after her proper time, enjoyed a young cock.

An unmarried boy
There was once a boy who was still unmarried. He was always longing

for girls but none would have him. There was a garden of flowers enclosed by a mud wall. In the wall was a tiny hole. One day the boy went to the garden and saw the hole. He said, 'I will put my tool in it.' So he put it in and coupled in the hole. It became a habit with him and every day he went and did it. In the village was a girl who was grown-up but still unmarried. One day she saw him working in the hole and after that she went each day to watch him. At last she put a thorn in the hole. The boy came and as he worked his organ the thorn went in. At first he did not guess what had happened. Then his thing swelled and he could not even piss. They tried to make him right with medicines but nothing did him any good and he told no one what had happened. Then the unmarried girl who had put the thorn said, 'I will cure him but if I cure him he must take me as his wife.' The boy said, 'Make me right and I will marry you.' Everyone was happy. Then the girl said, 'All of you must go outside.' So they went out. The girl took off her clothes, opened her thighs and sat down. She made the boy sit by her. The boy saw her privates and desire flared. His member stood up and he pressed her down and had her. As he fucked, his cock burst and the thorn came out. The boy got better slowly and when he was well, he made the girl his wife.

The boy and girl

There were two friends – a boy and a girl. The boy used to graze cattle and whenever he asked her the girl would pretend to gather cowdung and go to the grazing grounds. In this way the boy and girl were always meeting either by a bank in a paddy field or in a dried-up stream and whenever they met they wrestled with each other. One day it happened that although the boy had asked her to go to the high land where the cows grazed, for one reason or another, the girl did not go. The boy failed to fill his mind and was much upset. At noon he brought the cows home. The girl was standing in the road, watching the paddy dry and holding her elder brother's baby. When the boy came near the girl, he began to speak as if he were talking to the cows, 'Hyak, black cows, so you are looking away. Have you no memory today ?' The girl guessed he was reproving her so she said as if to the fowls, 'Little chicks, I did not get a chance.' Then in order to calm him and to hint at a place and time where they could meet, she began to dandle the child up and down and to say, 'Hitik' dan, tirin dan, das danetan, hetam dan, under the bar tree at noon.' The girl's elder brother happened to overhear her and began to turn over in his mind the words 'under the bar tree at noon'. So in order to see what would happen the brother went below the field and climbed a tree. At noon the boy and girl met. The girl said, 'When I did not go to the grazing ground, were you very angry with me? Do not fret or sulk. I had not forgotten you. I did not go because we boiled some paddy and I was busy drying it. I have come to you now and you can have me in as many ways you like. Enjoy me utterly.' When he heard her say this, the boy was overjoyed and taking each other in their arms, they kissed. Then they had each other in every possible way till only the goat's way was left. Then the girl said, 'You have done it all the other ways but you have still to have me from behind.' So the boy got ready and the girl knelt down. Then the boy pushed his head against her bottom, sniffed at her cunt and began to bellow like a goat in heat. At this, the girl's brother spoke out from the tree, 'Bah re, the ox has got six teeth.' When they heard this, the two sprang up. They rushed away and the girl cried, 'It is all because you made me come that he has shamed us. Never take me again.' But the boy replied:

471
The frogs have each other over and over
The he-goats copulate again and again
And I will never leave my love
I will see the axes and arrows
I will lose my home
But never will I leave my love.

The old man and the prostitute

Once some carters set out for trading in a distant country. They loaded their carts and halted for the night at the end of a village street. In that village lived a prostitute and when she saw their wares, she decided to entangle the carters and deprive them of their goods. All the carters save one were young. The woman strolled before them showing off her clothes and body. Seeing her flaunting before them, the boys said, 'Will you let us lie with you?' The prostitute said, 'If you can wear me out, you may lie with me free of charge but if I defeat you, you must give me everything you have. If you agree, you may start on me at once.' The boys reflected, 'There are so many of us we must surely defeat her.' So they said, 'We agree.' But though they worked their hardest they could not tire her and in the end they had to admit that she had won.

Among them was an old man. He did not know what the boys had been up to and only found out when the carts were being taken away. To save the carts he called the villagers but they all decided that the prostitute must keep them. Then the old man said, 'But she has not yet let me have her.' The woman agreed that this was so. So the meeting told him he might have his chance and by this time it was dark. In the old man's waist there was a purse for keeping money. The old man took the money out, put the purse on his penis and began to copulate. When he had rubbed her once or twice the prostitute screamed out, 'Stop, leave me.' The old man overcame her and the carts were saved. Then the old man said to the boys, 'Never do anything without first taking the advice of an old man.'

The great girl

There was once a girl who had a huge cunt. No one was coming for her so her parents searched for a boy. One day they saw a youth ploughing naked and prodding the bullocks with his prick. 'We must have you as our bridegroom,' they said. The boy replied, 'The other two are much larger. My middle brother is in the rice field eating Iowa berries. My elder brother is helping people to cross the river.' So the girl's parents went to the middle brother and found him on his back knocking down the berries with his tool and eating the fruit. Then they said, 'We must have you as our son-in-law.' The boy replied, 'I have an elder brother. Take him as your bridegroom. We have not yet found a bride for him.' So they went to the Mor river. There they found him with a great organ stretched from bank to bank and people crossing on it. Then they said, 'You indeed must be our bridegroom. We have a daughter who is not yet matched. You are the man for her.' The boy said, 'I am ready but how shall I get there? Bring twelve bullock carts and I will go in search of her.' So they brought the carts, loaded his organ on them and walked the man away. That night the two copulated and the spunk flowed through the village in a great stream. Lower down some weavers were living. As the semen flowed, they said, 'Whose rice-water is this?' and in a hurry they dipped a thread in it, and brushed it out. That is why whenever weaver's cloth is new, it always stinks.

The young husband

There was once a boy who being married when he was still very small did not know that he had got a wife. When he grew bigger he used to catch hold of the village girls but they only scolded him saying, 'Away with you, little one. Go to your own wife.' One day he said to his mother, 'Mother, is it true that you have married me?' His mother answered, 'Yes, son. We have given you a wife.' The next day the boy could restrain himself no longer. He cut off a bunch of plantains and set off for his father-in-law's house. After going for hours he crossed the village boundary. By the side of the path his father-in-law and brother-in-law were ploughing. They saw that a boy was going with a bunch of plantains. Neither recognised the other and the two did not see that it was their girl's husband. The young brother-in-law began to cry out, 'Father, ask him for a plantain.' Then the old man said, 'Boy, give us one of your plantains.' The boy replied, 'If you can press and bend my cock, I will give you one.' So what was there to do? The old man tried to bend it, but he could not. As he struggled, the organ slipped, struck his mouth and knocked out all his teeth. Then the boy gave them two plantains and went on. A little later the brother-in-law again saw the boy in their own house. He was about to say, 'Father, that is the boy who knocked out your teeth' when his father said, 'Do not talk about it. He is our daughter's husband.' Then everyone came privately to know that the young bridegroom's tool was very large and stout. As night fell, the members of the household did not sleep from fear and the grandfather sat near the couple. Then the boy began on his wife. The girl said, 'It is so big it is not going in. It is burning me like fire.' Near them in a niche was a pot of oil and the girl said, 'Take some oil and put it on your organ.' The boy dipped his tool in the pot and it stuck tight. Then the girl said, 'Go to the rice mortar in the corner and break the pot on it.' Her grandfather was sitting near at hand and when the boy went there he smashed the pot on the old man's head. The old man rushed out and said, 'Wait, grandson-in-law.' But the boy started on the girl again. Yet still it would not enter. Then the girl said, 'It is burning me like fire.' Then the girl's mother said, 'What? Are you playing with fire?' The boy went to her with his foreskin back and said, 'Mother, is this fire?' The mother-in-law said, 'No, my boy. My daughter always did make a fuss about nothing.'

Throughout the night, stories of this kind go on while, sitting in a separate spot, the dihri patiently hears appeals from regional courts. Parganas and their local headmen defend their decisions. Rates of bride-price are solemnly discussed. The state of tribal morals is investigated and the whole code of sex is re-affirmed. If necessary, the meeting goes on after dawn while attendance gradually thins and the hunters make for home. Sometime in the morning the dihri ends the session and at last the hunt is over.

3 THE RELEASE OF REPRESSIONS

This strange institution with its mixture of high seriousness and comic joking fulfills a number of functions in Santal life. On the council side, it is obviously both a 'High Court' and a 'Parliament'. We have seen that while the parganas and village headmen are responsible for day to day administration, it is the tribe itself which is the final authority. To exercise that sovereignty it is necessary that the people should meet and the annual hunt is the accredited way of bringing them together. 'Very few would come,' said Barka of Jhandaburu, 'if I invited them only for a council.' When the hunters 'go into committee', anyone who likes may attend, the dihri is at most a neutral president and it is the sense of the meeting which invariably prevails. Such councils seldom result in major changes but they have the great advantage of publicising the prevailing law and ensuring that the code is generally understood. They encourage in even the humblest Santal the feeling of active democracy and make him feel that the rules are his own creation and not a discipline brusquely imposed upon him by others.

But besides uniting Santals in a single vast gathering the hunt is also an important form of recreation. There is an 'August Bank holiday' feeling in the huge crowds combing the hillsides for exiguous game. There is the interest of new country, the freedom from women, the sudden break with routine, a faint but teasing sense of danger, and the fascination of the forest. These are things that get beneath a Santal's skin and give him keen satisfaction.

Yet even more significant is the air of sexual relaxation that suffuses every hunt. This is due to several causes. According to Santal theory, Pargana bonga is the guardian of the forest and the Rongo Ruji bonga is his sister. Since this latter bonga delights in sex, it is necessary to regale her with sexy songs and stories. 'If we talk sex at the hunt,' a Santal told me, 'the Rongo Ruji bonga will be pleased. She will give us many hares and peacocks. Pargana bonga will do whatever she says.' 'If we sing forest songs,' said Sibu of Tetaria, 'the Rongo Ruji bonga will keep us safe from tigers and leopards.' 'It is only with songs and tales of sex,' said Maisa, a dihri of the Jhandaburu hunt, 'that the Rongo Ruji bonga can be won. She is the sister of Pargana bonga and makes him give us whatever animal she wills.' To placate the Rongo Ruji bonga, therefore, the ban on sexual talk is lifted and words which if uttered in the village would be visited with fine and disgrace are not only permitted but enjoyed.

But besides the need for humouring a bonga, there is also a realisation of the deep if dimly conscious connection between hunting and the act of sex itself. This is doubtless based on the principle that like may influence like. Since a penis stabbing a woman is like an arrow plunging in a peacock, copulation is liable to neutralise the hunting. It would act as a substitute for killing and rob the hunters of every chance of game. Talk of sex on the other hand creates a favourable atmosphere. It is, as it were, an enactment of the slaughter – at only one degree from actual life. For this reason it is as vitally necessary for the hunters to talk sex as it is for them to avoid its actual practice.

Yet even more important than its role in getting game is the effect of relaxations on ordinary conduct. By providing a formal occasion when rules can be broken with propriety, the hunt makes infinitely easier their day to day observance. It would be surprising if Santals never felt the need to talk sex. It would be incredible if boys and girls were never attracted by forbidden relatives. If, as sometimes happens, an aunt is younger than her nephew, family affection may easily give place to something stronger. Equally a young uncle may be far from oblivious of a niece's charm. Yet in the circumstances of village life, each must smother their feelings and avoid the slightest act which might suggest a guilty relationship. Even the grosser forms of sexual deviation must sometimes trouble individuals and confront them with the need for iron repression. To all these stresses the hunt provides a joking outlet. Its atmosphere of bantering amusement, its droll distortions, its ludicrous exaggerations succeed to some extent in dissipating wishes, in putting them in their place, in laughing them out of court. The 'forest' songs sung at the hunt and the 'forest' stories told are full of wild absurdities. The woman who deceives her husband in his actual presence, the boys whose lechery leads them to encounter an old crone, the boy whose large organ breaks an old man's teeth – these are figures which might at certain points reflect a Santal's whims or fancies but in their actual Rabelaisian guise could not possibly occur in normal life. They serve, in fact, a function not unlike the English comic postcard. 'A recurrent, almost dominant motif in comic postcards', George Orwell has said, 'is the woman with the stuck-out behind. In perhaps half of them, even when the point of the joke has nothing to do with sex, the same female figure appears, a plump "voluptuous" figure with the dress clinging to it as tightly as another skin and with breasts and buttocks grossly over-emphasised according to which way it is turned. There can be no doubt that these pictures lift the lid off a very widespread repression, natural enough in a country whose women when young tend to be slim to the point of skimpiness. But at the same time the McGill postcard – and this applies to all other postcards in this genre – is not intended as pornography but, a subtler thing, as a skit on pornography. The Hottentot figures of the women are caricatures of the Englishman's secret ideal, not portraits of it.' It is precisely in this manner that 'forest' songs and stories ease a Santal's repressions. They do not hold up certain acts to approbation. They over-do them, they 'guy' their exponents and by their wilful humour, their subtle debunking they reinforce the tribal code.

CHAPTER XX

Death and Society

I THE FUNERAL CEREMONIES

During the Sohrae festival, at lagre dances and weddings or at meetings in the forest, Santals occasionally sing songs of death.

472

O my love
The life of man
Is only a gourd of water
Let it leak only a little
And all is gone.

473

With my eyes I saw
Gold and silver
But at my death
I shall not take them on
The wealth of your heart
The wealth of your life
But you die
And cannot take them on.

474

When the pot breaks, the mouth stays
When the cotton bursts, the pod remains
Father, in this great village
I have gone from end to end
But cannot find my brother.

475

When Rudu Ram was living
O my love
I would eat plates of rice
And drink

326

Bowls of milk
When Rudu Ram died
How I wept.

476

All my life
I shall talk and laugh
All my life
I shall laugh and dance
When my life goes
My mother will weep
My life's hope
Is in my golden body.

477

In life what is happiness?
In life what is joy?
To be in love with others
For when we die
We go with no one.

478

On your hand is a shield, boy
On your back a shield
But death may come
To anyone.

479

With a fan in the armpit
And from the roof some thatch
They took my girl away
O sun and moon
Had I but been a vulture
I would have hovered as she went
I would have closed in like a whirlwind
And stroked her like a fly.

When death actually occurs, the family breaks into bitter grieving songs. A mother sings of her dead child.

480

Parrot, parrot
My little parrot
Has flown away
O where shall I go
To see its face?

A girl bewails the passing of her mother.

481

'Haere haere'
O my milk-tree
It has fallen down
In the past
She covered us like a hen
Mother
You have left us
Like little chicks
When we came home
My mother sat at the door
She welcomed us
Like young starlings.

A young wife watches her husband go with blank despairing sorrow.

482

My side of an umbrella
Has blown away
Where shall I go
To see his face?
My dove, my love
The pair of doves is split
O where shall I go
To see my dove?

But besides grief at the death of a loved familiar person, there is also the knowledge that a sudden sinister crisis has occurred in the family and village. The world of bongas which normally impinges only intermittently on Santal affairs is abruptly brought into sharper focus. Death is a victory for all those anti-Santal forces which are represented by hostile bongas. It is an affront to the major bongas whose prime concern is Santal welfare.

It is as if the dead Santal has betrayed his trust, has failed in his main duty – to go on living. To die is therefore to pollute and for the moment the whole village is bereft of its tribal guardians and deprived of ghostly care. At the same time death subjects a man to violent unnatural change. He remains a Santal. He is still a member of his family but until he has safely reached the country of the dead, he is a man with a grievance. He can no longer do the things which Santals value most for he is abruptly deprived of sex and the company of his children. He is 'out of position'. He no longer 'belongs' and only the most careful conduct by his family can ensure his due demission. He is now much more a bonga than a man–a ghostly force invisible but intimately real. The danger which killed him still infects his person and until the funerary process is over, he must remain a source of menace to all the members of his family. When he has achieved the final status of ancestor, he has still a bonga nature and can on no account be ignored. He is not as obvious as living Santals but he is something to be reckoned with, a power with whom it is even more necessary to be on good terms than when he worked and went about the village.

Accordingly when a Santal dies, the family and village all co-operate in disposing of his body and mollifying its outraged spirit. The news is given by a drum beating three times. This is a call to action and while the women keen by the corpse, the men assemble at the house. Until the corpse is carried away, there must always be five men at hand. If a Santal has ended his life away from home or if, as in the case of a married woman who has died at her father's house, another village is involved, it is this latter village whose bongas are polluted and whose inhabitants must therefore rally to receive the body and perform its last offices.

When the villagers have gathered, the corpse is laid out on a cot and the women rub the body with oil and turmeric, wash the hands and feet and drip some water on the mouth. A little vermilion is dabbed on the forehead and the body is wrapped in a cloth. This cloth is often made of silk and only if the Santal is very poor is cotton used.

Some gear is then got ready–a winnowing fan, a leaf plate, a mattock, some charred cotton seeds, some charred paddy and a fowl. A handful of thatch is pulled from the dead man's roof and the end of a straw rope is kindled from a fire inside the house. When lighting this rope, no one may blow on it with his breath.

A number of articles are also sent out with the corpse. If the dead person is a man, some of his personal equipment – his battle axe, sword, bow and arrow, stick, flute or drum – is placed beside him while if the deceased is a girl or woman a few of her bangles, earrings, and other ornaments are

set down with her. In addition the following articles must also be offered–
a piece of cloth (new or old), a plate, bowl and drinking vessel (all of
brass), and a little money knotted in the cloth.

Besides these presents which are the minimum dues of the departed
and must be given from the family stock, each near kinsman is expected
to contribute a small token of mourning – a coin, a bowl or a plate. This is
not compulsory but is given out of family regard.

When the gifts are piled on the cot, four men lift it and with two others
holding the lighted rope and the winnowing fan they carry the corpse
out into the street. Ahead of them goes a third mourner strewing paddy on
the ground. The body is then taken down to a piece of water. If the dead
man owned a tank, he is carried to its side. Otherwise, he is borne down to
the bank of a river or stream.

Brands of firewood are then arranged and a pyre is built waist high. No
special wood is necessary and if the village has rights in firewood, the
wood is simply collected from the forest. If there is no forest, the Santal
conducting the funeral must procure it either by stripping some branches
from his own trees or buying it in the village or market.

When the pyre is ready, the chief mourner bathes and then with the
same bowl used by the women he washes the hands and feet of the corpse
and sprinkles water on its mouth. All those present bathe in turn and with
the same bowl each performs the same service to the dead.

The cot is now lifted by the four bearers who go three times round the
pyre and then place the cot with the head facing south. A man mounts
the pyre and looking to the west removes the cot from the pyre and sets the
body on the wood. He strips the corpse of everything except its silk shift
and all the presents are taken off the pyre and set on the bed. He now takes
the fowl, circumambulates the pyre three times, pins the fowl to an end
pole and heaps some logs over the corpse. A small fire is now kindled
from the lighted rope and when it is fairly ablaze, the chief mourner takes
in his right hand a burning stick and in his left a bit of sedge, on which are
wound some threads from the dead man's cloth. He lights the threaded
sedge with the burning stick and as the cotton smokes, he averts his gaze
and touches the mouth with the stalk. After that he lights the pyre with the
thatch taken from the roof and then in the names of the dead man's kinsmen, he throws one piece of wood after another on the pyre. Other
villagers cast bits of wood, the cot is put by the side and the pyre is set
ablaze. As they throw, they urge the corpse not to detain them but to
burn itself out quickly. 'O dead body, do not dally now. Go like the wind.
Burn like a flame. We have given you wood and fire. Be consumed and go.'

While the pyre is blazing, the villagers squat at a distance and shave their cheeks, the head of the chief mourner being shaved completely. When the blaze subsides and the body is consumed, the unburnt logs are taken out, the ashes are gathered and water is poured on the embers. The chief mourner then picks out three pieces of bone – one from the skull, one from the upper arm and a third from the collar bone. These are called the jan baha or 'flowers of bone' and as he holds them in his clenched fist oil and a little milk and ashy water are poured over them. He then knots the bones into a piece of cloth, taken from the dry shift. These bones are, as it were, the life index of the dead. It is here that the dead man halts and his soul is, for the time being, contained.

As the bones are being gathered, the men sing

483

On the high hill
The vultures hover
Show me the bones of my father
O she vulture
Take the gold from my ear
Show me my father's bones.

The burning scene is now tidied up. Each pall-bearer stands in turn on the winnowing fan and digs a hole round it. The bones are covered with the dug earth and the fan is mingled with the ashes and dug into the hole. The fragments of the cot are then broken and after purifying the whole scene by sprinkling cowdung with water on all the places associated with the rites, the charred cotton seeds and paddy are sprinkled at the spot where the end poles were stood. The mourners now move over to a tank or stream where all take baths. When they have finished, the main mourner sets out five leaves by the water's edge, puts a little earth used for soap and a tooth twig on each, ties the 'flowers of bone' into a cloth at his waist, enters the water and after bathing, squats before the leaves. He then sprinkles a little of the earth and addresses Maran Buru, Porodhol (the general ancestors), Pilcu Haram, Pilcu Budhi, and the dead man in turn. 'Pilcu Haram, this man has fallen. He is dead and gone. Do not consign him to ash. Keep him in your care. Bathe and wash your hair.' 'O dead one, today in your name we have bathed and rinsed our hair. Do not dwell in the ashes. You have left your home, your children and your cattle. When all is ready we shall bear you to your home.'

If the corpse is of a child from three to eight years old, the bones 'are made to swim' the same day. When the chief mourner goes to bathe, he consigns them to the water and makes the offerings as he comes out.

After this, all the articles taken to the pyre are either sold at once or made over to a villager for later sale. The proceeds go to the village as a whole and swell the little stock of funds which are reserved for village feasts.

As the party enters the village, some resin is burnt, and the mourners inhale the smoke. Then they go to their homes. Later in the night some of the older men go to the house and console the family. 'Do not grieve all the time,' they say, 'He has gone away. He is happy. We too shall one day have to go. If you cry too much, your body will grow thin. You will not do your work. While we live we must eat and drink. Go about your work. Put your soul under a flat stone. People say if you cry night and day the one who has gone before will butt his head like a young buffalo. In the next world they will say to him, "Come and dance. They are singing for you." Do not mourn for him or you will load him with care and grief.'

As the party disperses the leader takes a small but new earthen pot from the dead man's house and puts the 'flowers of bone' into it. He makes a lid for the vessel with a piece of broken pot, bores a hole in the middle – for 'the dead one to breathe' – and inserts the culm of a special grass (*Rollboellia perforata,* Roxb.) 'for the dead man to go in and out on'. The lid is then glued to the pot with turmeric paste and the pot with the bones is put in a shallow hole under a tree beyond the village. The top remains above the ground and is protected with a little heap of stones.

For the next five days, the dead one will remain with whatever hostile agency has killed him for until rice-beer is brewed and the house is ready for the dead, the killer cannot be dislodged and the dead must wait, dangerous and impatient, at the end of the village.

Cremation is the ordinary rule both for men and women, but there are certain circumstances in which resort is had to burial. If a Santal dies from leprosy, smallpox, phthisis, asthma or cholera his body must be buried and lest the touch of fire should infect the chief mourner, or the smoke carry the disease through the village, the placing of fire on the corpse's face is also forbidden. Similarly if a woman dies in pregnancy the foetus is removed from the belly and buried, but her own body is cremated. If a child dies 'before it learns to talk' it cannot announce the cause of its death and it is buried without further ceremonies. Finally in areas where forests are thin, firewood scarce and cremation impossible, burial is resorted to as the only feasible means of disposing of the body.

When burial is done as a substitute for cremation, the corpse is taken to the grave in the same manner as for burning. Instead however of piling up brands of firewood the villagers dig a long hole three feet deep, facing north to south and with two slots in each of its walls. A cloth is laid in the grave and the body placed on it. After that a chick is pinned inside the grave and the chief mourner sets fire to the mouth. Branches are slid down into the slots, other branches are laid over them and the body rests beneath a canopy of twigs. The cot is hacked to pieces and laid on top and then the leading mourner picks up a handful of earth and casts it on the boughs. The villagers throw earth after him and then more earth is shovelled up and the grave filled in. Finally boulders are laid over the mound like a shallow cairn and a maze of thorns is built to keep it free of animals. When the scene is purified with cowdung and water, the mourners move away.

Five days after the death, the ceremony of tel nahan (oiling and washing) is performed. The village men gather at the dead man's house, wrap up a little grain, rice, and three pieces of country bread, collect from the house sufficient rice for a village meal and then assemble where the pot of the departed was buried. The man who mounted the pyre then disinters the pot with the 'flowers of bone', takes out the culm and pours the bones into the hands of the chief mourner. The latter wraps them in their original cloth and a little fire is made at the place where the pot was buried. As the flames leap up, the men say 'The hut of the old woman is ablaze' and the party move down to the end of the village. Here they meet the women. Some ebony sticks are tied together and stood up like a tripod. The pot is set down on the top and the man who mounted the pyre goes round it three times, strikes the pot with a fourth stick and smashes it to pieces. This dislodges whichever enemy has killed the dead one and who until now has dogged his soul. Then the chief mourner holds out the bones in his hand and the women rinse his clenched fingers with turmeric, milk and water. He then knots the bones into his waist and the men go on to a piece of water beyond the frontiers of the village.

At this water the leader purifies a piece of ground, squats by the water, sets out five leaves and on each of them puts some grain and a piece of country bread. He then offers to Maran Buru, Porodhol, Pilcu Haram, Pilcu Budhi and to the dead, throwing into the water each leaf-plate in turn and addressing them 'O Pilcu Haram, Pilcu Budhi, today we have brought the fallen one from the village. We are bringing him back to the shadow of his house. Do not let him linger outside. Do not lodge him under the eaves. Take him by the hand and guide him to his rest.' 'O fallen one, today we are bringing you to the shadow of your house. Do not dwell outside it. Do not linger under the eaves.'

333

The men then bathe and rub themselves with oil and after that, they buy some fowls or a pig with money given by the chief mourner. These must be bought outside the village boundaries and are eaten with the rice before the party returns. By consuming this feast, 'in the presence of the bones,' the mourners associate themselves with the dead and coax him to return. While the men are away, the women also bathe. After sundown, the men return to the village and assemble at the dead man's house. Here the feet of the chief mourner together with those of his two companions are washed by the nearest female relatives and the 'flowers of bone' are consigned to a new receptacle. This is either the hollow handle of a new broom or a small but new earthen pot. The vessel of the departed is then taken inside a room and put up in the rafters beyond the reach of smoke.

If the dead person has been buried, and there are no 'flowers of bone' the villagers begin the day by going to the grave. The chief mourner collects a symbol for the bones by taking up a handful of earth from near the body. He then goes down to a place near water. There he burns the earth and puts it in a new earthen pot. The villagers return and the pot is put down on a tripod of ebony sticks at the end of the village. The women then gather, the pot is smashed as if it were a pot with actual 'flowers of bone' and the burnt earth is held in the hand and rinsed with turmeric, milk and water. After that the burnt earth is used as a proxy for the bones and the ritual is the same as in cremation.

The villagers now gather in the courtyard and the leading mourner assumes the role of the dead man while two villagers take the parts of Porodhol (the general ancestors) and Maran Buru. The actor for the dead demands water from all the dead man's kinsmen and the inmates of his house and when he is offered it, he demands water from all the villagers. 'Maran Buru' and 'Porodhol' are also given bowls of water which they drink. The three are then given bowls of rice-beer and the leader asks the dead man how he died. 'I went of my own will,' he says. 'Porodhol' is also asked and he replies, 'I was inside. I do not know.'

After that, the dead is asked if the future holds any danger. If there is danger he replies, 'Consult the ojhas and jan gurus. They will give medicines. They will prescribe the sacrifices. All will be well.'

The people then drink rice-beer and go to their homes. The dead person is now, as it were, in transit. He has lost the enemy that killed him but he has not as yet been admitted to the ancestors. He is still at one with the 'flowers of bone'. They are his temporary abode and he must now dwell for some time in his house until his kinsmen can arrange for his final passage.

With the ablutions of the people, the village bongas cease to be unclean and sacrifices can again be made to them. The house of the dead one remains 'in the shadow' but his kinsmen, outside the immediate family, are at liberty to perform weddings and make sacrifices.

While these ceremonies are proceeding and sometimes even on the day of death itself, the house of the dead person is visited by a jadupatua, a humble member of a Hindu painter caste. This individual combines the roles of itinerant minstrel and funerary beggar. He brings a few scrolls of paintings depicting the Santal myth of creation, the Baha festival, life in Death's kingdom and sometimes the goddess Kali and the Krishna cycle. He squats in the courtyard, unrolls his pictures, entones a recitative and finally produces a sketch in which the dead person is shown with blank and sightless eyes. In the corner of the drawing is a picture of a cow, a fowl, a bowl or a brass plate according as the jadupatua assesses the wealth of the family. At the end he exacts the animal or utensils as his tribute for restoring sight to the dead and only when it is given does he put the eyeballs in the sketch and leave the house.

The jadupatua's tribute is paid either from the dead person's own moveables or if he has left none, from the property of the joint household, his guardian or his heir.

Some weeks after the oil and washing ceremony, the chief mourner fixes a day for consigning the 'flowers of bone' to water. The villagers assemble at the house, drink rice-beer and the dead man, Maran Buru and Porodhol are again evoked and questioned. 'Today, we are taking you to the river. May no ache of belly or head rack us; keep us from all harm in the way', and the dead man replies, 'I shall keep all harm away. Go and come like the wind.' The leader then takes out the 'flowers of bone' in their little cloth and women pour turmeric, milk and water over his clenched hand. The ears of a fowl are chopped off and the blood stains some rice. If a date for the feast has been settled a cow is reserved for sacrifice and the blood is got by cutting a slit in the ear. The blood-smeared rice is then put in a leaf packet while in another leaf, a copper pice and some sindur are tied together. The leading mourner now puts on a new dhoti, and knots the 'flowers of bone' into his waist.

The party sets out. The man who mounted the pyre carries the pot or drags the broom, sweeping the earth as he goes. At the village end, the leader squats on the ground and the man who mounted the pyre offers a fowl, tears off its head, and throws the head and carcase away. The pot is then smashed or the broom thrown away.

If the former custom of taking the bones to the Damodar river is followed, the leader takes one or two villagers with him and goes on to the river. If however this is not done (and it is nowadays no longer usual to make such a long journey) the villagers go in a body to a river or stream. If the departed was the owner of a tank they go there but if there is no river close at hand, they scoop a hole and fill it with water. The chief mourner goes to the west, taking the bones with him and never looking back. At the water he 'buys the ghat' with a pice. Then he mixes the bones with the blood-besmeared rice and entering the stream consigns them to the water.

After the bones are immersed, offerings are made to Maran Buru, Porodhol, Pilcu Haram, Pilcu Budhi and to the dead himself. 'O fallen one, today we have washed ourselves in the great river. Do not linger outside the house. Do not dwell in the eaves. When we return we will arrange your last feast.' The new cloth is then discarded and abandoned. The offerings are eaten and the villagers go back.

On the way they buy fowls or a pig from a village not their own and after eating a meal with rice, they wait till sundown and then return. After that, the chief mourner gives them rice-beer and they go to their houses.

With this ceremony, the dead one is released from his temporary shell – the 'bones of flower' – and is now an acknowledged ancestor, a family bonga. But he is not yet fully of the dead, neither has he entered the realm of Jom Raja, King of the Dead. He must now dally in the family's bhitar or private shrine and await the feast when his kinsmen will take their last farewell and send him happy and honoured, to his long home.

This last feast which is known as bhandan cannot be performed earlier than nine days after the return from the river but is permissible at any later date. It is celebrated for all except small children and if the initiation ceremony of caco chatiar has not been performed this is included in it as part of the ritual.

The village men first bathe and shave and assemble in the house of the dead. They are given rice-beer and a meal. Then the chief mourner again sustains the role of the dead man, his companion is possessed by Porodhol and a third enacts Maran Buru. The dead man is re-identified. 'It is I,' he says. Then he demands water from all his immediate relations and after water is given he again declares the cause of his death. Finally rice is offered to him and the family say, 'Keep us in peace. Do not trouble us. Do not take anything away.' The three men then emerge from their roles and are given rice-beer.

The jogmanjhi now erects a sal branch in the courtyard and the chief mourner sacrifices a fowl by clubbing it on the head. The cow with the slit ear is then led in, tied to the branch and after dedication, it is felled by the jogmanjhi with the butt-end of an axe. After that the near kinsmen offer fowls, pigs or goats.

In cutting up the cow, the side on which it falls is carefully observed. The fore-leg of this side together with the head is allotted to the villagers, the neck is given to the barber and out of the rest three divisions are made. The first is cooked with rice and is eaten by all, i.e. the villagers and members of the house. The second is divided among the villagers who take the pieces to their homes. The third is kept by the dead man's family. The man who does the bhandan gets the hide.

A little later some cooked rice is brought out and sitting before the branch the chief mourner offers it first to the dead and then to the grand-parents. 'O dead man, today we have given you rice. Take and eat it gladly. Look to your children. Keep them from harm. Go your way gladly. Keep all sorrow or ill far from the house.' Rice-beer is then brought and offered in the same way.

After this the flesh is brought out and the chief mourner again sits before the branch. He faces east holding a dismembered leg of the cow and the man then recites the traditions of the ancestors. This recital often lasts the greater part of the night and ends, 'We have cleaned the head that was full of ashes and the mouth that oozed blood. He who was black as a crow is white as a swan.' With this recital the chief mourner is purified. The villagers drink more rice-beer. Then they dress the flesh and cook it with rice. The villagers' share is taken outside and eaten in the road while the family consume their portion in the house. These later provisions are mandatory for the village share is known as the 'feast of the street'.

When the bhandan is over, the impurity that has hitherto dogged the household ends and the family can again sacrifice to bongas, drink rice-beer, use vermilion and celebrate weddings. It is therefore of great import-ance that once a man has died his bhandan should be done with reasonable speed. If, for any reason, a family cannot do the ceremony quickly, a substitute bhandan is performed in its place. On the day of return from the river, a fowl is offered by the chief mourner. It is cooked with rice and offerings are made to the departed and the grandparents. The dead man is asked to accept the food and so make way for weddings and the placation of the bongas. After this the chief mourner is declared finally pure. The people are given rice-beer and go to their homes. Some months or even years later, a full bhandan is performed so that the spirit of the dead may be finally appeased.

3 THE MORA KARAM

In addition to the bhandan, a Mora Karam ('a Karam for the dead') is sometimes performed. This ceremony is done in either of three cases – if the dead man was a Karam guru, if a Karam seedling grows in his court-yard or on the site of the cremation and lastly, if during his lifetime, he was famous for his riches. The celebration resembles Jiwet' Karam – 'a Karam for the living' – except that the myth of Karmu and Dharmu is not recited, the two boys are not employed and the branch is first set up on the site of cremation before being taken to the mourner's house. When it reaches this place, it is installed in the village street and the guru recites the Mora Karam sermon. He begins by following the formal recital that accompanies a Karam for the living. He traces the story of the Santals from their stay in Hihiri Pipiri down to their founding of the village. He discourses on Madho Singh and relates the part played by Maran Buru in their wander-ings. After that he branches off and describes the life of the dead man, how he fell ill and at last died. Finally he explains how once a Karam tree sprouted from a man's head and then from the site of a cremation and stresses that because of this the Mora Karam is being celebrated.

When the sermon is over, the men dance and a cycle of songs are sung describing how a man is conceived and born and is at last, removed by death.

484

Together we lay down
Together we got up
My body of lotus leaves
Is turning into iron
O my body, my body
Is changing into iron.

485

Together we lay down
Together we sat
My body of lotus leaves
Is turning into flesh
Is turning into flesh.

486

With a stick in his hand
He searches for the midwife

A little hut
Has a door to the east
In the middle of the village
Is the house of the midwife
Sister, come at once
To ease her pain
Sister, I will give you
A stool of gold
I will give you
Betel nuts to eat
You shall have
The finest rice.

This is followed by a song describing the foetus and its growth.

487

It was made by Thakur
Born from the mother's womb
But in the father's body
Its form was water
It was made by Thakur
It was born from the womb
But in the mother's body
Its form was blood
Whether in two months or in three
The body of lotus leaves
Her body is changing
Whether in eight months or in nine
The body of lotus leaves
Her body made it man.

After this, a mother is supposed to describe an act of birth.

488

I have climbed a dry tree
How shall I descend?
Go by the branches
Descend by the leaves
I will catch you in my cloth.

Finally, the dead man is made to comfort his partner.

489

> *Do not cry, juri*
> *Do not mourn*
> *The house is full of children*
> *Let the sight of them*
> *Press your heart*
> *Juri, I cannot tell*
> *My children's heart*
> *How shall I get*
> *My daily food?*
> *The river is in flood*
> *The river has brimmed over.*
> *How shall I cross?*
> *How shall I go over?*
> *Juri, do not cry*
> *Or weep too much*
> *The warm sun*
> *Will keep you.*

When these songs are over, the men continue dancing and it is only at dawn that the parties disperse.

Later in the morning, a circling ceremony is performed, water, oil and milk are offered and the branch is given to the mourner. If he so likes, he plants it in the ground and if it then takes root, a second Karam must be staged, a year later, to celebrate its 'marriage'. At this Karam, a black goat is sacrificed and a branch from the newly sprouting tree is cut and thrown in water. If the mourner decides not to plant it, he takes the branch to a pool, plunges below the surface and releases it. He then returns with it to the villagers, rice-beer is drunk and the ceremony ends with rinja dancing.

4 THE DISMISSAL OF THE DEAD

Once the bhandan is performed, the dead man is finally gathered to his ancestors. He takes with him all the animals that were sacrificed. He enters Death's kingdom and is allotted a round of daily tasks by Jom Raja. If he was the first to mark a girl with vermilion, their deaths unite them in the after world and even if they have parted while on earth, they must now resume a conjugal routine. Children however are separated from their

340

mothers 'for in the life on earth they sucked their blood'. For much of the day, the ancestors must devote themselves to Jom Raja and to executing his behests. If they have treated others harshly, they are given savage punishments. They bear rotting meat on their head, wrestle with huge worms or sit immersed in excrement. If however they have lived kind and honest lives and not departed radically from the tribal code, they are gently dealt with. They reside in 'Santal' villages, cultivating their fields, living, in fact, in a way that is scarcely different from their life on earth. Moreover, just as in normal Santal life, work gives place to leisure, the ancestors are often free from tasks and can come for short periods to their villages. Even when they are involved in various duties, they can see and hear all that is happening and can hurriedly take leave and intervene. For a generation they take an active interest in village matters, sitting with the living, assisting at births, weddings and at caco chatiar ceremonies, and helping to settle village problems. Only in fact when a generation has completely replaced the old familiar figures and their names are lost to memory do they merge in the multitude of the venerable dead and inter-vene no more. Until this happens, they insist on only one prerogative – that their family should not ignore them. If they are speedily forgotten or conventional tribute is withheld, they are liable to visit the family with sick-ness, loss and worries. For this reason, the immediate ancestors must constantly receive oblations and whether it is a time of drinking water or rice-beer, eating a meal, celebrating a festival, a birth or a wedding or placating the bongas the recent dead must be given their small offerings. At the Sohrae, Baha and Erok' festivals, special sacrifices must be made to them and at the Sohrae festival the village decides whether to perform 'the play of the cattle' according as death has or has not visited the village. If anyone has died the preceding year, a limit is set to jollity and the 'play' is abandoned. For this reason, also, if there is no male member of the household qualified to sacrifice, an agnate of the dead must be charged with this duty. If a daughter is married to a ghar jawae, neither the girl herself nor her husband can offer to the dead and unless a brother or uncle of her father agrees to do it freely, she is expected either to provide the rice and fowls each year or to set aside some land as curuc' cawale to pay for the offerings. The grant of such land lies purely within her discre-tion and none of her relatives can demand it as of right. It is made after her father's death when the occasion first arises. If it is not given the agnates can at most refuse their services and murmur at the girl's impiety. Occasionally at the time of according its approval to her marriage, the village may specify how much land should ultimately be given. Such land is usually only a small plot – 'it is given to the dead father. It is for him.' The relative holds it for his lifetime and after that it merges in his property and is taken by his heirs.

If these rites are completed, the dead dwell peaceably, content with what life gave them and glad that others should now pursue the Santal way of life.

NOTES AND COMMENTS

1 *The Santal Parganas*

During the period to which this book relates, the years 1942 to 1946, the Santal Parganas district in Bihar contained six subdivisions each of which was administered by a subdivisional officer responsible to the Deputy Commissioner. The district lay on the easternmost side of the province, blending partly with the Bengal district of Birbhum, the home of Rabindranath Tagore, and partly with another Bengal district, Burdwan. The broad stream of the Ganges bounded its grassy hills on the north, while far to the south, the river Damodar – the 'sea' in Santal legend – lay just outside a portion of its vast area. The district was 5,400 square miles in size and may perhaps be compared to several English counties merged into one. The capital, Dumka, was a small township forty miles from the nearest railway station and without telephones or electricity. It was the administrative centre of the district but also the headquarters of a subdivision. 'Supposing Dumka to be London', wrote Carstairs, an early Deputy Commissioner, 'the other subdivisional headquarters are Godda at Bedford, Deogarh at Aylesbury, Jamtara at Basingstoke, Rajmahal at Bury St Edmunds and Pakaur at Colchester. The district's greatest length, north and south, is from Guildford to Ely and east and west, from Ipswich to Oxford.'

2 *The Santali Language*

According to Grierson's Linguistic Survey, Santali is an Austro-Asiatic Language, closely related to Mundari and Ho. As the Santals had no written language, the roman character was generally adopted in the nineteenth century by the early missionaries who first reduced it to writing. The resulting script was heavily interlarded with diacritical marks. During my time in the Santal Parganas all printed books in Santali still followed this method. For general readers, signs of this sort are apt to be unintelligible while those who know Santali will readily recognise the words without them. In the interests of readability, I have therefore omitted diacriticals retaining only the apostrophes used after the four checked consonants – c', k', t', and p'. The complexities of Santali as a language are alluded to by Macphail in his brief but charming, fictional *The Story of a Santal*.

3 *'The ever-singing Santals'*

Besides T. H. Lewin, E. G. Man (an Assistant Commissioner in the Santal Parganas) sensed the important part played by poetry in Santal life:

'There is a dash of poetical feeling in the composition of the Sonthals [he wrote in 1867] which shows itself in their traditions. Their songs generally allude to birds and flowers and unlike the lyrics of their neighbours are remarkably free from obscenity. The tunes also which they play on their flutes are often attempts at imitation of the notes of birds or have a wild melancholy cadence, which heard in the depths of the jungle, sounds pleasing on the ear. The following is the song of a love-sick girl:

> The osprey's voice is heard on the mountain
> Then the people feel pity
> Oh, mother, at midnight, the peacock's tail
> Can be seen on the top of the hills and in the valley
> My brother observes the white flower
> Upon the dried-up tree
> The parrot has her young ones
> Oh, aunt, when will you dandle my children?
> When will you, my aunt?
> The cock crows in the morning
> The turtle-dove builds its nest in the garden
> Oh, my mother, come and see it
> From the steep sides of the mountain
> I hear a pair of flutes
> And below in the valley
> The beating of a drum.'

This was not the only song that Man recorded. During a camp at Simra he attended a Santal wedding and as a consequence passed a sleepless night 'for as soon as the males had become too unsteady in gait or voice to dance and sing, the women took their places and until long after cock crow refrains were borne to my unwilling ears as I lay and tossed on my cot.'

The full meaning of these songs was not perhaps realised by Man and it is also obvious that a whole category of Santal poetry – the Bir Seren or Forest Songs – escaped him. None the less, in referring to 'a dash of poetical feeling in the composition of the Santals', he had made a crucial point.

4 *Santali poetry*

Printed collections of Santal songs in the original Santali are listed in the Bibliography – the chief collections being *Hor Seren* and *Don Seren*, published jointly by Gopal Gamaliel Soren and myself in 1943. *Hor Seren* comprises 1676 songs which are sung at festivals or dances, *Don Seren* 1824 songs which are sung at weddings. A further 129 cultivation songs are included in the second volume. The majority of these songs are ancestral but it is part of the vitality of Santal poetry that new songs are sometimes made up on the spur of the moment. There is no special class of poet, singer or bard, and the songs are accordingly communal in origin and inspiration. Songs connected with the induction ceremony of Caco Chatiar and with the ritual of Karam are given in Stephen H. Murmu's *Karam ar Caco Chatiar* (published 1945). The special songs, known as Bir Seren, which are sung in the privacy of the forest, are as yet unpublished. A manuscript collection amounting to almost one thousand is with me and I hope in due course to deposit it in the India Office Library, London. Songs of this kind are characterised by a bold use of sexual terms and for this reason are banned in Santal villages. They fall into two categories – those which are tender, sensitive and charming, the prerogative of women, girls and lovers and those which are coarse and bawdy, the 'music-hall' entertainments which are put on at bitlahas and at annual hunts. Bir Seren, intended primarily for lovers, could well be termed 'Forest Love Songs', Bir Seren which are primarily jocular could be termed 'Forest Hunt Songs'. Since the same title covers both sorts, it is no surprise that, as one Santal expressed it, 'to the old, Bir Seren are jokes but to the young, they are beauty'.

All Santal songs, whether 'forest' or 'village', have certain characteristics. Rhyme is not employed and the form of the song, the length of its lines and indeed its whole structure is determined to a great extent by the tune or melody. Few songs have more than ten or twelve lines; any that are longer have usually a ritual purpose. In some cases the fourth line repeats the second but more normally every line is different and the song achieves its effect by a subtle combination of assonance, rhythm and imagery. In one important respect, the use of unexplained symbols, Santal poetry is very close to that of the Uraons, samples of which I translated in my books, *The Blue Grove* and *The Dove and the Leopard.* Just as in English slang, 'girls' are called 'birds', so in Santali 'girls' are often 'peacocks', children 'little parrots', mothers 'milk-trees', boys 'flutes' and so on. It is to the vivid character of particular symbols that many Santal songs owe their poetic brilliance.

For translation, I have adopted the following principles. When working on Uraon poetry, I had modelled myself on Arthur Waley and believing, like him, that 'images were the soul of poetry', I had refrained both from using rhyme and from 'either adding images of my own or suppressing those of the original.' The same method had been independently arrived at by Verrier Elwin, first in his *Songs of the Forest*, a collection that he published with Shamrao Hivale in 1935 and later in *The Baiga.* We were aware however that not every previous translator adhered to these principles and when in 1942 we began to edit the Indian journal of anthropology, *Man in India*, I was led to preface a short anthology of Indian folk-poetry with the following editorial:

'If translations are to be of value, it is obvious that they should conform to certain standards. The most evident is that the translation should itself be a poem. If it is not a poem, if it does not create the effect of poetry, it is merely a degradation of its original, an act of murder. The second requisite is that the translation should correspond with the original. If it does not correspond, it loses all claim to scientific value. It ceases to be the translation of a poem. It becomes a poem by a translator. Such a poem may have value as poetry but it has none at all as science. The problem of translating Indian folk poetry is in essentials how to produce a version which contains all the elements both of poetry and science.

'It will be evident that to this problem no solution will be perfect. A poem is a combination of certain images, certain rhythms and certain effects of music, and only if a translation could provide an exact parallel for each of these elements could it be perfect. In actual fact, a translation from a tribal language into English can parallel only one of these elements. Differences of verbal structure are so great that if parallel images are retained, the rhythms will be different. If the rhythms are maintained, the images will suffer, while no form of English can reproduce the musical effects of Hindi, Uraon, Gondi or Mundari. "Certain things," said Ezra Pound, "are translatable from one language to another, a tale or an image will translate; music will practically never translate." A translation becomes possible, therefore, only when there is no attempt at all at *complete* correspondence.

'We believe that the best solution so far reached is that of Arthur Waley. In translating from the Chinese, Arthur Waley was faced with problems that are identical with those of Indian languages. His solution has been a series of versions in which the literal meaning of the translation corresponds with the literal meaning of the original. In particular, the images are never added to and never subtracted from. The poem as a system of images remains in translation what it is in the original. Instead, however, of attempting a duplication of rhyme, rhythm or music, his versions use the rhythms and sound effects which come most naturally to the English. The original form is abandoned and instead the effort is to create a new form which is valid for a contemporary sensibility. We believe that in terms of this solution translations of Indian folk poetry can preserve all the elements essential for anthropology while still retaining all the ingredients of poetry.'

This editorial was published in March 1943, four months after I reached the Santal Parganas. I cannot hope that all the present versions successfully achieve these standards. But they do, at least, attempt to reach them. I have not distorted the literal meaning of any of the originals and I have not added or left out any image or symbol.

There remains the question of how best to present these versions. It would have been possible to group them according to the occasions on which they were used and to add notes explaining their imagery. But this, I think, would have weakened their impact. Santal poetry is Santal life; Santal life is Santal poetry. I decided, therefore, to employ two methods and to alternate between them. If a song illustrated with special vividness a particular aspect of Santal living, I have used it as evidence of thought, feeling or behaviour and removed it from its social context. In the accounts of marital and pre-marital love, for example, I have freely inserted wedding, Sohrae and Forest love songs. If, on the other hand, certain songs or stories are essential parts of a ceremony such as the Karam, or of a festival such as the Baha, I have presented them in their original setting. The result may not be wholly satisfactory but the following chart will, I hope, make clear my underlying method.

Chapter I: The Santals
Cultivation songs (Horo Rohoe): 1–4

Chapter II: Early Years
Forest song (Bir Seren): 5

Chapter III: Induction to the Tribe
Caco Chatiar songs: 6, 7

Chapter IV: Social Dances
Lagre songs: 8–15
Dahar songs: 16–22
Golwari songs: 23–30
Dasae songs: 31–46

Chapter V: The Rules of Sex
Marriage songs (Don Seren): 47–49

347

5 Santal pre-marital infertility

During my time in the Santal Parganas, the problem of pre-marital infertility was still puzzling all those who knew the tribes of Middle or Eastern India well. It was common knowledge that occasionally – very occasionally – an unmarried girl of fifteen years became pregnant but what surprised everyone was the rarity of such cases. The Santals took it for granted that for several years before marriage, every boy and girl had regular sexual intercourse. Why was it, however, that children so rarely resulted? Santals with whom I discussed the matter could offer no real explanation and suggestions of coitus interruptus, contraceptive devices and so on were always brushed aside. What was true of Santals appeared equally true of Uraons, Mundas, Kharias, Hos, Gonds, Baigas and Murias.

In 1946, the problem still appeared to defy solution but in 1947 Verrier Elwin included a detailed discussion of it in his massive study, *The Muria and their Ghotul.* 'The most satisfactory general explanation,' he wrote, 'is in the theory of a period of adolescent sterility.' He cited Hartman whose experiments in the nineteen-thirties had established the fact that 'there is not only a very high incidence of non-ovulatory cycles in young mammals but that human beings also have an infecund period for some years after the ménarche.' He also quoted a lucid summary by Ashley-Montague of this and subsequent literature on the subject. 'It has long been known,' Ashley-Montague wrote, 'that puberty is by no means coincident with the development of the reproductive powers, that in the girl menstruation may long precede the more important function of ovulation, and that in the youth ejaculation may long precede the process of spermatogenesis.' Although much further field-work is needed and what is true of tribal India may not necessarily apply to other countries and peoples, there seems little doubt, on present evidence, that a sterility interval of the kind described is the most likely solution to the problem of Santal pre-marital infertility.

6 Santal Polygamy

Polygamy is not regarded by Santals with much enthusiasm and a number of proverbs deprecate its rather dubious joys. 'A pair of dogs always bite.' 'A co-wife pricks like spear grass.' 'Pecking hens never agree.' 'Sparks fly from a co-wife like an ebony branch flaming in the rains.' Yet occasionally circumstances make it desirable. If a woman is sickly, it is kinder to bring another wife as housekeeper rather than divorce the first wife and send her away. Similarly if a younger sister is taken, the result may be a happy domestic set-up.

If an elder brother dies, his widow often remains a part of the household. She may already have allowed her husband's younger brother access to her person and if he takes her as a co-wife, the terms of marriage excuse him from paying a further bride-price. There is now the advantage of common cultivation. Her children remain to assist in the home and if his first wife likes her company, the household continues as a smoothly working unit. Even if his first wife is opposed, their conventional intimacy may prompt him to install the woman as a wife.

Besides these family adjustments, the need of a wife in the world to come may sometimes impel a Santal to experiment with plural marriage. Chota Murmu of Lakhibad was first married to a girl who had already been divorced. Later he decided that he must also have an unmarried girl as his wife so as not to be alone in the after world. His wife's younger sister was still unmarried and he therefore took her.

In Jitpur, a wedding had been arranged between Kadu Tudu and the elder daughter of Alma Kisku. Before the marriage took place another man put vermilion on the girl and thus made her his wife in the world of the dead. The girl, however, declined to marry him and it was finally decided that Kadu would take her, but would also marry her younger sister.

Finally, a sense of personal prestige sometimes results in a Santal expanding his ménage. In Asanbona, Lakhan Tudu had seven wives 'because he was a pargana' and I was told how he used to ride round every night visiting each woman in turn. In Mahulbona the headman took a second wife 'so that he might boast of his wealth'.

When one or more extra wives are taken, it is the attitude of the first wife that usually decides the composition of the household. If she is indifferent or even agreeable to the arrangement, the new wife is admitted to the house. Singhrai Marandi of Karmai was a big cultivator with a large house. He had five wives all of whom lived with him in the same courtyard. Nimai Murmu of Rajpokhar also had five wives and kept them in a single house. In Titria, Bhadu Murmu had four wives and they too lived together.

If, on the other hand, the second wife is regarded as a rival, she is sometimes given a completely separate house and allowed to run her own affairs. In Ghanti, Ghata Marandi took a girl against his first wife's wishes. He already had a number of children so in order to avoid friction he installed the girl in his father's house lower down the village lane.

7 *Additional forms of Santal marriage*

Besides the standard form of wedding (dol bapla) described in Chapter X, four other kinds of Santal wedding are from time to time resorted to:

(1) Tunki dipil—'bearing on the head a small basket'. This is a standard wedding stripped to bare essentials with most of the celebrations telescoped into one. It is adopted when both parties are poor and the minimum of expenses must therefore be incurred. The chief difference is that vermilion is put on the girl's brow in the boy's house rather than in the girl's.

(2) Golaeti—'exchange'. This also is an economy-type wedding but with fewer savings. It involves the double wedding of a brother and sister in one family to a brother and sister in another. Under this arrangement there is a single 'viewing' of each household and although two separate ceremonies are held they are greatly simplified. The party of the eldest boy moves first and goes to his bride's house where sindurdan and the circling ceremony are performed. The boy's party then returns home taking the girl with them and is followed shortly after by the party of the girl's brother. A second sindurdan and circling ceremony are then performed in the house of the first boy. In this way one wedding follows on the heels of another and since the villagers are entertained on only one occasion, much expenditure is saved.

(3) Ghardi jawae—'the serving son-in-law'. This is an arrangement by which a bridegroom becomes a serving son-in-law for a limited period of from five to seven years. He lives in his father-in-law's house, is excused the payment of a bride-price, is kept in food and clothes and at the end of his term returns to his own village, taking with him his wife, and children and the basic necessities for starting a new home. The ceremony differs sharply from that of a dol bapla since it takes place in the girl's house and, instead of the boy's party going for the bride, the girl's father and some old villagers go for the boy. The bridegroom, in fact, is treated like a girl and the girl's party that brings him is called 'the boy's train of followers'. When the boy arrives with the party, there is no mock combat in which the two parties face each other in warlike lines. The boy is merely brought to the village and after the girl has been lifted in the bridal basket and he has put vermilion on her, he is quietly installed.

Ghardi jawae weddings are usually resorted to when a Santal father finds himself growing old with no sons of an age to keep him or when his wife has borne him only daughters, but there is still the possibility that she may bear him a son. Boys who become serving sons-in-law are normally drawn from poor families.

(4) Ghar jawae—'daughter into son'. In contrast to a ghardi jawae who tides a Santal through a short but difficult period, a ghar jawae is essentially a long-term solution of a different and more basic problem. As a father grows old, it is imperative for him to have a man about the house – to supervise the family affairs and carry on the cultivation. If he has no sons and marries his daughters in the usual way, he may end his days, ill and lonely in an empty house. Moreover, the older a man gets the more he values children. In fact between the very old and the very young there is often a strange bond of sympathy. To be old and have no children, playing and chattering in the house – that is a fate from which a Santal shrinks. If in addition he has a crippled son or a favourite or deformed daughter, these are merely extra reasons for so arranging a girl's marriage that her husband comes to live permanently in his father-in-law's house.

This permanent reversal of the ordinary assumptions of a marriage has a number of revolutionary corollaries. The first and most vital consequence is that so far as her father's land is concerned, the daughter now becomes a son. During her father's lifetime, she cannot claim a partition but on his death she inherits his land to the exclusion of all her other relatives. If she has a brother the normal rule is that she shares equally with him and it is only if a smaller share is expressly allotted to her at her marriage that she inherits less. Like a son, she may also adopt a child provided that the villagers agree.

As far as movable property is concerned, marriage to a ghar jawae gives a girl not perhaps the full status of a son but something closely approximating to it. If she has a brother she will share equally unless a smaller share has been expressly reserved for her. If she has no brother but her father has left agnates, she will inherit all the movables but if the agnates perform her father's funeral, they are entitled to recover their expenses. If there are neither brothers nor agnates, the girl inherits all her father's property.

For achieving this new status, the ghar jawae acts only as a catalyst. He himself acquires no right of inheritance in his father-in-law's property but is merely the means by which his wife secures these rights. As soon, in fact, as the boy has entered the house, the girl approximates to a son and even though she divorces her husband, her rights as a special kind of inheriting daughter persist. She is required, however, to remain in her father's house and on his lands and if the boy dies and she marries again, she must take another ghar jawae as her new husband. Should she marry again and leave the village, such a union cancels her special status and she once again becomes an ordinary daughter.

Similar changes occur with regard to her children. If the girl is now a son in respect of her father's land, she becomes to a great extent a father in respect of her children. All offspring by the ghar jawae are brought up in her father's house and if she divorces her husband, they continue in her custody. Their names are chosen as if she were a son and it is only in matters of religion that her status dwindles to that of an ordinary wife and mother. Her children take the clan of the ghar jawae and in a similar manner, the girl herself is debarred from worshipping her father's bongas and must now assist in the worship of her husband's. Apart from this, she is virtually a son.

This strange reversal of roles has corresponding implications for the boy. The first requirement of the union – that he should forsake his father's house and reside permanently with his father-in-law – gives him an immediate resemblance to a girl and there are even further ways in which this analogy is developed. His status, in the household, is that of a wife. He is entitled to maintenance in food and clothing and to treatment in sickness and when he dies the family must meet the expenses of his funeral. When questions of divorce arise, an equally feminine role is filled. It is the ghar jawae and not the girl who is sent home while if the boy is at fault, the girl can claim divorce money. Similarly if the girl commits adultery, the ghar jawae is scarcely different from an injured wife. He can make the incident an excuse for separation but apart from divorce money can demand nothing else.

It is in fact in three respects only that he remains a man. He takes the dominant part in cultivation. He retains the rights of a son in his father's land and movables while, so far as religion is concerned, his bongas continue as before. He can neither sacrifice to his father-in-law's bongas nor learn their names. Similarly while he can share his father-in-law's sacrificial meat (except the head), he can only do so in respect of sacrifices within the house. Even at funerals, his role is comparatively unimportant and it is only as a last resort that he can touch the corpse of his father-in-law with the ceremonial fire.

Such a marriage requires, as a first essential, the agreement of the villagers.

Lotho Soren of Bichkora had eight sons while his younger brother had two daughters. The brother wanted to bring a ghar jawae but Lotho objected on the ground that if he wanted assistance, he could easily adopt a nephew. The villagers thought Lotho's viewpoint very reasonable and accordingly withheld consent.

On the other hand, in Nawadih, Dabra Marandi had a son, Barka, by his first wife. The woman died and he married again. By his second wife he had two daughters of whom the first was married in the ordinary way and for the second he proposed to take a ghar jawae. Barka was very much against it but since he was not treating his father well, the villagers over-ruled him and a ghar jawae was brought.

In another case, Phoce Hansdak' of Baghsol had two daughters while his elder brother had three sons. When Phoce proposed to bring a ghar jawae, his brother strongly objected. Phoce replied, 'I am not giving my daughter your land. I am only giving her my own.' The villagers supported him and in due course the arrangement was made.

When their approval has been given, the next step is to choose a daughter and arrange a boy who will marry her. A daughter with brothers is eligible and neither the brothers nor other ghar jawaes have any power of veto. One or more daughters can be given ghar jawaes and there are cases in which every daughter has been married in this manner. Moreover the fact that a daughter has been married once in the ordinary way and has then been divorced or widowed is not in itself a bar to a second marriage in this form. If there are no sisters and a widowed daughter is alive, she can herself arrange a ghar jawae provided that the villagers agree.

Equally, almost any boy can be accorded this status. It is of no consequence whether he is a bachelor, a divorcee or a widower with children and provided he is already married in the same family, even a married boy can become a ghar jawae.

Jalpa Tudu of Dundin was married to a girl of Turka. His wife's younger sister became a widow and Jalpa was then married to her in ghar jawae form. Jalpa and his two wives then lived together on his second wife's land.

Once the principle has been accepted, the form of marriage is determined by circumstances. If the girl has not been married before and a public wedding is proposed, the arrangements closely follow the lines on which a ghardi jawae is wedded. There is the same engagement of a matchmaker, the same viewing of the houses and the same betrothal without a presentation of clothes. If the families so desire, the girl's party visits the boy's house and gives him a dhoti but this is not at all compulsory. Similarly on the wedding day, there is the same fetching of the boy, his same installation in the girl's house and the same exemption of the bride-price. As in the wedding of a ghardi jawae, the bridegroom must bring the vermilion, the basket and a cloth for the bride but there is otherwise great flexibility in the presents.

There is, however, one important addition to the ritual. On the morning after the wedding, the girl's father and the village officials conduct the bridegroom through the fields and he is shown the family lands. If there is already another ghar jawae in the house or an adult son, the new ghar jawae is shown only the share which he himself will cultivate. Similarly if at the time of his induction certain lands have been reserved for the agnates, these are excluded from the showing.

This inspection of the lands is in almost all areas a normal aspect of a ghar jawae wedding and it is everywhere a valuable indication of the boy's status. It is not however an essential of a valid wedding. In some cases Santals omit it 'because they forget'. In others they leave it out 'because it is not strictly necessary' while in certain villages it is reduced to a nominal gesture. When Chunda Soren was taken as a ghar jawae of the Sibtala headman, the headman merely gave a jerk with his chin, Chunda looked over his shoulder and the showing was done.

If this kind of wedding is the usual and best form, it is sometimes preceded by an arrangement known as agu hatar or 'bringing in'. This enables a ghar jawae to enter his father-in-law's house without waiting for a formal celebration. When this happens, his status as a ghar jawae is fully understood and if any of the parties should die before the formal wedding is performed, his position is in no way affected.

In 1945 Thakur Hansdak' of Ranidinda obtained the approval of his village to the bringing of a ghar jawae. By the time everything was settled the wedding season was over and Thakur himself was also short of money. As he needed the boy for helping him in the fields, he brought him to his house and the following year performed the wedding.

Besides arranging the marriage in either of these ways, a Santal father can convert an existing son-in-law into a ghar jawae. If the boy is already serving as a ghardi jawae or has married the girl by 'intrusion' or 'discovery', all that is necessary is to call the villagers, secure their approval and ratify the arrangement by drinking some rice-beer.

If his daughter is living at her husband's house, his son-in-law can be made into a ghar jawae by the process known as agu mit' ('taking him in'). Here also the villagers are consulted and if they agree, the daughter simply returns to her father bringing her husband with her. The couple live in his house and the fact of village recognition gives the son-in-law this new status.

8 Santal laws of inheritance, rights in property, etc.

I have discussed these topics in detail in three reports – *Civil law in Santal society*, *Bitlaha: a report on Santal criminal law*, and *Civil justice in tribal India* (with special reference to the Santal Parganas). I have deposited manuscript copies of these papers in the India Office Library and Records, London.

9 Acknowledgments

I cannot conclude without recording my deep indebtedness to those who assisted me in the final preparation of the text: to my wife, Mildred Archer, who with our son, Michael and daughter, Margaret savoured the delights of living in the Santal Parganas, to Professor Christoph von Furer-Haimendorf, who visited me in Dumka, took photographs (some of which he has kindly allowed me to use) and who over the years has discussed with me many facets of tribal India, and to Jane Boulenger, Peter Hill, and John and Lorraine Parker who read the manuscript with critical care and gave me most helpful opinions.

BIBLIOGRAPHY

Abbreviations

J.B.O.R.S.   Journal of the Bihar and Orissa Research Society.
J.(R.)A.S.B.   Journal of the (Royal) Asiatic Society of Bengal.
Mem.(R.)A.S.B.   Memoirs of the (Royal) Asiatic Society of Bengal.
B.C.R.I.   Bulletin of the Cultural Research Institute, Chinwarah,
                  West Bengal.
B.A.S.I.   Bulletin of the Anthropological Survey of India.
Q.J.M.S.   Quarterly Journal of the Mythic Society.

i ENGLISH

Allanson, H. Ll. L. *Final Report on the Survey and Settlement Operations in the District of Sonthal Parganas 1898-1910* (Calcutta, 1912).
   Contains a detailed account of measures to keep the Santal on his land as well as notes on Santal village officials.
Archer, Mildred. 'The Folk-tale in Santal Society', *Man in India*, XXIV (1944), 224–32.
   Indian Miniatures and Folk Paintings (Arts Council, London, 1967).
   Discusses and illustrates scroll-paintings by jadupatuas of Santal subjects.
   Indian Paintings from Court, Town and Village (Arts Council, London, 1970).
   Illustrates further examples of scroll-paintings by jadupatuas of Santal subjects.
Archer, Mildred and Archer, W. G. 'Santal Painting', *Axis*, Autumn 1936, 27–8.
Archer, W. G. 'Santal Poetry', *Man in India*, XXIII (1943), 147–53.
   'Betrothal Dialogues', *ibid.*, XXIII (1943), 147–53.
   'An Indian Riddle Book', *ibid.*, XXIII (1943), 265–315.
   'Festival Songs', *ibid.*, XXIV (1944), 70–74.
   'More Santal Songs', *ibid.*, XXIV (1944), 141–4.
   'The Illegitimate Child in Santal Society', *ibid.*, XXIV (1944), 154–69.
   'The Forcible Marriage', *ibid.*, XXV (1945), 29–42.
   'The Santal Rebellion', *ibid.*, XXV (1945), 223–39.
   'Santal Rebellion Songs', *ibid.*, XXV (1945), 207.
   'Santal Transplantation Songs', *ibid.*, XXVI (1946), 6–7.
   'Ritual Friendship in Santal Society', *ibid.*, XXVII (1947), 57–60.
   'The Santal Treatment of Witchcraft', *ibid.*, XXVII (1947), 103–121.
   India and Modern Art (London, 1959).
   Discusses and illustrates the treatment of Santal subjects in modern Indian painting.
Bishwas, P. C. *Primitive Religion, Social Organization, Law and Government amongst the Santals* (Calcutta, 1935).
Bodding, P. O. 'Some Remarks on the Position of Women among the Santals', *J.B.O.R.S.*, II (1916), 239–49.

The Traditions and Institutions of the Santals. Second Edition of *Horkoren Mare Hapramko reak' Katha* with a foreword by P. O. Bodding (Benagaria, 1916).

Materials for a Santali Grammar (Benagaria, 1922).

'A Chapter of Santal Folk-lore', *Indian Institute publications, Royal Frederick University, Kristiania* I (1924), 41–119.

Studies in Santal Medicine and Connected Folk-lore. Part I, 'The Santals and Disease', *M.A.S.B.*, X (1925), 1–132.

Part II, 'Santal Medicine', *M.A.S.B.*, X (1927), 133–426.

Part III, 'How the Santals live', *M.A.S.B.*, X (1940), 427–502.

Santal Folk Tales, 3 vols. (Oslo, 1925–29).

'The meaning of the words Buru and Bonga in Santali', *J.B.O.R.S.*, XII (1926), 63–77, 286–8.

A Santali Grammar for Beginners (Benagaria, 1929).

'Notes on the Santals', Census of India, 1931, I, India, Part III B, 98–107.

A Santal Dictionary, 5 vols. (Oslo, 1932–36).

A masterpiece of learning.

Santal Riddles (Oslo, 1940).

Witchcraft among the Santals (Oslo, 1940).

The Traditions and Institutions of the Santals, being a translation of *Horkoren Mare Hapramko reak' Katha* (Oslo, 1942).

Bolton, C. W. *Notes on the Settlement of the Sonthal Pergunnahs (Zamindari portion) 1874–9* (Calcutta, 1880, Deputy Commissioner's Record Room, Dumka).

Bompas, C. H. *Folk-lore of the Santal Parganas* (London, 1909).

Includes translated accounts of witches and of bonga lovers supplied to Bodding.

Bonnerjee, B. 'The Social and Ceremonial Life of the Santals', *The Indian Antiquary*, LIX (1930), 57–60, 88–92, 95–100.

Bradley Birt, F. B. *The Story of an Indian Upland* (London, 1925).

Buchanan, Francis (ed. Banerji-Sastri, A.). *An Account of the District of Bhagalpur in 1810–11* (Patna, 1939).

Campbell, A. *Santal Folk Tales* (Pokhuria, 1899).

Collected in the Manbhum district of West Bengal.

'The Traditional Migration of the Santal tribes', *The Indian Antiquary*, XXIII (1894), 103–4.

A Santali English Dictionary (Pokhuria, 1899).

'Rules of Succession and Partition of Property as observed by the Santals', *J.B.O.R.S.*, I (1915), 21–25.

'Superstitions of the Santals', *J.B.O.R.S.*, I (1915), 213–28.

'The Traditions of the Santals', *J.B.O.R.S.*, II (1916), 15–29.

A variation of the myth as recorded in *Karam ar Caco Chatiar* and *Horkoren Mare Hapramko reak' Katha.*

'Santal legends', *J.B.O.R.S.*, II (1916), 191–200.

'Santal Marriage Customs', *J.B.O.R.S.*, II (1916), 304–37.

'Death and Cremation Ceremonies among the Santals', *J.B.O.R.S.*, II (1916), 449–56.

Carstairs, R. *Letter No. 1394 dated 8.7.1892 to the Commissioner, Sonthal Parganas, forwarding J. A. Craven's Settlement Report* (Deputy Commissioner's Record Room, Dumka).

The Little World of an Indian District Officer (London, 1912).
An account of his work by one of the greatest of 'Santal' Deputy Commissioners.
Harma's Village (Pokhuria, 1935).
A novel of the Santal Rebellion.
Cole, F. T. 'Santali Riddles', *The Indian Antiquary*, IV (1875), 164.
'Santali Folk-lore', *ibid.*, IV (1875), 257.
'Santal Ideas of the Future', *ibid.*, VII (1878), 273–4.
Craven, J. A. Settlement Report (1892) (with forwarding letter No. 1394 dated 8.7.1892 to the Commissioner, Santal Parganas from R. Carstairs) (Deputy Commissioner's Record Room, Dumka).
Crooke, W. *Religion and Folklore of Northern India* (Oxford, 1926).
Culshaw, W. J. 'Some Notes on Bongaism', *J.R.A.S.B.*, V (1939), 427–31.
'Some Beliefs and Customs relating to Birth among the Santals', *J.R.A.S.B.*, VII (1941), 115–27.
'Lars Olsen Skrefsrud, 1840–1910', *International Review of Missions*, XXXI (1942), 347–53.
A biographical sketch of a missionary who was also a pioneer of Santal studies.
'The "Folk Consciousness" of the Santals', *Essays in Anthropology presented to S. C. Roy* (Lucknow, 1942), 219–27.
'Santal Songs', *Proceedings Asiatic Folk-literature Society*, I (1944), no. I.
'Early Records concerning the Santals', *Man in India*, XXV (1945), 191–3.
Gives extracts from early reports of the Freewill Baptist Foreign Missionary Society ranging from 1838 to 1847 and includes a vivid reference to Santal dancing.
'The Santal Rebellion', *ibid.*, XXV (1945), 218–23.
Tribal Heritage: a study of the Santals (London, 1949).
An account of the Santals of the Bankura district of West Bengal.
Dalton, E. T. *Descriptive Ethnology of Bengal* (Calcutta, 1872).
Dutta, Kali Kinkar. *The Santal Insurrection* (Calcutta, 1940).
Elwin, Verrier. *Folk-tales of Mahakoshal* (Bombay, 1944).
A brilliant collection of folk-tales with notes and references to Santal and other folk-lore.
Loss of Nerve (Bombay, 1941).
The Aboriginals (Bombay, 1943).
The Tribal Art of Middle India (Bombay, 1951).
Describes and illustrates Santal wedding litters.
Gait, E. A. *Census of India, 1901, Bengal* (Calcutta, 1902).
Gantzer, J. F. *Final Report on the Revision Survey and Settlement Operations in the District of Santal Parganas, 1922–35* (Patna, 1936).
Gausdal, J. *Contributions to Santal Hymnology* (Bergen, 1935).
'The Khunt system of the Santals', *J.B.O.R.S.*, XXVIII (1942), Part IV.
The Santal Khunts (Oslo, 1960).
Ghose, Sudhin N. *Cradle of the Clouds* (London, 1951).
A novel of rare charm describing a young Bengali's sensitive reactions to Santals in West Bengal.
Grierson, G. A. *Linguistic Survey of India, IV, Munda and Dravidian Languages* (Calcutta, 1906).
Guha, B. S. *Racial Elements in the Population* (Bombay, 1944).

Hearn, W. N. 'Notes on the Santals', *Census of India, 1931, I, India, Part III B*, 108–9.

Hoernle, E. S. *A Brief Introduction to the Administration of the Santal Parganas* (Benagaria, 1929).

Hunter, W. W. *The Annals of Rural Bengal* (London, 1868).
A Statistical Account of Bengal: the Sonthal Parganas (Calcutta, 1872).
Reproduces the section in Dalton.

Lacey, W. G. 'The Santals', *Census of India, 1931, I, India Part III B*, 97–98.
Census of India, 1931, VII Bihar & Orissa Part I Report.
Contains a survey of recent Santal migrations with notes on Santal astrology, musical instruments, agricultural implements, bows and arrows and the life after death from notes by P. O. Bodding.

Lewin, T. H. *The Wild Races of South-eastern India* (1870).

Macphail, J. M. *The Story of the Santal* (Calcutta, 1922).

Macphail, R. M. 'Notes on Santals', *Census of India, 1931, I, India, Part III B*, 109.

McAlpin, M. C. *Report on the condition of the Santals in the Districts of Birbhum, Bankura, Midnapore and North Balasore* (Calcutta, 1909).

McPherson, H. *Note on the Aboriginal Races of the Santal Parganas* (Calcutta, 1908).
Final Report on the Survey and Settlement Operations in the District of Santal Parganas, 1898–1907 (Calcutta, 1907).
The fullest account of the history and administration of the district.

Man, E. G. *Sonthalia and the Sonthals* (Calcutta, London, 1867).

Martin, Montgomery, *Eastern India* (London, 1832).
Contains a garbled version of Buchanan's note.

Majumdar, S. C. 'Some Santal Songs', *The Visva-bharati Quarterly*, III (1925), 67–9.

Mitchell, J. M. 'Santali Songs with Translations', *The Indian Antiquary*, IV (1875), 342–4.

Mookherjee, H. N. 'Ceremonies associated with the agricultural operations of the Santals', *Folk-lore*, VIII (1967), 86–94.

Mukherjea, Charu Lal. *The Santals* (Calcutta, 1945).

Mukherji, C. C. 'Notes on the Santals and Kherias of Manbhum District', *Census o, India, 1931, I, India, Part III B*, 110–12.

Naqavi, S. M. 'Santal Murders', *Man in India*, XXIII (1943), 236–52.

O'Malley, L. S. S. *Bengal District Gazetteers: Santal Parganas* (First edition, Calcutta, 1910; second edition, revised by S. C. Mukherji, Patna, 1932).
Reproduces a section on the Santals from the first edition but adds extra notes by P. O. Bodding on methods of cultivation, musical instruments and weapons. Adds an inaccurate note on gharjawae and includes some incorrect sentences on inheritance.
(ed.) *Modern India and the West* (London, 1942).
Contains a discussion of Santals by J. H. Hutton.

Orans, Martin. *The Santals: a Tribe in Search of a Great Tradition* (Detroit, 1965).
An account of the Santals of Jamshedpur, Bihar and of Mayurbhanj, Orissa.

Phillips, J. *An Introduction to the Santali Language* (Calcutta, 1852).

Prakasi, K. and Mukherjee, B. N. 'Marriage and fertility among the Santals', *B.C.R.I.*, VIII (1969), 26–31.

Puxley, E. L. *A Vocabulary of the Santali Language* (London, 1868).

Risley, H. H. *The Tribes and Castes of Bengal* (Calcutta, 1891).
The section on Santals includes the first statement in English of the Santal law of inheritance.

The People of India (Calcutta, 1908).
Reproduces the section on Santals originally published in *The Tribes & Castes of Bengal*.

Rochar, V. K. 'Kinship terms and usages among the Santals of Bolpur, Birbhum', *B.A.S.I.*, XII (1963), 47–56.
'Family Spirits and Deities among the Santals and associated Rituals', *J.A.S.B.*, V (1963), 59 seq.
'More Village Bongas of the Santals', *Folk-lore*, V (1964), 448–53.
'Ghosts and Witches among the Santals', *Q.J.M.S.* LV (1964–5), 47–52.
'Village deities of the Santals and associated rituals', *Anthropos*, LXI (1966), 241–257.
'Village organisation among the Santals', *B.C.R.I.*, V (1966), 11–19.
A series of papers based on researches in Birbhum, West Bengal.

Roussos, T. 'Santal Marriage Customs', *New Review*, XVI (1942), 148–57.

Rowat, F. 'Other Notes on the Santals', *Census of India, 1931, I, India, Part III B*, 107–8.

Saha, N. K. 'Husband, Wife and Children in a Santal Village', *B.C.R.I.*, VIII (1969), 97–102.

Sen Gupta, S. K. 'Some Aspects of a Santal Village', *Folk-lore*, VI (1965), 109–113.

Sherwill, W. S. 'Notes upon a Tour through the Rajmahal Hills', *J.A.S.B.*, XX (1851), 544–606.

Shore, John. 'Some Extraordinary Facts, Customs and Practices of the Hindus', *Asiatic Researches*, IV (1795), 345 seq.

Skrefsrud, L. O. *Introduction to the Grammar of the Santali Language* (Benares, 1873).

Sutherland, H. C. *Report on the Management of the Rajmahal Hills dated 8 June 1819* (Deputy Commissioner's Record Room, Dumka).

Thompson, E. and Garratt, G. T. *Rise and Fulfilment of British Rule in India* (London, 1934).
Contains a commentary on the Santal rebellion.

Waddell, 'The Traditional Migration of the Santal Tribe', *The Indian Antiquary*, XXII (1893), 294–6.

ii SANTALI

Archer, W. G. and Murmu, Stephen H. *Hor Kudum* (Dumka, 1944).

Archer, W. G. and Soren, Gopal Gamaliel. *Hor Seren* (Dumka, 1943).
Don Seren (Dumka, 1943).

Deshmanjhi, Chotrae. *Chotrae Deshmanjhi reak' Katha* (Benagaria, 1938).

Haram, Kolean and Skrefsrud, L. O. *Horkoren Mare Hapramko reak' Katha* (Benagaria, 1887).

Murmu, S. C. *Gam Kahani* (Dumka, 1944).

Murmu, Stephen H. *Karam ar Caco Chatiar* (Dumka, 1945).
Hor Bapla Puthi (Benagaria, 1961).

Murmu, Solomon. *Hor Gidra Enec'* (Dumka, 1946).

Rapaz, R. R. Kisku. *Harmawak' Ato* (Dumka, 1946).

GLOSSARY

I. SANTALI

Abge bonga   Sub-clan spirit.

Ag muk   The funerary ceremony of touching the mouth of a corpse with fire.

Agu hatar   A ghar jawae by anticipation.

Agu mit'   A son-in-law brought back to be a ghar jawae.

Apangir   Elopement.

Arak'   Pot herbs.

Atnak'   *Terminalia tomentosa*, W. & A. A tree.

Ato   Village.

Ato bapla   'A wedding by the village', symbolic term for bitlaha.

Baha   A flower.

Bahu   Bride.

Bahu jawae   'Bride and bridegroom', also the leaf emblems depicting the sexual organs.

Bajra   *Sorghum vulgare*, Pers. A millet.

Bapla   A wedding.

Baske   A Santal clan.

Besra   A Santal clan.

Bhandan   Final funerary feast.

Bhelaoja   A plant used at the Karam ceremony.

Bhinsar   Dawn or day-break; a certain way of drumming, dancing or singing commenced at day-break.

Bhitar   Private family shrine.

Bidhanta   Controller of destiny; allocator of the soul and sex of a male child.

Bidhi   Controller of destiny; allocator of the soul and sex of a female child.

Bidhua   A bastard whose father is unknown.

Bir kitauri   *Plumbago zeylanica*, Willd. A jungle plant rather like sugar cane with red flowers.

Bir   Forest.

Bir sendra   Annual hunt.

Bitlaha   A punitive mass gathering for major tribal offences.

Bital   Outcaste.

Bol   To enter or intrude.

Bonga   Spirit.

Bonga tala. To bring into the bongas, i.e. formally adopt.

Buru Hill or mountain.

Caco chatiar Ceremonial purification of young children; the tribal induction ceremony.

Catom arak' *Oxalis pusilla*, Salisb. A plant used in Santal medicine.

Caulia *Ruellia suffruticosa*, Roxb. A bush.

Chadua A divorced man.

Chadui A divorced woman.

Chata Umbrella; also the umbrella festival.

Chat pat *Evolvolus hirsutus*, Willd. A creeper.

Chatiar Ceremonial purification.

Cela Disciple, pupil.

Codgoc' *Ophicephalus gachua*, Buch. A fish.

Cok khunti A pole set up in celebration of festivities.

Core A Santal clan.

Dadi A spring.

Dahar A quick-step dance.

Dan Witch.

Dangua Unmarried.

Danta A type of dance performed by men at the Sohrae festival.

Dar Branch or twig.

Dare Tree.

Dasae daran September wanderings.

Dataoni A twig of a sal, or nim tree used as a toothbrush.

Deger A small kettle-drum.

Deper (der) To copulate.

Deshmanjhi Pargana's deputy and assistant.

Dharwak' Branch; sending round a dharwak', a summons.

Dhub *Cynodon dactylon*. Pers. Reg. A sacred grass of fine texture.

Dibi Santal term for the Hindu goddess, the Devi.

Dihri Hunt-master; president of the annual hunt.

Disom duk Epidemic.

Disom hor Men of the country, the Santals of the area.

Dol Company, party.

Dol bapla A full-dress or party wedding.

Dom enec' Wedding dance with drummers of the Dom caste.

Don The wedding dance.

Don seren Wedding songs.

Dunger Dance by nude jokers at annual hunts and bitlahas.

Durumjak' A form of street dance performed when turning at the end of the street.

Enec' Dance.

Erba *Setaria italica*, Kunth. A cultivated grain or jungle corn.

Erok' Sowing; also Sowing festival.

Ghangra *Dolichos catjang*, Willd. A cultivated bean.

Ghar jawae A permanent serving son-in-law who stays for good in his father-in-law's house.

Ghardi jawae   A serving son-in-law who works for a limited term in his father-in-law's house.

Ghugri   *Gryllus gryllotalpa*. The mole cricket.

Godet   Headman's messenger, a village official.

Golaeti   Marriage by exchange of sons and daughters.

Golwari   A type of social dance with pantomime gestures.

Gulanj   See *gulechi* (Hindi).

Gonon pon   Bride-price.

Gundli   *Panicum miliare*, Lamarck. A millet.

Gunjar   A type of dance performed by men especially during the Sohrae and Karam festivals.

Guru   Religious teacher or preceptor, deliverer of sermons; also doctor or physician.

Hanapuri   The afterworld.

Handi   Rice-beer.

Haram   Old man.

Haram budhi.   Old woman; an old man's wife.

Hariar   Green, verdant.

Hapram   Ancestor.

Hansdak'   A Santal clan.

Hembrom   A Santal clan.

Hesel   *Anogeissus latifolia*, Wall. A common forest tree with hard wood used for axles, ploughs, and other implements.

Horec'   *Dolichos biflorus*, L. A small leguminous plant.

Iputut'   The forcible application of sindur (vermilion) to the forehead of a girl.

Ir arpa   Gleanings.

Iri   *Panicum crus-galli*, L. A cultivated millet.

Jaher   Sacred grove.

Jaher Era   Lady of the Grove.

Jan   Bone.

Jan baha   'Flowers of bone'.

Jan guru   Witch-finder.

Janam   Birth.

Janthar   Offerings in connection with the first fruits.

Jatra   A gathering of villages for mass dancing. In the nineteen-forties already obsolescent.

Jatur   A form of dance performed by men mainly at the Baha festival.

Jawae   Bridegroom or husband.

Jiu (Jivi)   Life principle; soul.

Jobrani   Force or violence.

Jogmanjhi   Superintendent of youth and guardian of morals, proctor.

Jog paranik   Jogmanjhi's assistant.

Johar   Salutation.

Jom raja   The King of the dead.

Jormohol   A jungle root.

Jugi	Mendicant, ascetic, devotee.
Juri	Friend, companion.
Karam	*Adinia cordifolia*, Hook. A tree, associated with good luck; also a festival in celebration of it.
Karamdar	'Karam twig'; a form of friendship among girls.
Kend	A tree with long pod-like fruits.
Kuntau	Tie to a post or tree; especially used in connection with the Sohrae festival when the cattle are baited.
Khunt	Sept or sub-clan.
Khuntut'	Tree stump.
Kisar bonga	A brownie.
Kisku	A Santal clan.
Kode	*Eleusine corocana*, Gaertn. A millet.
Kudam	Rear side, the back of the house.
Kudam naeke	A 'field' priest chiefly employed for placating bongas on the village outskirts as distinct from the main or 'national' bongas
Kudum	A riddle.
Kulhi	The village street.
Kulhi durup'	A sitting in the street, i.e. a village meeting.
Kulhi enec'	A street dance.
Kundal napam	Marriage by openly living together with village acquiescence.
La	To dig.
Lagre	The standard social or recreational dance.
Landa sagai	A joking relationship between relatives.
Lar (jom lar)	A gigantic climber, *Bauhinia Vahli*, W and A., the leaves of which are used for leaf-plates and leaf-cups.
Langta	Nude.
Lita	Maran Buru in the guise in which he appeared to the first Santals.
Loa	*Ficus glomerata*, Roxb. The fig tree.
Lopon	*Terminalia belerica*, Roxb. A forest tree with fruits shaped like a penis.
Mandargom	*Anona squamosa*, L. The custard apple.
Manjhi	Headman.
Manjhi budhi	Headman's wife.
Manjhithan	Shed dedicated to the village founder.
Maran Buru	'Great Mountain', major bonga of the Santals.
Marar	*Erythrina undica*, Lam. The Indian coral tree.
Marandi	A Santal clan.
Matkom	See Mahua (Hindi).
Matwar mucet'kher	A final dance performed by men chiefly at the Sohrae festival.
Meral	*Phyllanthus emblica*, L. A tree used in Santal medicine.
Mersa loa	A kind of fig tree of which the leaves are a little smaller than those of the loa proper.
Mora	Dead.
Mora Karam	A Karam ceremony for the dead.
Moreko Turuiko	'The Five-Six', a leading bonga.

Munga *Moringa olcifera*, Lam. The horse-radish tree.

Murmu A Santal clan.

Naeke Priest, a village official in charge of offerings and sacrifices to the principal bongas.

Naihar bonga Spirit of the wife's parents' house.

Nim dak' mandi Rice-gruel mixed with nim leaves; also a term applied to the name-giving ceremony.

Nir bolok' Marriage by intrusion; a girl or woman who intrudes or installs herself in the house of a man as his wife.

Ojha Medicine-man, exorcist.

Or ader 'Pulling in', marriage by capture.

Orak' House, home.

Pai A little over half a pound in weight, a pinch of something.

Paik Stick dance performed by men chiefly at weddings.

Pante A line or row.

Pante begar 'Separation from the line'; the minor form of excommunication.

Paranik Deputy headman.

Pargana Chief, leader of a group of villages, chairman of a bench of five headmen.

Pata The hook-swinging festival.

Pauriya A Santal clan.

Porodhol The general ancestors.

Raghop' boar The fish which is supposed to have brought up earth from the bottom of the sea at the creation of the world.

Ranu A ferment made from roots and bark used in brewing rice-beer.

Rinja A dance performed by men.

Rol *Terminalia chebula*, Retzius. A large forest tree, the bark of which is used in Santal medicine.

Raher *Cajanus indicus*, Spring. A kind of pulse.

Rongo Ruji bonga. The female bonga identified with sex.

Sabai *Ischaemum angustifolium*. A silky grass cultivated in the Santal Parganas for papermaking.

Sadai bapla A proper or standard wedding.

Saket The tutelary bonga of an ojha.

San Plants and bushes with edible tubers.

Sarjom See *sal* (Hindi).

Sec' Side or direction.

Sendra Hunt.

Seren Song.

Sid Initiation.

Sima Boundary.

Sin Cando. The sun; also by usage the Creator.

Sirom *Andropogon muricatus*, Retz. A grass.

Sogoe A rustling sound of cloth.

Sohrae Harvest festival.

Sondhaeni *Tylophora longiflora*, Wight. A plant used in Santal medicine believed to cause amnesia.

Soren   A Santal clan.

Sunum bonga   Divination by means of oil and leaf.

Tamak   Dancing drum with hide-covered bowl.

Tandi catom arak'   *Oxalis corniculata*, Willd. A plant of which the root is sometimes used for procuring abortions.

Tarop'   *Buchanania latifolia*, Roxb. A tree.

Tel   Oil.

Tel nahan   A purification ceremony performed five days after a death.

Tetri kuri   Maid-of-all-work at a wedding.

Thakur Jiu   The Creator.

Than   Place, usually a sacred place.

Tudu   A Santal clan.

Tumdak'   Dancing drum made from a cylinder of burnt clay.

Tunki   Small basket.

Tunki dipil   'Bearing on the head a small basket'; a type of poor man's wedding.

Upas   Fasting.

2 HINDI

Akhara   A village place of assembly often used as a dancing ground.

Baghaut   A man killed by a tiger.

Bar   *Ficus bengalensis*, Linn. Banyan tree.

Bel   *Aegle marmelos*, Correa. Wood-apple; a tree with large smooth and rounded fruits, and orange-coloured aromatic pulp.

Ber   *Zizyphus jujuba*, Lam. A tree with orange-coloured fruit.

Bhogta   'The sufferer' or devotee who is swung on hooks at the hook-swinging festival.

Bigha   A measure of land in the Santal Parganas, equivalent to about a third of an acre.

Dhenki   Rice-pounder.

Dhobi   A washerman.

Dhoti   A cloth worn round the waist and passing between the legs. Loincloth.

Ghat   Any approach, steps or path to a pond, tank, stream or river, used for bathing, washing clothes or fetching water.

Gulechi (Frangipani)   *Plumeria acutifolia*, Poir. The Pagoda tree.

Gur   Molasses.

Haribol   'Hari be praised'. Hari, a pseudonym for Vishnu. A shout raised at the *sindurdan*, the application of vermilion to the forehead of a bride.

Imli   *Tamarindus indica*, Linn. Tamarind tree.

Jadupatua   Village painter.

Jaithan   Shrine.

Jamun   *Eugenia jambolana*, Lam. The black plum.

Laddu   A ball of sweetmeat composed of cream, gram and sugar.

Lota   Brass vessel.

Magh   The tenth Hindu month – the second half of January and the first half of February.

Mahua   *Bassia latifolia*, Roxb. A tree that provides food, oil and spirits.

Mantra   Charm, prayer or magical formula.

Nahan   Bathing.

Nilgai   A big white-footed antelope, known as 'blue cow' from its bluish grey colouring.

Nim   *Melia indica*, Linn. A tree of which the leaves, bark and oil are used medicinally.

Palash   *Butea frondosa*, Roxb. The Flame of the Forest. A tree with coral-red flowers which blossoms at the onset of the hot weather.

Palki   A palanquin or litter.

Phul   Flower.

Pipal   *Ficus religiosa*, Linn. The fig tree sacred to the Hindus.

Sal   *Shorea robusta*, Gaerta. One of the most important timber trees in India.

Sindur   Vermilion.

Sindurdan   Bestowal of sindur on the forehead of a bride.

INDEX OF IMAGERY

GENERAL INDEX

(All references are to page numbers)

Abge bongas, protectors of sub-clan 28
Abortion 160, 161
Abstinence before a hunt 305
Abuse, permissible forms of 50, 51
  punishable forms of 50, 51
Adoption, rules of 275–278
Adultery, rarity of 216
Afterworld, ideas of 216, 340, 341
  rewards and punishments in 55, 341
Agriculture, the year's pattern 21–23
Aldington, Richard 232, 233
Amaru 11
Archer, Mildred 353, 354
Ashley-Montague, F. H. 348
Aunts and nephews, songs about 314, 315

Baha festival: dances 239, 249
  origins of 238–240
  promotion of fertility 238, 240
  ritual 240–255
  songs at 237, 239, 241–255
Baiga tribe 73, 348
Brahmin caste 96
Bastardy, permanent form of 168, 169
Bauri caste 84
Bestiality 96, 97, 309
Betrothal, ceremony of 171–173
  dialogues at 171
  implications of 173
Bhuiya tribe 94, 96
Birhor tribe 59
Birth, ceremonies after 34, 35
  processes of 33, 167
Bidhi Bidhanta, role in conception 160, 238

Bitlaha, attitudes to 100–103
  ceremony of 93–96
  leaf emblems at 93, 95
  rules for 90
  significance of 96–100
  songs at 96–98, 102, 103
  symbolism of 95–100
Bodding, P. O. 11, 354, 355
Bompas, C. H. 34, 167, 168, 299, 355
Bondo tribe 109
Bongas 25–31
  as allies 27, 31, 64
  dispensers of illness 27
  enemies 27, 31
  guardians of tribal integrity 27, 31
  husbands of witches 27, 294
  lovers 279–289
  protectors of sub-clans 28
  teachers of singing and dancing 238
  association with springs and streams 67, 284
  attitudes to 25–31
  different types of 26–28
  food of 53, 283
  physical characteristics of 280, 283
  susceptibility to pollution 31, 33, 53
  vulnerability to kicks and to blows on head 280, 282, 285
  world of 25–28, 280, 283
Broom, symbolism of 98, 99
  use of at bitlahas 96
  use of by witches 295
Boulenger, Jane 353
Buchanan, F. 28
Buru Beret' festival 60